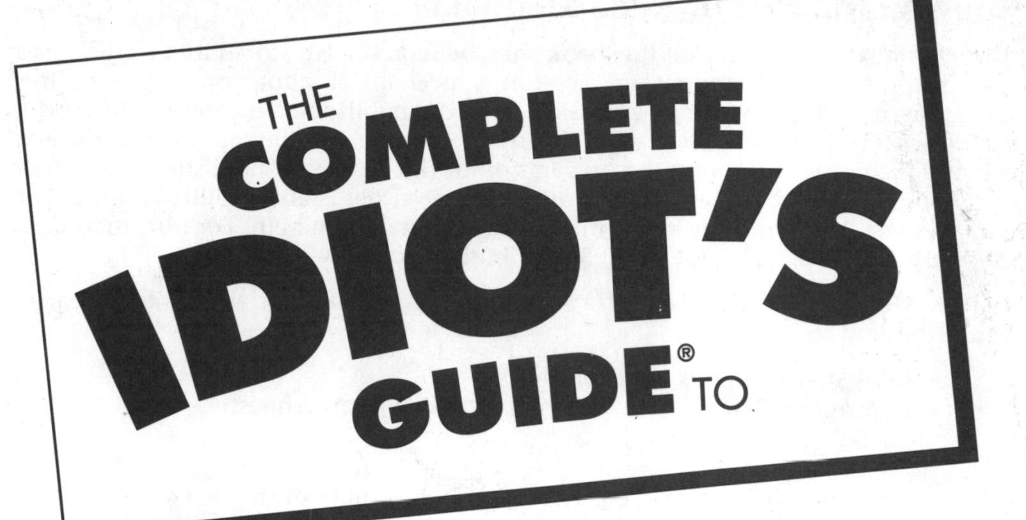

Writing Poetry

by Nikki Moustaki

alpha
books

201 West 103rd Street
Indianapolis, IN 46290

A Pearson Education Company

International Standard Book Number: 0-02-864141-8
Library of Congress Catalog Card Number: Available upon request.

03 02 01 8 7 6 5 4 3 2 1

Interpretation of the printing code: The rightmost number of the first series of numbers is the year of the book's printing; the rightmost number of the second series of numbers is the number of the book's printing. For example, a printing code of 01-1 shows that the first printing occurred in 2001.

Printed in the United States of America

Publisher
Marie Butler-Knight

Product Manager
Phil Kitchel

Managing Editor
Jennifer Chisholm

Senior Acquisitions Editor
Randy Ladenheim-Gil

Development Editor
Suzanne LeVert

Senior Production Editor
Christy Wagner

Copy Editor
Jan Zunkel

Illustrator
Jody Schaeffer

Cover Designers
Mike Freeland
Kevin Spear

Book Designers
Scott Cook and Amy Adams of DesignLab

Indexer
Angie Bess

Contents at a Glance

Appendixes

Contents

Part 1: What Is Poetry and How Do I Write It?

Appendixes

Foreword

A few years ago I passed a bookstore window in which was displayed a pyramid of books that had "Idiots" or "Dummies" in the title. I immediately had the thought of composing, perhaps in collaboration with my chum Jim, just such a primer on America's most famously "difficult" poet. My poem of the day—I was experimenting with writing a poem every day, a procedure I recommend highly to aspiring writers—began with the lines, "Maybe Jim Cummins and I / will write *John Ashbery / for Dummies,*" followed with a sequence of other "Maybe" clauses. This seemed to me the perfect exposition of the idea, rendering superfluous the composition of the actual book.

A book on writing poetry aimed at the "idiot" audience seems, on the other hand, not only a reasonable proposition but an inevitable development, one to be welcomed, especially when the writer turns out to be as energetic and imaginative as Nikki Moustaki. The intended reader of *The Complete Idiot's Guide to Writing Poetry* is neither a complete idiot nor a partial one but an open-minded person of good will who will tolerate being called anything if you'll just consent to speak in plain English that cats and dogs can understand. The fact that one day on a visit to John Ashbery I saw *The Complete Idiot's Guide to the Internet* on the coffee table may prove my point.

It seems to me that the single best thing a book like the one you hold in your hands can do is to generate enthusiasm and provide you with ideas for how to convert that enthusiasm into poetry. I have long believed that inspiration comes not as a lightning bolt but as the result of the workings of our hearts and minds. The secret of poetic composition is that you can create your own inspiration, and a clever way to do that is with exercises and assignments—such as the ones you will find in this book. Nikki Moustaki has borrowed the ideas of estimable poet friends such as Catherine Bowman, Denise Duhamel, Campbell McGrath, Maureen Seaton, Reginald Shepherd. What assignments do they give themselves to jump-start their imaginations? You will find poems for imitation, practical advice on everything from revision to reading in public, an introduction to poetic terms and conventions, and answers to questions the idiot side of your brain has always wanted to ask: "Why are there so many rules in poetry?" "How do you know if what you are writing is 'good'?" "What is meter?"

Good writing begins with good reading and is followed by work—hard, disciplined, sometimes daily labor. There is no denying the element of truth in Thomas Alva Edison's definition of genius as 10 percent inspiration next to 90 percent perspiration. Yes, but sometimes the work can be fun. That's the ultimate logic behind the whole range of poetic regulations from the complicated rules of the sestina form to the uses of metaphor and simile: These are some of the ways in which the imagination turns a feat of labor into an activity yielding pleasures both immediate and long-lasting.

Enjoy the ride.

David Lehman

David Lehman is the author of four poetry books, including *The Daily Mirror: A Journal in Poetry,* which includes a selection of 150 of the poems he wrote after resolving to write one a day. Lehman initiated *The Best American Poetry* in 1988 and continues as the series editor of this distinguished annual anthology. He has served on the core faculty of the graduate writing programs at Bennington College and the New School since the inception of the programs. He also teaches a "Great Poems" honors course at New York University.

Introduction

"A journey of a thousand miles begins with a single step."

—Confucius

The art of poetry has been around for thousands of years—a poet beginning today has a lot of catching up to do! To write poetry is to become a part of a very large clique composed of some of the greatest thinkers and writers of all time. When you write poetry, you're casting a spell that conjures all of them. You're a member of a pretty big party now!

Can writing poetry be taught? Or, an even more pressing question, can you learn to write poetry from reading this book and following its suggestions? Yes to both questions. Poetry is made of a certain skill set, that, when executed well, creates poetry. Sounds a little like car mechanics, doesn't it? I'll admit there's a lot more to it than just using the skills well, but you have to begin somewhere, and here's as good a place as any.

This book is designed to tap into your creativity and to teach you the initial skills (and then some!) to get you well on your way to becoming a poet. You'll find a lot to *do* in this book—poetry exercises, poetic forms to try, valuable tips designed to put your creativity into action, and more. I hope you enjoy the journey. Sharpen your pencil and dig in!

What You'll Learn in This Book

This book is divided into four parts that take you though the process of developing your poetic potential. You'll learn about the whys and wherefores of poetry, discover the basic skills needed to write it, and get practical tips on publishing your own poems. Here's what the four parts of this book cover:

In **Part 1, "What Is Poetry and How Do I Write It?"** you'll learn the basic elements of poetry, how to get started, how to conquer the fear of the blank page, journaling, and more. You will see if you "have what it takes" to be a poet, and you'll get a lot of encouragement along the way.

Part 2, "Opening the Stanza's Door: Entering Poetry," teaches you the set of skills that a poet practices to create his or her art: metaphor, repetition, music, meter, and more. This part details these skills and gives you practical advice on how to use them. You will also find a lot of exercises to get you using the skills right away, and examples to help you see if you're doing them right.

Part 3, "Popular Types of Poems and How to Write Them," verses you in a variety of ways to write poems, from the love poem to the sonnet. You will get a crash course on popular fixed forms, as well as tips and hints on writing other types of conventional poems. There are thousands of ways to write a poem—here are a few.

In **Part 4, "Poetry and Practicality,"** you'll learn how to avoid poetry's pitfalls, obtain valuable revision techniques, get advice on workshops and graduate schools, and gain some enlightenment on the wonderful world of publishing your own poems, including a complete how-to section and an "insider's look" at getting published. You'll also find a chapter of original exercises from poets who teach, as well as a short course in appreciating poetry. Finally, a Frequently Asked Questions chapter will answer those little things you still need to know.

There's a glossary of poetic terms following Part 4 that explains key terms and gives their definitions. Finally, there's an appendix containing the information to valuable resources such as books, magazines, and Web sites specially created for poets.

More for Your Money!

In addition to the solid advice you get in each chapter of this book, there are places other than in the text where you can get information to make it even easier for you to unlock your creative potential and learn how to become a great poet. Here's how you can recognize these features:

Roses Are Red

The information here will key you in to valuable tips and advice to make your writing easier and better—you'll get the inside edge on what it takes to write better poems.

Touchstones

A touchstone tests the purity or value of something, usually gold, but, for our purposes, we're testing poetry. Here's where you will find quotes from well-known poets that will help you come to a new understanding of this ancient art.

Let Me Count the Ways

Here you will find interesting anecdotes and trivia about the art of writing poetry.

Dodging Doggerel

Doggerel is defined as trivial or bad verse—something you want to avoid. The information contained here will help you steer clear of poetry pitfalls.

Poetically Correct

Like every other art, poetry has its own jargon. Here's where you will find definitions to important words that you should know.

Acknowledgments

I would like to thank my family for indulging me all these years in "this poetry thing"; my professors, without whom I would be lost; my agent on this project, Lee Ann Chearney; my patient acquisitions editor, Randy Ladenheim-Gil; my extra-special super-duper editor, Suzanne LeVert; all the other people at Alpha Books who made this book possible; all of the poets and poet-friends who contributed to this project; and everyone who listened to my angst during the writing of each chapter of this book—you know who you are. Much love and thanks to you all.

Special Thanks to the Technical Reviewer

The Complete Idiot's Guide to Writing Poetry was reviewed by an expert who not only checked the technical accuracy of what you'll learn in this book, but also provided invaluable insight and suggestions.

Roger Mitchell is the author of six books of poetry, including *Letters from Siberia and Other Poems* (New Rivers Press, 1971), *Moving, a Clear Space on a Cold Day, Adirondack* (BkMk Press, 1988), *The Word for Everything* (BkMk Press of the University of Missouri—Kansas City, 1996), and the recently released book-length poem *Braid* (The Figures, 1997). Mitchell has also written a book of nonfiction, *Clear Pond: The Reconstruction of a Life* (Syracuse University Press, 1991). His reviews and essays appear regularly in a variety of journals, including *Ploughshares, The Nation, New Republic, Poetry, Prairie Schooner, Poetry Northwest, New England Review, Redbook, American Poetry Review, Times Literary Supplement* (U.K.), *The New York Times, New Review* (U.K.), *Beloit Poetry Journal, North American Review, Harvard Magazine,* and many others.

His poems have been included in *Poetry Comes Up Where It Can: An Anthology of Poems from the Amicus Journal 1990–2000,* ed. Brian Swann (University of Utah Press, 2000). In addition, his writing has won several awards, including the Midland Poetry Award, the Borestone Mountain Award, the John Ben Snow Prize, the Chester H. Jones Award, two Arvon Foundation Awards, as well as creative writing fellowships from the Indiana Arts Commission (1999 and 2000) and the National Endowment for the Arts.

Contributor Notes and Poem Acknowledgements

The author would like to thank the following contributors.

Exercise and Poem Contributors

Diann Blakely's new volume, *Farewell, My Lovelies,* is available from Story Line Press. Her current project is a cycle of "duets," or call-and-response poems, with the 33 known songs of the great bluesman Robert Johnson. Blakely serves as a poetry editor for *Antioch Review* and works as a book and music reviewer for the Nashville Scene / Village Voice Media Group.

Richard Blanco's first book of poetry, *City of a Hundred Fires,* is winner of the 1997 University of Pittsburgh Agnes Starrett Prize. Richard has been featured as a guest poet on the National Public Radio show *All Things Considered,* and was a fellow of the 2000 Breadloaf Writer's Conference. His work has appeared in *The Nation, Indiana Review, Michigan Quarterly Review, TriQuarterly Review,* and several anthologies, including *The Best American Poetry 2000, Breadloaf Anthology,* and *American Poetry: The Next Generation.* Blanco is Assistant Professor and Poet in Residence at Central Connecticut State University where he teaches Creative Writing and U.S. Latina/o Literature.

Catherine Bowman is the author of the poetry collections *1-800-Hot-Ribs* (Gibbs Smith, 1993) and *Rock Farm* (Gibbs Smith, 1996). Her writing has been awarded a New York Foundation for the Arts Fellowship in Poetry, the Peregrine Smith Poetry Prize, the Kate Frost Discovery Award for Poetry, and the Dobie Paisano Fellowship. Her poems have appeared in the 1989, 1994, 1995, and 1997 editions of *Best American Poetry,* as well as many other literary magazines and journals, including *The Paris Review, TriQuarterly, The Kenyon Review, River Styx, The Los Angeles Times, Ploughshares, Crazyhorse, Sycamore Review, Conjunctions, 13 Ways of Looking at a Poem,* and the anthology *Real Thing: Pop Culture Poems.* In addition, Bowman reports on poetry for National Public Radio's *All Things Considered.*

Richard Cecil is the author of three collections of poetry: *Einstein's Brain, Alcatraz,* and *In Search of the Great Dead.* He teaches in the Honors Division and the Department of English at Indiana University, Bloomington.

Denise Duhamel's most recent poetry titles are *The Star-Spangled Banner* (winner of Crab Orchard Award in Poetry, Southern Illinois University Press, 1999) and *Kinky* (a book of poems devoted to Barbie dolls, Orchises Press, 1997). Her other books and chapbooks include: *Girl Soldier, The Woman with Two Vaginas, How the Sky Fell,* and *Smile!* Several poems from each of these volumes will appear in *Queen for a Day: Selected and New Poems,* due out in April 2001 from the University of Pittsburgh Press.

Stephen Dunn is the author of 11 collections of poetry, including the recently published *Different Hours* (Norton). A new and expanded edition of his *Walking Light: Essays and Memoirs* will be published by BOA in April, 2001. He teaches at Richard Stockton College of New Jesey.

Lola Haskins' work has appeared in such periodicals as *The Atlantic Monthly, The Christian Science Monitor, The London Review of Books,* and *Georgia Review.* She has published five full-length collections of poetry, the most recent of which is *Extranjera*

(Story Line, 1998). Story Line also reissued *Hunger,* which won the Iowa Poetry Prize in 1992, and will publish *Desire Lines, New and Selected Poems* in May, 2001. A further volume, *The Rim-Benders,* is forthcoming in October, 2001 from Anhinga Press. Ms. Haskins has taught Computer Science at the University of Florida since the late 1970s. She lives on a farm outside Gainesville with her husband, two dogs, two cats, and a large number of fish.

Dean Kostos is the co-editor of *Mama's Boy* (Painted Leaf Press, 2000), the author of the book *The Sentence That Ends with a Comma* (Painted Leaf Press, 1999), and the chapbook *Celestial Rust* (Red Dust Press, 1994). His poems have appeared in *Boulevard, Southwest Review, The James White Review, Barrow Street, Poetry New York, Blood and Tears: Poems for Matthew Shepard* (anthology), Oprah Winfrey's Web site Oxygen, and elsewhere; his translations from the Modern Greek have appeared in *Talisman;* his essay in *American Book Review.* He is the co-director of the Greek-American Writers' Association. He has taught poetry writing at Pratt University, The Gotham Writers' Workshop, and The Great Lakes Colleges Association.

David Lehman is the author of four poetry books, most recently *The Daily Mirror: A Journal in Poetry*. Lehman is the co-director of the KGB Bar reading series in New York City and is the co-editor of the *KGB Bar Book of Poems* (HarperCollins, 2000). He has served on the core faculty of the graduate writing programs at Bennington College and the New School since the inception of the programs. He also teaches a "Great Poems" honors course at New York University. A Guggenheim Fellow, he succeeded Donald Hall as general editor of the University of Michigan Press's *Poets on Poetry Series*. David initiated the *Best American Poetry Series* in 1988 and serves as the series editor.

Lyn Lifshin, whose most recent prize-winning book, *Before It's Light* (Black Sparrow Press, 1999) following the publication of *Cold Comfort* (1997), has published more than 100 books of poetry, won awards for her nonfiction, and edited four anthologies of women's writing, including *Tangled Vines, Ariadne's Thread,* and *Lips Unsealed*. Her poems have appeared in most literary poetry magazines, and she is the subject of an award-winning documentary film, *Lyn Lifshin: Not Made of Glass*. Her poem, "No More Apologizing," has been called "among the most impressive documents of the women's poetry movement." For interviews, samples of work, and more, please visit www.lynlifshin.com.

Campbell McGrath is the author of four books of poetry, most recently *Road Atlas* (Ecco/HarperCollins, 1999). His most recent award is a MacArthur Fellowship. He teaches in the Creative Writing Program at Florida International University, and lives with his family in Miami Beach.

David Rivard's most recent book is *Bewitched Playground* (Graywolf, 2000). *Wise Poison* was the winner of the 1996 James Laughlin Award from the Academy of American Poets. He teaches at Tufts University.

Maureen Seaton's fourth book of poetry, *Little Ice Age,* is forthcoming from Invisible Cities Press in April, 2001. She won the Iowa Prize and the Lambda Literary Award for her third collection, *Furious Cooking*. She has been the recipient of an NEA Poetry Fellowship, an Illinois Arts Council Grant, and the Pushcart Prize.

Reginald Shepherd's books of poems are *Some Are Drowning* (1993 AWP Award), *Angel, Interrupted* (finalist for a 1997 Lambda Literary Award), and *Wrong,* all from the University of Pittsburgh Press. His fourth book, *Otherhood,* will also be published by Pittsburgh. He has received an NEA fellowship and many other grants and awards.

Maura Stanton has published four books of poetry, *Snow on Snow, Cries of Swimmers, Tales of the Supernatural,* and *Life Among the Trolls.* She has published a novel, *Molly Companion,* and a collection of short stories, *The Country I Come From.* Her poems and stories have appeared in many magazines including the *American Poetry Review, Poetry, Crazyhorse, Ploughshares, The Chicago Tribune, The Paris Review,* and *The New Yorker.* She teaches in the MFA Program at Indiana University, Bloomington.

Charles Harper Webb's most recent book, *Liver,* won the Felix Pollak Prize and was published in 1999 by the University of Wisconsin Press. He has also received the S.F. Morse Poetry Prize, the Kate Tufts Discovery Award, and a Whiting Writer's Award. He teaches at California State University, Long Beach. *Tulip Farms and Leper Colonies,* a new collection of his poems, will be published by BOA Editions in 2002.

Acknowledgments

The author would like to thank the following poets and their publishers for permission to use their original work:

Chapter 1:

AMERICAN POETRY © Louis Simpson, reprinted with permission from the author.

Chapter 4:

ON THE RELATIONSHIP BETWEEN SCIENCE AND POETRY © Richard Cecil, reprinted with permission from the author.

DECEMBER 7th © David Lehman, from *The Daily Mirror* (Scribner), reprinted with permission from the author.

Chapter 6:

SHAVING © Richard Blanco, from *City of a Hundred Fires,* reprinted with permission of the author and The University of Pittsburgh Press.

Chapter 7:

EL JUAN © Richard Blanco, from *City of a Hundred Fires,* reprinted with permission of the author and The University of Pittsburgh Press.

HERE'S A PILL © Nikki Moustaki, reprinted with permission of the author.

THE ROAD TO ACUNA © Catherine Bowman, from *1-800-HOT-RIBS* (Gibbs Smith), reprinted with permission of the author.

Chapter 9:

BOUNCITY FLOUNCITY © M. M. DeVoe, reprinted with permisson of the author.

Chapter 10:

NIGHT PLUMBER © Nikki Moustaki, reprinted with permission of the author.

THE YEAR OF MINIMUM WAGE © Guillermo Castro, reprinted with permission of the author.

LOON © Roger Mitchell, from *The Word for Everything* (BkMk Press), reprinted with permission of the author.

SCISSORS © Nikki Moustaki, reprinted with permission of the author.

Chapter 11:

PAPA'S BRIDGE © Richard Blanco, from *City of a Hundred Fires,* reprinted with permission of the author and The University of Pittsburgh Press.

THE WARNING © Robert Creely, from *Selected Poems,* reprinted with permission of the author and the University of California Press.

BELL PEPPER © Dean Kostos, reprinted with permission of the author.

ANOTHER LOVE AFFAIR/ANOTHER POEM © E. Ethelbert Miller, reprinted with permission of the author.

DAVID LEMIEUX © Denise Duhamel, reprinted with permission of the author.

SKIRT © Nikki Moustaki, reprinted with permission of the author.

THE DEATH OF SANTA CLAUS © Charles Harper Webb, from *Reading the Water,* reprinted with permission of the author and Northeastern University Press.

Chapter 12:

THE VETERINARY STUDENT © Nikki Moustaki, reprinted with permission of the author.

POSTCARD TO W.C. WILLIAMS FROM CIENFUEGOS © Richard Blanco, from *City of a Hundred Fires,* reprinted with permission of the author and The University of Pittsburgh Press.

Chapter 13:

THINGS MY FATHER SENDS ME VIA U.S. MAIL © Laura Howard, reprinted with permission of the author.

DIRECTIONS FOR A THURSDAY AFTERNOON: HOW TO KEEP ME WHOLE AND UNBROKEN © Laura Howard, reprinted with permission of the author.

Chapter 14:

ELK ISLAND © Phil Metres, reprinted with permission of the author.

MY CONFESSIONAL SESTINA © Dana Gioia, from *The Gods of Winter: Poems* (Graywolf Press), reprinted with permission of the author.

MI ROSA Y MI SAL © Richard Blanco, reprinted with permission of the author.

PRAELUDERE © Ron Drummond, reprinted with permission of the author.

GHAZAL FROM MOSCOW © Phil Metres, reprinted with permission of the author.

4 HAIKUS © Alfred Corn, reprinted with permission of the author.

POSTCARD FROM THE PARK © Guillermo Castro, reprinted with permission of the author.

TRIOLET © Connie Roberts, reprinted with permission of the author.

Chapter 15:

READ DOWN © M. M. De Voe, reprinted with permission of the author.

AUBADE © Julie Carr, reprinted with permission of the author.

From CENTOS © Nikki Moustaki, reprinted with permission of the author.

VALENTINE FOR TERRY RAY © Ron Drummond, reprinted with permission of the author.

AUNT TOODUM'S EMAIL © Ron Drummond, reprinted with permission of the author.

A DOVE © Campbell McGrath, from *Road Atlas,* reprinted with permission of the author and Ecco Press.

Chapter 16:

SUICIDE'S NOTE © Langston Hughes Estate, reprinted with permission from Alfred A. Knopf Publishers.

YOU FIT INTO ME © Margaret Atwood, from *Power Politics* (House of Anansi Press), reprinted with permission of the author.

Chapter 17:

PINK FLAMINGOES © Maura Stanton, reprinted with permission of the author.

Chapter 18:

THE SOUND OF METAL © Gary Mex Glazner, reprinted with permission of the author.

Chapter 21:

STORY HOUR © Diann Blakely, reprinted with permission of the author.

A PORTRAIT OF THE ARTIST'S BEDROOM © Richard Cecil, from *In Search of the Great Dead* (Southern Illinois University Press, 1999), reprinted with permission of the author.

THE LAST PAGE OF A JENNY CRAIG SEMINAR BOOKLET © Denise Duhamel, reprinted with permission of the author.

TO PLAY PIANISSIMO © Lola Haskins, from *Forty Four Ambitions for the Piano,* reprinted with permission of the author.

STACCATO © Lola Haskins, from *Forty-Four Ambitions for the Piano,* reprinted with permission of the author.

ROSE DEVORAH © Lyn Lifshin, reprinted with permission of the author.

THE ALL NIGHT WAITRESS © Maura Stanton, from *Snow on Snow* (Yale University Press), reprinted with permission of the author.

Chapter 22:

I TOLD YOU I WAS SICK © Denise Duhamel, reprinted with permission of the author.

Every effort has been made to secure permissions for use of the poems appearing in this book. Please contact the author at betterverse@aol.com in the case of an oversight. Thank you.

Trademarks

All terms mentioned in this book that are known to be or are suspected of being trademarks or service marks have been appropriately capitalized. Alpha Books and Pearson Education cannot attest to the accuracy of this information. Use of a term in this book should not be regarded as affecting the validity of any trademark or service mark.

Part 1

What Is Poetry and How Do I Write It?

True poetry makes things happen.

—Robert Graves

When asked what poetry is, poet Ben Jonson replied, "It is much easier to say what it is not. We all know what light is; but it is not easy to tell what it is."

To begin any art you have to know what the product is. A painter must learn what a painting is and a composer should be able to recognize a song. In this part, you will discover the basic elements that poetry is made of, learn how to get started, and find out how to conquer the fear of the blank page. You will see if you have what it takes to be a poet, and you'll get a lot of encouragement along the way.

Chapter 1

What Is Poetry and How Do I Begin to Write?

In This Chapter

- Where poetry comes from
- What is a poet?
- What does talent have to do with it?
- Good uses for a poem

Poetry is ...? That's a question for the ages, isn't it? Answering what "poetry is" is like answering what love is, or what life is, or, more precisely, what art is.

A better question might be "what does poetry do?" though even a gaggle of poets would be hard pressed to definitively answer that question in a space smaller than Yankee Stadium. So, we'll concern ourselves primarily with learning how to write poems and leave most of the worrying about "what poetry is" to the poetry critics and philosophers.

This book is designed to help you "break the poetry code," to teach you what it takes to be a poet and to discover how writing poetry works in this modern age. Poetry as a popular art has gained some ground, it seems, with car companies using lines from Robert Frost's famous poem, "The Road Less Traveled," to sell their product, and The Gap hiring poets to read aloud on their television ads. The truth is, poetry has never gone out of style, though its primary function has changed a little bit.

Where Does Poetry Come From?

Fragment

What is poetry? Is it a mosaic
 Of coloured stones, which curiously are wrought
 Into a pattern? Rather glass that's taught
By patient labor any hue to take
And glowing with a sumptuous splendor, make
 Beauty a thing of awe; where sunbeams caught,
 Transmuted fall in sheafs of rainbows fraught
With storied meaning for religion's sake.

—Amy Lowell

Poetically Correct

A **mnemonic device** is an element used to help the memory.

Let Me Count the Ways

The first recognized poet in Anglo-Saxon culture was a herdsman named Caedmon, who lived around 670 B.C.E. Caedmon dreamed one night that a spirit told him to sing of the *Beginning of Created Things*. He later became a monk and wrote some of the earliest Old English Hymns.

From what we know about poetry's roots, poetry is presumed to be older than written history, as well as one of the oldest arts. Ancient storytellers probably sat around the fire relating the historical journey of the tribe, and that story was passed down through the ages orally until the written word was invented and those stories became what we know now as poetry. Elements of verse, such as rhyme and repetition, were *mnemonic devices* that helped our ancient ancestors to remember the tales of the tribe and pass them down from generation to generation. Poetry is story condensed; it can help us to understand with one phrase how we came to be, what we are, and what we will be in the future. You've probably heard the term "a picture is worth a thousand words." Well, one good image or phrase is worth far more than that.

Let there be light.

Well, this is heavy stuff, isn't it? It doesn't have to be. Writing and reading poetry is fun, enlightening, soul-filling, and wonderfully good for you, far more enjoyable than many other activities, and you won't even break a sweat—well, not a literal sweat, anyway! Poet Gwendolyn Brooks said that poetry is "life distilled." So, writing a poem may be likened to taking a large quantity of life and boiling it down to its essence, the product being far more powerful than the original substance. For example, a fourteen-line poem may indicate the beginning, middle, and end of a long love affair. Poetry only has use for the important stuff and leaves out the rest.

Poetry is an ancient art, and becoming a poet is to ally yourself with some of the most important thinkers and writers in world history. Each culture has its own type of poetry, but, ultimately, all poetry tries to do the same thing: Poetry says, "This is what my (or our) experience is like—I hope you can learn something from it or see the world in a new way from this minute forward."

Poetry uses a certain kind of language and set of skills to make a poet's ideas accessible to others. Take a look at the poem "American Poetry" by Louis Simpson.

American Poetry

Whatever it is, it must have
A stomach that can digest
Rubber, coal, uranium, moons, poems.

Like the shark, it contains a shoe.
It must swim for miles through the desert
Uttering cries that are almost human.

This poem addresses the subject of "American poetry," as we can see from the title. The poem indicates that American poetry must be hardy, enduring, and suffer a bit, among other things. Ideas like these come from inside our brains and our bodies, and to show them to the reader, a poet uses things from the outside, such as rubber, coal, a shark, and a shoe. This is how poetry uses the world—engulfing everything, just like that metaphorical shark swimming through the desert with a belly full of moons and poems.

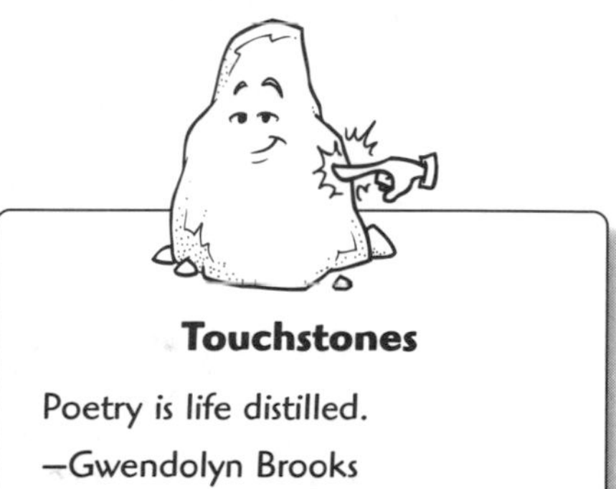

Touchstones

Poetry is life distilled.

—Gwendolyn Brooks

Using the world around you, the things and actions of your everyday life, is the stuff that much of contemporary poetry is made of. Poetry doesn't have to come from "on high" to be poetry; using the everyday things around you will help your readers understand your intention. Using obscure symbols and heightened language, on the other hand, may only serve to alienate or confuse your reader.

Touchstones

Poets were the first teachers of mankind.

—Horace

How Does Poetry Function?

Poetry used to be a crucial, utilitarian art. Poets held an important place in religious and political life and were an integral part of the society in which they lived. They led their communities in chants and rituals for a better harvest or a victorious battle, and they wrote poems to chronicle wars, the rising and falling of power, and to serve the gods and the muses. One famous Roman emperor's first decree after taking power was, "Kill all the poets." Poets were powerful, and their voices held the attention of the people.

Poetically Correct

Poetry is a verbal art written in verse, using a heightened sense of language to convey feeling, experience, meaning, and consciousness.

Today, poets are still political, but they don't have the power or utility they once held. *Poetry* is now considered a pure art, written only for the sake of writing it. We are inundated with other, louder voices now, like MTV and *People* magazine. Nevertheless, poets continue to be jailed and killed for expressing their feelings in countries where free expression is squelched. Poetry is powerful indeed.

Poetry also functions to keep language alive. Poets are inventive folks, always looking for an original word or phrase. What better way than to invent words themselves? Shakespeare is credited with having invented hundreds of words that we commonly use today. If you can't find the right word, make one up! That's what Lewis Carroll did—remember the poem "Jabberwocky" from *Through the Looking Glass?* (You can find that poem in Chapter 8, "The Sound of Music.")

How a Poem Functions

A poem functions; a poem *does* something—it creates out of being created. A poem is like a machine that acts upon the world and makes a product much the way the heat from an oven helps combine ingredients to make a casserole. Here's a "recipe" for writing a poem:

1. A few dozen words (use more or fewer if necessary)
2. Line breaks (to taste)
3. Metaphor
4. A pinch of rhyme (use sparingly)
5. A concept (something to say)
6. Blend all ingredients well and place in a well-greased pan.
7. Heat oven to 350 degrees and bake for a few years. Serve chilled.

If you've blended well, your reader will leave the table satisfied. If not, you can always revise and bake it again! (We discuss the revision process later in the book.)

As a poet, you'll have the power to create not only the poem, but also feelings the poem invokes in your readers. Have you ever felt a certain way after reading a poem? Perhaps a feeling of joy, of sadness, or of having come to a deeper level of thought? That feeling is the result of the poem, not the *poet*. The poet may have intended you to feel a certain way, or may not have thought of you at all, but there you are, feeling *something*—the poem has done its job. It's amazing to think that you can create something that has a life of its own once you've written it.

Like a casserole, if you make it right, you've got a great meal, and your guests will come back for seconds. A poem should satisfy, yet leave the reader wanting more.

Touchstones

Poetry is like fish: if it's fresh, it's good; if it's stale, it's bad; and if you're not certain, try it on the cat.

—Osbert Sitwell

Reading and Writing

Your job as a poet is not only to write, but to read as well. Indeed, good poets read other good poets. That's a fact. You will never, ever, *ever,* learn to write poetry if you don't read it. To write good poetry, you have to pay homage to the poets who came before you. They will teach you how to write. They are your mentors and your muses. Don't ignore them.

You shouldn't even attempt to write poetry if you aren't reading it. Poetry begets more poetry. You will find yourself inspired. Reading equips you to write, gives you ideas, delights and challenges you. Reading other poets can only help your writing. Don't worry about being influenced—influence is *good*. You want the good stuff to rub off. That's what it's there for!

I'm going to add something to my plea to get you reading poetry: Read modern and contemporary poets. Read poets living today. Find something you love in their work. Let what delights you about their work help to form your own poems. Reading older poets is great, but if you're not careful, you may begin using archaic techniques, which could make your own work sound dated and even silly.

Dodging Doggerel

To keep your own poetry fresh, read as many contemporary poets as you can. Subscribe to a literary review and read it cover-to-cover the day it arrives!

Roses Are Red

Hundreds, perhaps thousands, of poetry lists and forums are on the Internet today. These are great places to read poems—www.poems.com will even e-mail you a poem a day when you sign up—no effort involved!

Reading contemporary poets, poets who are writing *today,* will help you to see what the current poetic conventions are, and will prepare you to break them someday if you decide that's what you want to do. Before you invent your own style, you have to know what style is. Even Picasso painted realistic portraits before he worked in the style of cubism. If you mix your reading of contemporary poetry with older poetry, you'll see how contemporary poets developed the poetry written today.

Finally, reading other poets helps to solidify your taste in poetry and in your own writing. No one writes in a vacuum. Part of being a poet is *listening*. If you think you're the most important person with the most important things to say, and that other poets don't matter, I can just about guarantee that your poetry is going to suffer. Read. It's simple and it's gratifying.

What Is a Poet?

A poet is someone who writes poems. The ancient Greeks believed that the poet was a seer, someone to whom ideas and inspiration came from a source beyond him or herself, someone on which a higher power was bestowed. The poet was kind of "possessed" with poet-ness, and had muses to call upon for inspiration. I like this notion!

Touchstones

To be a poet is a condition rather than a profession.

—Robert Graves

What a "poet" is, is largely defined by the culture in which the poet lives. Today, in the Western world, we often think of poets as pale men and women in black turtleneck sweaters with cigarettes dangling from their bottom lips. Perhaps they have a bongo between their knees. These people don't smile or eat meat or enter the world when the sun is shining. They read esoteric poems to herds of their clones and scoff at the "normal" people for their shallowness. They are "monetarily challenged" and drink a lot of coffee.

We also think of poets as professionals locked in the Ivory Tower of Academia, looking down their bespectacled noses at the poor unfortunates who don't have tenure and books for sale on Amazon.com.

These stereotypes are no longer wholly true—okay, the coffee part is usually accurate—but poets are all around you, in every profession, in every neighborhood, and of every age and ethnicity. There are poet factory workers, dog walkers, and store clerks. There are poets picking produce in the supermarket right next to you, and you don't even know it.

Is everyone a poet? Not really. Poets are people who are able to render their feelings and thoughts into verse, such that a reader is able to understand and feel clearly what the poet meant. Poets may also see connections and notice things where others don't. Take, for example, this poem:

Complete Destruction

It was an icy day.
We buried the cat,
then took her box
and set fire to it
in the back yard.
Those fleas that escaped
earth and fire
died by the cold.

—William Carlos Williams

Let Me Count the Ways

Pablo Neruda, the famous Chilean poet immortalized by his beautiful poems and a recent feature-length fictionalized movie called *The Postman,* once said, "There is no advice to give young poets." Perhaps he meant that young poets would not take advice. Nevertheless, if you only take one piece of advice from this book, it is this: Read poetry.

Williams is paying attention to the world in this poem, noticing things as small as the fleas on a dead cat. Part of writing poetry is about finding the small things and making them important.

Do You Have to Have Talent to Write Poetry?

Nope, none, nada. Talent is a crock. People with talent often waste it with procrastination, drinking, doubt, whatever. Persistence, patience, practice, and the willingness to learn is the key to writing poetry. Everything else is icing.

Do you have to have talent to write good poetry? Well, that's a different question altogether. Since talent is so indefinable, I'd rather use the word inclination. Yes, I believe that you have to possess some kind of poetic inclination to write good poetry.

Touchstones

The poet makes silk dresses out of worms.

—Wallace Stevens

Touchstones

I could no more define poetry than a terrier could define a rat.

—A. E. Houseman

Roses Are Red

Memorizing poems is a great way to internalize poetry. When you memorize a poem it becomes part of you—its rhythm, words, and meaning filter into your being and into your poems. Try to memorize six poems this year—they don't have to be long. The only requirement is that you like them enough to live with them for the rest of your life!

Perhaps everyone has this inclination, the way everyone has muscles. You know that muscles don't take on definition if you sit around eating bon-bons all day. It's the same with poetry. You need to flex your poetry muscles to see what shape you can get them into. And the truth is, some people will never get huge muscles, no matter how often they go to the gym, while others will become giants by expending only half the energy. The only way you're going to find out the level of your poetic inclination is by "working out." This means reading poetry and writing poems. No one becomes a good poet without sweating.

Do some people have more natural "talent" for writing poetry than others? Probably. Being a good poet is being able to see the world differently or more clearly than other people do, being able to make strange and wonderful connections. But much of what we see as "talent" is really just hard work in action. Regardless of the common notion, poetry doesn't come winging down out of the ether to strike you in the head. Poetry can come from a small, still place—all you have to do is listen.

The question of talent always compels me to ask a person's reason for writing poetry. There are as many reasons for writing poetry as there are individual poets. Writing poems can be a personal art or a highly public one—what you do with your poems and what you hope to gain by writing them makes all the difference as to how "talented" you need to be. For now, don't worry about talent. Just write.

Poet W. H. Auden had this to say about potential young poets:

> "A marked gift for any occupation is not very common. What is surprising is that such a high percentage of those without any marked talent for any profession should think of writing as a solution. One would have expected that a certain number would imagine that they had a talent for medicine or engineering and so on, but this is not the case. In our age, if a young person is untalented, the odds are in his favor of his imagining that he wants to write."

I say, talented or untalented, if you want to write, go ahead. You're not going to hurt anyone. But realize that the delight of writing poems should be your first reason for writing them.

Touchstones

Everyone has talent. What is rare is the courage to follow the talent into the dark place where it leads.

—Erica Jong

Why Write Poems?

The Poet and His Songs

As the birds come in the Spring,
We know not from where;
As the stars come at evening
From depths of the air;

As the rain comes from the cloud,
And the brook from the ground;
As suddenly, low or loud,
Out of silence a sound;

As the grape comes to the vine,
The fruit to the tree;
As the wind comes to the pine,
And the tide to the sea;

As come the white sails of ships
O'er the ocean's verge;
As comes the smile to the lips,
The foam to the surge;

So come to the Poet his songs,
All hitherward blown
From the misty realm, that belongs
To the vast unknown.

His, and not his, are the lays
He sings; and their fame
Is his, and not his; and the praise
And the pride of a name.

For voices pursue him by day,
And haunt him by night,
And he listens, and needs must obey,
When the Angel says: "Write!"

—Henry Wadsworth Longfellow

Your own motivation for writing poems will tell you how much time to spend on your craft. You have to decide what you want from your poetic life, and what kind of life you want your poems to have. This will help you determine what kind of poet you will be. In the above Longfellow poem, the poet writes because he is haunted by the voices of his poems, and just as the stars emerge at night and the rain comes from the clouds, the poet *must* write—that's a great reason!

These are the most common reasons that I have heard over the years as to why people begin their poetic endeavors:

- **You want to be a famous poet.** To begin with, the phrase "famous poet" is an oxymoron. There ain't no such animal. You and your friends might discuss poets X, Y, and Z, but that's because you love poetry, I hope. Poets simply do not get recognized at the post office, nor do their publishers take them out for lavish dinners. Most poets, in fact, write poetry between teaching, watching their kids, and picking up after their dogs. Poetry will not make you famous, so forget your dreams of fame and fortune. You may have to wait until you're dead, and then what good will it do you? Being famous is overrated, anyway. Famous people get stalked, sued, and chased by paparazzi. You're much luckier—you're a poet!
- **You want to use writing poetry as therapy.** Poetry is a great way to get your feelings on paper, to explore what's going on with your "insides." There is a whole group of people, the "confessional poets," who approach poetry in this way. But while writing poetry looks a bit like therapy, it's not. Poetry is an art, not just a jumble of feelings slapped together and called "a poem." Of course you can express your feelings—that's a wonderful side-effect of poetry—but just do it with craft and originality. Poetry alone isn't going to improve your mental health, but it may give you an outlet for some of your feelings.
- **You have something important to say.** Great! So do the rest of us. Poetry is a wonderful way to communicate, but that's not all it's good for. Poetry used merely for communication might as well be journalism. Again, a specific art is involved here. Practice your art—read, write, enjoy—then say what you have to say. If you are burning with desire to communicate, write a letter to the editor of *The New York Times*.
- **You want a path to another career, such as teaching.** You can find easier ways to become a teacher. Write poetry because you love it—only then can you make a good poetry teacher. Besides, it's not easy to get a gig teaching poetry. Thousands of graduates of creative writing programs compete each year for just a few jobs—not great odds there. But poets are resourceful creatures. Wallace Stevens was an insurance lawyer and William Carlos Williams was a doctor. Shakespeare was an actor. You don't have to teach to live as a poet, though teaching does provide some free time to concentrate on writing, and you do get to talk all day long about what you love.

- **You can't paint, draw, take photos, throw pottery, create jewelry, act, or make things out of Silly Putty.** Poetry as an alternative art—it's worth a try. Poetry is cheap: All you need is a pencil and a surface to write on. You can take poetry anywhere just by memorizing it. No one can take poetry away from you. You already own the building blocks of poetry—words. Now all you need to do is learn how to put them in a pleasing, original order, and voilà! Poetry! Sounds easy, doesn't it? But read on ...
- **You're bad at math.** The good news is that poets don't have to do much math. This is a terrific by-product of being a poet. However, if you want to write formal poems and poems in meter, you will have to possess minimal counting skills. (That's the bad news!)
- **You write because you can't *not* write.** This is probably the best reason for writing poems—because you have to. Something compels you to write them, regardless of what kind of life they will have once they're written. Remember, poet Emily Dickinson spent her whole life writing poems that never saw publication while she was alive. She was a shut-in and so were her poems—and she's the Mother of American Poetry.

Touchstones

Art teaches nothing, except the significance of life.

—Henry Miller

While these are some common reasons for beginning to write poetry, they are not generally the reasons that people make poetry a way of life. Poets write poetry because they love it, they live it, and they look at the world with it in their eyes. Poetry, for serious poets, becomes the fiber from which they are made. If you have this kind of dedication and passion, you are one of the chosen few. Limber up those fingers and get to writing!

Poet

To clothe the fiery thought
In simple words succeeds,
For still the craft of genius is
To mask a king in weeds.

—Ralph Waldo Emerson

Touchstones

A work of art is good if it has sprung from necessity. In this nature of origin lies the judgment of it: There is no other. ... I know no advice for you save this: to go into yourself and test the deeps in which your life takes rise; at its source you will find the answer to the question whether you *must* create.

—Rainer Maria Rilke, from *Letters to a Young Poet*

Uses for a Poem

You can do several things with a poem after you've written it. Here are a few:

- Take it to a workshop for critiquing.
- Give it as a gift to a loved one.
- Use it as kindling for the barbeque grill.
- When folded into a tight square, a poem makes a great doorstop.
- Line your parakeet's cage with it.
- Write it a companion poem so it won't be lonely.
- Read it at a poetry reading, even if your Mom is the only person in the audience.
- Send it to a literary journal and hope it gets published, or at least not used as a parakeet cage liner by the editor!

Exercises

At the end of every chapter, including this one, you'll find exercises designed to help get you thinking about what you've just read and hopefully learned in the chapter. Here are some exercises to get you started in your role as a working, writing poet:

- Go to the bookstore and browse the literary journals. Read one straight through and choose a poem that you really like. Buy the journal or copy the poem out of it and tape it to your refrigerator for a week. Try to discover what it is you like about the poem. Once you've figured it out, try to use that same technique in a poem of your own.

- Go online and check out some poetry forums. Hint: About.com has a wonderful poetry forum where you can ask questions and post poems and ideas, and it has hundreds of useful poetry links.
- Memorize a poem written by someone else. Hint: Sonnets and rhyming poems are easier to memorize.

The Least You Need to Know

- Poetry is difficult to define but that isn't a concern to you right now—just start writing.
- A poet is defined as someone who writes poems.
- Talent isn't as important as the desire to write.
- Writing poetry is fun, but it won't make you famous.
- Reading good poetry is crucial to writing good poetry.

Chapter 2

Exposing Poetry's Bones: What Poetry Is Made Of

In This Chapter

- "Skeleton" terms defined
- The "short course" on the basic types of poems
- Poem checklist
- Putting it all together
- Fun exercises to get you thinking about the elements of poetry

Just as a building has a skeleton that provides its underlying structure, so does a poem. A well-built poem has the capacity to endure time, the elements, and criticism, while a poem with shoddy construction may not make it beyond kindling for the fire-place!

To build a poem well, you must have a working knowledge of its elements. Just as a construction worker knows how many beams it takes to create the skeleton of a sound building, a poet knows how to use his or her "beams" to make the poem work.

This chapter offers you a "short course" on the elements that make up a poem, elements you'll learn more about throughout the book. There is far more to poetry than just these "beams," but they are the biggies, the ones you will use most often.

Rivets and Beams

Here are some important terms that are most often associated with poem-making. Indeed, it would be difficult to write a good poem without using them!

Imagery

Poet William Carlos Williams said that there are "No ideas but in things." By this, he meant that poetry should be made up of the things of the world, not just of ideas. Of course, ideas are important—you have to have a concept to write about. However, to convey your idea to a reader, it's most effective when you attach your idea to a "thing."

Touchstones

It is absurd to think that the only way to tell if a poem is lasting is to wait and see if it lasts. The right reader of a good poem can tell the moment it strikes him that he has taken an immortal wound—that he will never get over it. That is to say, permanence in poetry, as in love, is perceived instantly. It hasn't to await the test of time. The proof of a poem is not that we have never forgotten it, but that we knew at sight that we never could forget it.

—Robert Frost

For example, the following "abstract" words have certain associations that are somewhat universal in Western culture (we call these clichés—you don't want to use them in your writing):

- Love = a red heart, face of a loved one
- Death = the grim reaper, coffin
- Mercy = a religious figure
- Justice = a blindfolded woman holding a scale

See how a concept can equal a thing? When you're writing your poems, you want to think about using visual imagery to convey your meaning. Remember, your reader can't *see* "pain," but if you use concrete terms to describe it, "a needle through the fingertip," the reader will be able to empathize with you. We'll learn more about imagery in Chapter 5, "Painting with Words: Imagery."

Metaphor

Metaphor is a comparison between two dissimilar things. For example, here's a poem by Emily Brontë:

Love and Friendship

Love is like the wild rose-briar,
Friendship like the holly-tree—
The holly is dark when the rose-briar blooms
But which will bloom most constantly?

The wild-rose briar is sweet in the spring,
Its summer blossoms scent the air;
Yet wait till winter comes again
And who will call the wild-briar fair?

Then scorn the silly rose-wreath now
And deck thee with the holly's sheen,
That when December blights thy brow
He may still leave thy garland green.

You can see how Brontë makes the connection between love, an abstract thing, and a wild rose-briar, and does the same with friendship and the holly tree. Poets do this type of thing to add power and meaning to their writing. What if Brontë simply wrote:

Love is difficult and often doesn't last that long;
Friendship is kind of easier and is more long lasting.

Isn't that terrible? It conveys something, but it's certainly not the art of poetry in action. Metaphor is one of the poet's finest tools. An original metaphor is a delight to read and will stay with the reader far after the page is turned. We'll find out how to create great metaphors in Chapter 6, "Metaphorically Speaking."

Repetition

Poets use repetition to convey a sense of urgency or importance, or to add music to their writing. A repetitive word, phrase, metrical pattern, syllable, or sound tells the reader to pay attention to that aspect of the poem or adds a certain tone to the writing.

Repetition is an effective formal element used in the earliest of poems. Read aloud from Genesis in the Old Testament and you will understand how repetition works. Your ear gets caught up in the sound, and before you know it you've learned how the earth was made and who begat whom!

Look for the repetitive device in the following poem. Read this poem aloud for the best effect:

How Do I Love Thee?

How do I love thee? Let me count the ways.
I love thee to the depth and breadth and height
My soul can reach, when feeling out of sight
For the ends of Being and ideal Grace.
I love thee to the level of every day's
Most quiet need, by sun and candlelight.
I love thee freely, as men strive for Right;
I love thee purely, as they turn from Praise.
I love with a passion put to use
In my old griefs, and with my childhood's faith.
I love thee with a love I seemed to lose
With my lost saints, — I love thee with the breath,
Smiles, tears, of all my life! — and, if God choose,
I shall but love thee better after death.

—Elizabeth Barrett Browning

Touchstones

The courage of the poet is to keep ajar the door that leads into madness.

—Christopher Morley

In repeating, "I love thee," so many times in such a short space, this poem takes on a chant-like quality and impresses on the reader (and the recipient, the poet's husband!) the quantity and depth of her love. Note that this poem is also a sonnet and has metrical and musical repetition as well. Can you find these repetitions? See Chapter 7, "Repetition, Repetition, Repetition."

Music

Poetry was originally sung to music. You will hear poetry called an "aural" art, meaning that it is supposed to be heard. When you attend a poetry reading, you are actually participating in a ritual that pre-dates the ancient Egyptians.

While most poetry today is not sung, it has many musical elements, such as repetition, meter, pitch, and tone. Read the following lines from Thomas Hardy's poem, "The Voice":

> Woman much missed, how you call to me, call to me,
> Saying that now you are not as you were
> When you had changed from the one who was all to me,
> But as at first, when our day was fair.

Can you hear the music in those lines? Okay, they're not rock lyrics, but they are "lyrical." Musical poetry uses rhyme, alliteration, consonance, assonance, meter, and many other poetic elements to create a certain "sound." We'll learn more about these things in Chapter 8, "The Sound of Music."

Language

If you take a poetry workshop or hang out with practicing poets, you'll probably hear a lot of talk about this mystical thing called "language."

When poets talk about language, they mean a "heightened" language, not the language you use, say, to order a hot dog. Poetic language is original, "fresh," and distilled. Poets like to convey meaning in as few words as possible. If you just want to fill up a page with words, you might want to write a novel.

Poets are also fond of nouns (things) and verbs (actions). They have less use for the adjective (words used to describe nouns) and abhor the adverb (words used to describe verbs). Poetic language is something that workshop groups and editors look for in a poem. They will evaluate whether or not the poet is conscious of using the most precise and original language possible.

Line

Line is the element that makes up the verses, or stanzas, in a poem. A line is not necessarily a sentence like it is in prose. A line is a unit of meaning that stands all by itself for a moment, before the reader goes on to the next line. Because of this, it's important that a beginning poet understand that line breaks are one of the most significant elements of a poem, and deciding where line breaks belong is among the most important decisions a poet makes.

Touchstones

Poetry is language surprised in the act of changing into meaning.

—Stanley Kunitz

A poet doesn't break his or her lines indiscriminately; there is a certain logic to the breaking of a line. Poetry isn't prose chopped up like meat: Poets try to write with line in mind. Where the lines break in a poem creates pauses, which help show the reader where to breathe, and creates emphasis and transitions.

To become skilled at great line breaks, read a lot of poetry and learn by example. There's no real formula for breaking lines; you'll get a "feel" for it the more you practice. Some poets pay close attention to line length to create a certain look and feel to the poem, maybe making all the lines the same length or wildly different lengths; some poets are concerned with the word or idea that begins and ends a line; poets using form break their lines according to the convention of the form, on a certain rhyming or repeating word, for example.

Poetry has two basic types of line breaks: enjambed and end-stopped. Enjambed lines break in the middle of a sentence or phrase, while end-stopped lines end with punctuation.

Here are two enjambed lines from the poem "Blessed Be" by Catherine Bowman (the last line is end-stopped):

Blessed are the man and the woman who fall
easily to sleep. Who each night slip
into suits of iron and drop seven leagues.

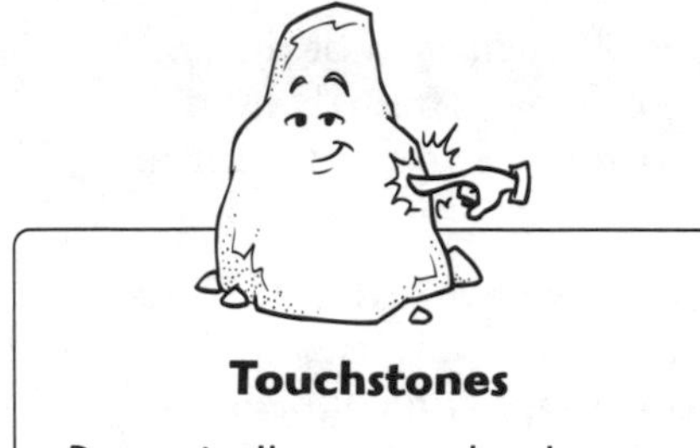

Touchstones

Poetry is all nouns and verbs.

—Marianne Moore

The two enjambed lines have a provisional meaning. In the first line, you imagine the man and the woman actually *falling,* but by the second line you see that they are just *falling asleep*. The same goes for the second line with the word *slip*. The poet intended the lines to have a meaning, momentarily, different from the larger meaning of the sentence unit.

Here is a stanza of end-stopped lines from the poem "The Rainy Day" by Henry Wadsworth Longfellow:

The Rainy Day

The day is cold, and dark, and dreary;
It rains, and the wind is never weary;
The vine still clings to the moldering wall,
But at every gust the dead leaves fall,
And the day is dark and dreary.

In these end-stopped lines, the reader has to pause for a moment before going on to the next line. End-stopped lines use our normal patterns of speech and breath to create a line. End-stopping slows down the reading of the poem; it's a technique you might want to use if your subject warrants it.

Many poets use a mixture of these two line breaks. Doing so creates variation and texture.

Stanza

Stanza, literally, is an Italian word meaning "room." In poetry, a stanza is a group of lines, often fixed in terms of number of lines, rhyme scheme, and metrical pattern, but not necessarily. Some poems are all one big "stanza," while others are broken into a number of stanzas. Poets often use stanzas to create and maintain a rhyme scheme or to give the poem visual space on the page. Some forms require certain stanza lengths.

- Monostiche = one line stanza
- Couplet = two line stanza
- Tercet = three line stanza
- Quatrain = four line stanza
- Quintet = five line stanza
- Sestet = six line stanza
- Septet = seven line stanza
- Octave = eight line stanza
- Spenserian Stanza = nine line stanza

Nuts 'n' Bolts

Now that we've looked at the "skeleton" of a poem, let's look at some of the nuts 'n' bolts that poets use to craft their art. These are the finer points of the art, the less obvious but equally important elements a poet uses to create great poems.

Speaker

The *speaker* is the voice we hear in a poem. Even if the "I" in a poem seems synonymous with the poet, we can't assume that it is. Poets often use *personas* or write about things they never experienced. If you felt you could only write about your own experiences, you'd limit your creativity, devalue your research capacities, and lose out on a fun part of writing poems: imagining!

Thinking of the speaker and the poet as separate entities becomes crucial in understanding a poem; this is especially important in a workshop setting when you're discussing someone else's poetry, where you'll refer to the voice in a poem as the "speaker." Thinking about the poem's voice as separate from the poet will help you to make a clearer assessment of a poem—if you are hung up on the poet and the "I" being the same person, you might miss an important part of the poem.

Symbol

A symbol is a thing or action in a poem that has meaning beyond itself. For example, when a poet writes about an apple, a reader from the Western tradition might think of the fall of Eden and all of the complexities of that story: the snake, the rebellion, the consequences. And the poet accomplished that with one little reference to an apple!

Some symbols are *personal* and some are more *universal,* like the apple. Don't be surprised if your readers don't "get" your private symbols; you might have to do some work to explain them in your poems. It's not a wise practice to rely too heavily on universal symbols unless you can manage to use them in a new and fresh way.

For example, the moon is often the symbol for female/fertility, the spring for rebirth, lambs for innocence, and birds for freedom. If you turned these commonly associated symbols "on their heads" and did something new with them, then you might get away with using them as symbols. For example, here's a poem by Percy Bysshe Shelly that changes the symbolic association of the moon as a fertile female:

The Moon

I

AND, like a dying lady lean and pale,
Who totters forth, wrapp'd in a gauzy veil,
Out of her chamber, led by the insane
And feeble wanderings of her fading brain,
The moon arose up in the murky east,
A white and shapeless mass.

II

Art thou pale for weariness
Of climbing heaven and gazing on the earth,
Wandering companionless
Among the stars that have a different birth,
And ever changing, like a joyless eye
That finds no object worth its constancy?

Poet Ezra Pound said this about symbols: "I believe that the proper and perfect symbol is the natural object … use them so that their symbolic function does not obtrude; … so that … the poetic quality of the passage is not lost to those who do not understand the symbol as such, to whom, for instance, a hawk is just a hawk." That's good advice: Don't make the symbols weigh so heavily on the understanding of your poem that a reader who doesn't understand your symbol will be lost.

Try writing a poem that uses a familiar symbol (for example, the moon as a fertile female) and "turn it on its head," as Shelly does in his poem "The Moon."

Irony

Irony occurs when the poet or speaker in a poem indicates the opposite of what they actually mean. Here's part of a fun poem by Lewis Carroll that uses comic irony throughout:

The Walrus and the Carpenter

"The sun was shining on the sea,
 Shining with all his might:
He did his very best to make
 The billows smooth and bright —
And this was odd, because it was
 The middle of the night.

The moon was shining sulkily,
 Because she thought the sun
Had got no business to be there
 After the day was done —
"It's very rude of him," she said,
 "To come and spoil the fun."

The sea was wet as wet could be,
 The sands were dry as dry.
You could not see a cloud, because
 No cloud was in the sky:
No birds were flying overhead —
 There were no birds to fly.

The Walrus and the Carpenter
 Were walking close at hand;
They wept like anything to see
 Such quantities of sand:
'If this were only cleared away,'
 They said, 'it would be grand!'

'If seven maids with seven mops
 Swept it for half a year,
Do you suppose,' the Walrus said,
 'That they could get it clear?'
'I doubt it,' said the Carpenter,
 And shed a bitter tear.

Dodging Doggerel

Don't get carried away with any one element of poetry in a single poem. It's easy to get delighted with what you're writing and not see that you're writing with a "heavy hand." As you become a better writer you will recognize what's working and what's not. All it takes is practice!

'O Oysters, come and walk with us!'
 The Walrus did beseech.
'A pleasant walk, a pleasant talk,
 Along the bring beach:
We cannot do with more than four,
 To give a hand to each.'

The eldest Oyster looked at him,
 But never a word he said:
The eldest Oyster winked his eye,
 And shook his heavy head —
Meaning to say he did not choose
 To leave the oyster-bed.

But four young Oysters hurried up,
 All eager for the treat:
Their coats were brushed, their faces washed,
 Their shoes were clean and neat —
And this was odd, because, you know,
 They hadn't any feet.

You can see the small ironies here in the beginning of the poem—the sun is shining in the middle of the night (it can't be night if the sun is shining—well, unless you're in the Arctic!), the Walrus and the Carpenter are distressed because there's sand on the beach (a beach isn't a beach without sand), etc. The narrative of the poem goes on to show how the Walrus and the Carpenter dupe the young oysters into taking a long walk with them, promising them a nice chat, when all the while the Walrus and the Carpenter intend to eat them—irony—they say one thing while their actions are quite different.

Hyperbole and Understatement

Hyperbole is figure of speech that uses overstatement for emphasis, surprise, or humor. Understatement functions much the same way and is generally ironic.

Here are a few lines from William Blake's poem "The Auguries of Innocence"—this poem uses hyperbole in every other line (and goes on like this for at least a hundred lines beyond this section):

A Robin Red breast in a Cage
Puts all Heaven in a Rage.
A dove house fill'd with doves & Pigeons
Shudders Hell thro' all its regions.
A dog starv'd at his Master's Gate

Predicts the ruin of the State.
A Horse misus'd upon the Road
Calls to Heaven for Human blood.
Each outcry of the hunted Hare
A fibre from the Brain does tear.
A Skylark wounded in the wing,
A Cherubim does cease to sing.

This is also the poem that begins with the famous hyperbolic lines:

To see a World in a Grain of Sand
And a Heaven in a Wild Flower,
Hold Infinity in the palm of your hand
And Eternity in an hour.

Here's a poem by Robert Frost that uses understatement to tell the story of the death of a child. Imagine how Frost could have narrated this gruesome story and its aftermath if he hadn't chosen this method. Indeed, the power of this poem is in its understatement:

"Out, Out—"

The buzz-saw snarled and rattled in the yard
And made dust and dropped stove-length sticks of wood,
Sweet-scented stuff when the breeze drew across it.
And from there those that lifted eyes could count
Five mountain ranges one behind the other
Under the sunset far into Vermont.
And the saw snarled and rattled, snarled and rattled,
As it ran light, or had to bear a load.
And nothing happened: day was all but done.
Call it a day, I wish they might have said
To please the boy by giving him the half hour
That a boy counts so much when saved from work.
His sister stood beside them in her apron
To tell them "Supper." At the word, the saw,
As if to prove saws knew what supper meant,
Leaped out at the boy's hand, or seemed to leap—
He must have given the hand. However it was,
Neither refused the meeting. But the hand!
The boy's first outcry was a rueful laugh,
As he swung toward them holding up the hand
Half in appeal, but half as if to keep

The life from spilling. Then the boy saw all—
Since he was old enough to know, big boy
Doing a man's work, though a child at heart—
He saw all spoiled. "Don't let him cut my hand off—
The doctor, when he comes. Don't let him, sister!"
So. But the hand was gone already.
The doctor put him in the dark of ether.
He lay and puffed his lips out with his breath.
And then—the watcher at his pulse took fright.
No one believed. They listened at his heart.
Little—less—nothing!—and that ended it.
No more to build on there. And they, since they
Were not the one dead, turned to their affairs.

Allusion

Allusions are references in a poem to people, places, and events that have significance outside of the poem. You may find words and references in a poem that you don't understand—get out the dictionary and the encyclopedia! A poet may refer to mythological figures, ancient battles, or biblical people and events.

For fun, choose your favorite mythological or biblical figure and write a poem using him or her (or it!) as the central figure or metaphor, and don't mention anything about the story surrounding the figure—let your reader do some work.

Content (What Are You Going to Write About?)

Poetry today is basically a content free-for-all—anything goes. However, some subjects are tougher to write well about than others, such as love, death, and unicorns, for example. You've got to be a pretty great poet to write a fresh, nonhackneyed poem about unicorns.

But any subject is valid if you can get away with it—that is, if you're a good enough poet. I drove cross-country recently and heard an on-air radio poetry contest featuring local "poets" competing for, well, nothing other than the validation of the three hosts. One caller read a poem that featured "toe jam" as its primary subject matter. Not only was I a little queasy at listening to a poem about "toe jam," but the poem wasn't well rendered either. Indeed, his was a poem that should never have been written. (But the poem won the contest—go figure!)

Are there some subjects poets shouldn't use? I think, perhaps, that poems of a racist or bigoted nature, and poems that attack other members of your workshop (who will inevitably see the poems), are better left unwritten or folded neatly and placed underneath your socks in a drawer. Write them if you must, but do us all a favor and keep these to yourself.

Poems do not have to be about "big" things like justice, war, and pain. Try writing a poem about a seashell, a stray dog, a puddle of melted wax on a table—you may come to find a metaphor in these ordinary things that will help you to write about the "big" stuff.

Touchstones

A poet always writes of his personal life, in his finest work out of tragedy, whatever it be, remorse, lost love, or mere loneliness.

—W. B. Yeats

Basic Types of Poems

The beginning poet would like to believe that poetry is more "loose and free" than other arts—that anything goes. This is far from the truth. Why would universities, libraries, and scholars devote so much time and energy to a formless thing? They wouldn't. Here are three basic types of poetry popular today.

Formal Poetry

Formal poetry has been around for thousands of years and follows certain conventions of the time in which the particular forms were invented. For example, in Shakespeare's time poets were writing in meter. That is, counting and measuring the syllables in their writing and making sure that their meter conformed to the style of the day.

You'll find multitudes of poems that are considered "forms." To write one of these types of poems, you follow the rules of the form like you'd follow a recipe, but more creatively! The fun part is getting good at a form and then "tweaking" the form to make it yours.

When I was in graduate school, one of my poetry professors once said to my class that form was like moonlight reflecting on a lake: Moonlight lies over the water, inseparable from it, but doesn't penetrate that far beneath. Form should not be the *point* of the poem—the form and the content should compliment each other, like moonlight on the surface of a lake.

Form shouldn't be considered daunting, but challenging. Think of form as a puzzle or a game. You'll learn how to write some fun forms later in the book.

Touchstones

Free verse is like free love; it is a contradiction in terms.

—G. K. Chesterton

Free Verse

Free verse is poetry not written in a fixed form. Free verse seems to lack structure, and indeed it is less structured than formal poetry; but free verse does have a structure just by the very fact that it is a poem using poetic conventions, and may even contain some formal elements.

Touchstones

Writing free verse is like playing tennis with the net down.

—Robert Frost

Sound complicated? It isn't. All poems have structure and follow some poetic conventions. What people really mean when they talk about *free verse* is that the poet using free verse worries a little less about line, stanza structure, rhyme, and meter than he or she would when writing a formal poem.

Paul Fussell, in his book *Poetic Meter and Metrical Form,* has this to say about free verse: "The first problem [with free verse] is the very term free verse. If we are persuaded with T. S. Eliot that 'there is no freedom in art,' the term free verse will strike us as a flagrant oxymoron … A lot of people take the term free verse literally, with the result that there is more bad free verse written today than one can easily shake a stick at."

Basically, whatever the terminology, the old adage "nothing is free" works in poetry as well as in the rest of the world.

Performance Poetry

Performance poetry is meant to be performed, obviously, in front of a crowd (if a poet is lucky enough to have that many friends who are willing to show up!).

Performance poets may not care as much about how their poem looks on the page as how it sounds when they read it, though this is not always the case. Performance poets may spend time practicing reading their poem and place their emphasis on their performance.

Poetry's roots are in performance. We often forget that poetry originated as an oral and aural art.

How Do I Put All These Things Together?

Ah, that is the question! Practicing and writing every day will help you to learn these techniques. You will probably find that you are good at one thing and not so good at another—that's fine. Keep practicing.

Practicing one skill over and over is a good way to learn these techniques. For example, set out to write 10 original metaphors a day. They don't have to be great, just original. Eventually you'll become good at metaphor. Don't expect any of these tools to come easily without practice.

Finally, don't get "heavy handed" with any of these skills. They are great when blended at the proper percentage, but when there's too much of one thing the mixture can become volatile! Bad poetry!

Roses Are Red

Does the start of every line in your poem begin with the same part of speech? If so, break your lines so that the left side of your poem has some word variety (especially if they are all words like *and, the,* and *or*).

Exercises

Here are some exercises that will get you started learning to use some of the skills you've discovered in this chapter.

- Write a 20-line poem describing the objects on your end table or in your kitchen "junk" drawer.
- Write a poem in two sections: In the first section enjamb every line, and in the second section end-stop every line. For fun, you can make the two sections the same.
- To practice line breaks, take a section of prose from a magazine or a how-to book and break it into poetic lines. Look at the result—has it become a poem because it's now in lines instead of sentences?
- Write a poem using irony: Say the opposite of what you mean. For example, write a poem about a fisherman who is happy that he hasn't caught any fish.
- Write a poem using different stanza lengths: couplets, tercets, etc. Play with line breaks and rhyme.

The Least You Need to Know

- Poetry is made up of a specific skill set particular to its art.
- Imagery is based on the concept, "No ideas but in things."
- Poetry has roots in music and performance.
- Don't get too carried away with any one single skill or tool in a poem.
- Practice makes perfect? Almost!

Chapter 3

Getting Started (and Over the Fear of Starting!): The Poetic Process

In This Chapter

- The poet's toolbox
- Invoking the muse
- Breaking habits
- How to know if your writing is "good"
- Exercises to get you started

When you hear other poets talking about the poetic "process," they're talking about the process of writing and all that comes with it: location, attitude, inspiration, writing utensils, time of day, revision, and sometimes what they are wearing. Some poets may even have certain rituals they perform before writing.

Poets as individuals are habitual and generally prefer to write in a certain milieu. You will often find poets writing in a coffee shop (now *that's* a cliché!), under a tree on a sunny day, or huddled over a notepad in their smoky studio apartment at 3 A.M. There's no one right way to *do* "process." You will eventually find a place and a time to write that simply feels good.

Process also refers to the way that a poet "approaches" a poem. How is the poet going to say exactly what he or she means, say it originally, and with the fewest words possible? The act of working and reworking a poem is part of the poetic process, too.

The Poet's Toolbox

Poets are fortunate in that they can practice their art anywhere, with a minimum of tools. Painters have to lug around an easel, paint, brushes, thinner, a palate, and canvases, among other items. You can practice your art with what you can fit in your back pocket: a pencil and a sheet of paper.

As a poet, you should never be far from a writing utensil and a scrap of paper. Keep several notebooks handy: a small one for your pocket, one for the glove compartment of your car (pull over before writing, please), one by your bedside for middle-of-the-night inspiration, and one near the "throne," if you do some good thinking there.

Practicing poets don't wait to write something down. They will get out of bed in the middle of the night in January when the heat's out to write down a good line. Inspiration won't wait for the change of seasons.

Writing Utensils

Many poets feel that the actual act of writing, of holding a pencil or pen and moving it across paper, enables them to be closer to the poem, to be a mechanical part of the poem-making. The act of typing words into a computer, where they "magically" show up on the screen, just doesn't do the trick for many poets. That's a highly personal decision and one you should take care to make consciously. Use your favorite type of writing utensil, something that feels good in your hand. If you're using pencils, keep plenty sharpened and ready to write. If you like writing in ink, keep lots of pens around, and make sure that you have another handy if the one you're using starts to fade. You don't want to miss a word!

Touchstones

Don't write with a pen. Ink tends to give the impression that the words shouldn't be changed.

—Richard Hugo

Once you've composed your poem on paper and done some tweaking, you can enter it into your computer, and in doing so, you might revise it as you type. This can be considered part of your writing process.

Some poets feel comfortable composing on a typewriter or right into the computer. Using a computer has its disadvantages, however. Unless you save each version with care, you will not be able to preserve all of your drafts, and you might lose "moves" and material that you want to preserve. If you do work on a computer, try to print out each draft or save it in another computer file as you write it.

Write On!

You can compose your poem on anything that feels comfortable to you: a special journal, a regular spiral-bound notebook, loose-leaf paper, or a laptop computer. Poet A. R. Ammons composed a long, skinny poem, "Tape for the Turn of the Year," entirely on a roll of adding machine tape.

Keep in mind, however, that, like it did in Ammons's poem, what you write on can influence the shape of your poem. William Carlos Williams, poet and doctor, used to write poems on his prescription pad, and many of them are short as a result. If you write on a giant artist's sketchpad, you may find that the poem you're creating develops long lines or keeps going and going.

A Room of One's Own

Poets, and writers in general, need privacy and solitude to create their art. It's difficult enough to write, and near impossible with someone looking over your shoulder. Find a place to write where you feel comfortable and will be undisturbed.

Where you write can also influence what you're writing. You will notice that you write differently sitting in an urban coffee shop than you do on a mountain in the High Sierras. Find various writing spots where your writing can flourish. You may have one or two "best" spots for creating, but your poems may benefit from a change of locale now and again.

Other Essentials

Beginning and novice poets will benefit from carrying around a dictionary and a thesaurus. If you're stuck for just the right word, you can turn to one of these references. Beware of becoming too reliant on these tools, however. Sometimes a really interesting word you find in the thesaurus simply isn't the right word for your poem.

Other reference books, from encyclopedias to books of bird or plant species, are also wonderful resources for a poet. Take a trip to your local used bookstore and stock up on them. Even if you only use one detail from a book, it's worth the purchase.

Roses Are Red

Check out www.thesaurus.com for an online thesaurus—the perfect word is right at the click of your mouse. It's great to be a poet in the modern age!

The Blank Page

Not much is more frightening to a writer than the blank page. The blank page represents the great void, an immeasurable space that is the writer's job to fill. That's a lot of responsibility for one person, isn't it?

Well, it doesn't have to be *that* scary. You can do plenty of things to get that first letter onto the page. Often, it's a matter of thinking about your task in a different way. Let's take a look at how poets become inspired.

Waiting for the Muse

Who is this Muse, anyway, and what does she have to do with me? Well, in Greek mythology, the Muses are the nine daughters of Zeus and Mnemosyne (the goddess of memory). Each Muse has a certain artistic talent attributed to her, and it was believed that artists could "invoke" the Muses and ask for their help in creating their art. Indeed, many contemporary poets and artists still pay homage to the Muses with invocations and poems.

Touchstones

The fact is that blank pages inspire me with terror. What will I put on them? Will it be good enough? Will I have to throw it out? And so forth. I suspect most writers are like this.

—Margaret Atwood

Should you wait for the Muse to write? Not really. But it doesn't hurt to try to call them with an invocation. Why not? As a poet, you're going to need all the help you can get. But don't wait for the Muse to sit on your shoulder—write without her, even when you are daunted by the blank page.

Choose your Muse:

- **Calliope:** Muse of epic or heroic poetry
- **Clio:** Muse of history and lyre-playing
- **Erato:** Muse of love poetry, hymns, and lyre-playing
- **Euterpe:** Muse of tragedy, flute-playing, and lyric poetry
- **Melpomene:** Muse of tragedy and lyre-playing
- **Polymnia:** Muse of hymns, pantomime, and religious dancing
- **Terpsichore:** Muse of choral dancing and singing, and flute-playing
- **Thalia:** Muse of comedy
- **Urania:** Muse of cosmological poetry

Reading for Inspiration

Reading is a wonderful "Muse." When you read poetry, you become filled with ideas, rhythms, and music. Your random thoughts will congeal and you will want to write. Poems beget poems.

Try this: Pick up a book of poems, turn to any page, read a poem to yourself, and then read it out loud. Let the words and the rhythms fill you. Now, take a single line from that poem and write it on the top of the page and begin a poem with that line. Write a whole page of lines. You have the beginning of a poem, one that didn't exist before. You have officially let another poet inspire you. Dedicate the poem to the poet whose line you used. Voilà! You've conquered the blank page!

Touchstones

O! For a Muse of fire, that
would ascend
The brightest heaven of
invention

—William Shakespeare, from *Henry V*

Freeing Yourself of the Ordinary

Freeing yourself of the ordinary is something that many poets do when they're faced with the blank page. Here are a few ways to get yourself going:

Touchstones

Poets or artists are sometimes married happily to their muse; and sometimes they have a very difficult life with her.

—W. H. Auden

- **Use a different kind of paper.** I know this sounds simple, but when you change what you're writing on, it frees you to write differently. Write on a horizontal pad, graph paper, or on dark blue paper with a gold pen. Whatever works to get you writing.
- **Change your locale.** Again, this seems simple, but it takes some effort. Take a bus ride around town, or go to a different coffee shop. If you can, take a weekend trip or a longer vacation to some place you've always wanted to go. Changing your location is often the spark that you need to get started.
- **Write a letter in verse.** You probably have a letter to write anyway, don't you? Now's your chance to get back to someone who has been on your mind. You don't have to send the "letter." This is just an exercise to get the words on the page. Of course, some people would be happy to receive a poem in the mail!

- **Get up in the middle of the night and compose a poem.**
- **Find a form you like and write a poem using it.** Take no longer than half an hour to do so. This will force you to begin and end a poem fast, and will take care of the fear of the blank page. After all, no one said it has to be good; it just has to get written. You can revise later.

A Note on Practice

The more you write, the better a poet you will become. A beginning pianist doesn't expect to play a symphony in the first weeks of practicing, and you shouldn't expect to write the "perfect" poem in the beginning stages of your writing, either. Practice. Write every day if you can, and if you can't, at least read poetry every day. Make poetry your habit.

Great Openings

Your first line should make the reader want to read the second line. It should begin close to the central action of the poem. Find and read Elizabeth Bishop's poem "The Fish" (it's widely anthologized and easy to find). The action of the poem involves the speaker catching a fish, admiring him, and letting him go. It's a gorgeous poem, one that many other poets admire for its imagery and original language. If the poem had begun with the speaker driving to the lake, rowing the boat, and baiting the hook, that would have been an essay, not poetry. Getting there isn't the point of the poem.

Touchstones

A poem begins with a lump in the throat: a homesickness or a love sickness. It is a reaching out toward expression: an effort to find fulfillment. A complete poem is one where an emotion has found its thought and the thought has found the words ... My definition (if I were forced to give one) would be this: words that have become deeds.

—Robert Frost

If you can, try to use an image somewhere in the opening of your poem. Imagery is the basic fabric of good poems. Try to get a concrete noun—a thing—in your first line. This is advice for beginning poets; as you get better and read more poetry, you can fudge these "rules." Every poem is different and will need a different kind of opening, but every poem will want an opening that begs the reader to keep reading. A boring, imprecise opening may not do that.

Sometimes, a line or a stanza in the middle of your poem or toward the ending can be moved up to the top of the poem during the revision process. As you write a poem, you get "warmed up," your words and thoughts get better and more powerful and the poem begins to gel. When you're revising, look for powerful places in the poem and try them as the poem's opening—often, rearranging a poem can make more effective.

Dodging Doggerel

It's easy to get carried away with the thesaurus: There are so many wonderful words to choose from! Remember, in poetry, the cliché "less is more" is good, practical advice. Opt for one concise word over three "pretty" words.

Closure

While we're looking at beginnings, we might as well look at endings as well. Ending on an image is often a good way to go, because an image sticks in a reader's mind more readily than an idea or concept does.

However, if the body of your poem is full of imagery, you may be able to end with an idea. Take a look at this famous poem's high-concept ending:

The Road Not Taken

Two roads diverged in a yellow wood,
And sorry I could not travel both
And be one traveler, long I stood
And looked down one as far as I could
To where it bent in the undergrowth;

Then took the other, as just as fair
And having perhaps the better claim,
Because it was grassy and wanted wear;
Though as for that, the passing there
Had worn them really about the same,

And both that morning equally lay
In leaves no step had trodden black
Oh, I kept the first for another day!
Yet knowing how way leads on to way,
I doubted if I should ever come back.

I shall be telling this with a sigh
Somewhere ages and ages hence:
Two roads diverged in a wood, and I —
I took the one less traveled by,
And that has made all the difference.

—Robert Frost

Why do we like this ending so much? First, Frost "gets away" with the ending because he does such a nice job at creating imagery in the other stanzas; readers can imagine themselves at that fork in the road. Second, Frost has chosen a subject that can be a metaphor for many things, and readers can relate this poem to many events in their lives. It really doesn't matter what Frost meant as the metaphor; we are allowed to make our own interpretation.

How to Know If What You Are Writing Is "Good"

In poetry there is no real "good" but there certainly is bad. Good is subjective. Bad is universal. To know if something you are writing is good, you can follow some basic criteria. You can't ensure that your poem is good, but following these steps will, at least, help you to begin to see the quality of your work.

Touchstones

A perfect poem is impossible. Once it had been written, the world would end.

—Robert Graves

The Five Senses

Using the five senses is crucial to making a "good" poem. Remember, if you use sensory images, your reader will be able to imagine that they see, hear, smell, taste, and touch what you are trying to convey. Concepts and ideas are not as effective as images. See Chapter 5, "Painting with Words: Imagery," for more detail about the five senses.

Have You Said What You Wanted to Say?

Many beginning poets want to know when their poem is done. A poem is not a pot roast. You might write a poem that never gets done, or, you might write a poem in 15 minutes that gets published in *The New Yorker*. (Is it even done once it's published in *The New Yorker?* Some poets would answer that it wasn't, but I'd say to leave that one alone and move on!)

Once you've said all you've wanted to say in a poem, it's time to move on to the revision process or time to set that poem aside for awhile to rest. If you feel that your poem is missing something, keep at it until the intention of the poem is all there—until you've said all that you want to say.

Touchstones

Prose = words in their best order;—
poetry = the best words in their best order.
—Samuel Taylor Coleridge

Words, Words, Words ...

Word choice is crucial to writing a "good" poem. Have you used the best words you could find? Have you been specific enough? Beginning poets tend to write in a kind of code that only they understand, using private symbolism and confused syntax to create what they think poetry is "supposed" to sound like. Your reader should not have to decipher your poems—no one wants to work that hard. If you're writing about your sister, simply write "my sister" instead of writing "rainbow girl" or "evil twin"—a reader won't know who "evil twin" refers to, but a reader will understand the relationship between siblings automatically—two people having the same parents. It's up to you, as the poet, to then clarify the nature of the relationship for the reader.

Roses Are Red

Gotham Writers' Workshop (www.writingclasses.com) in New York City has poetry classes both live and online. Online classes take the pressure off showing up at a certain time and place, and they are great for poets who keep irregular hours or who have heavy work schedules.

Using a precise word will go a long way toward revealing your meaning for your reader. Great poets are masters of *detail*. Instead of writing "flower," write "red aster," and instead of writing "bird," write "African grey parrot." One precise word or detail conveys your intended meaning far more than five less precise but "pretty" words.

Show Your Writing to Someone Else

Enroll in a poetry workshop in your area, or find one on the Internet. Showing your poems to people also engaged in writing poems is a great way to hone your skills and your poems.

Showing your poems to a few people whom you trust will help you to see your poems more clearly. Poets must be willing to take criticism and suggestion with a smile; even if you use only 2 percent of what you hear in the workshop, that's 2 percent you didn't have before!

Exercises

Here are a few exercises to help you get that blank page filled with poems:

- Open your dictionary to a random page and point to a word. Do this 10 times and write a poem using at least eight of the 10 words. Don't cheat. You have to stick with the words you choose, even if they're difficult.
- Buy a box of fortune cookies (or go to a Chinese restaurant). Open two cookies and use one fortune as the opening line of a poem, and the other as the closing line.
- Write a poem of at least 20 lines in which you use one specific word in each line. Make the word distinctive (in other words, don't use *and* or *the,* for example). If you can write longer than 20 lines, great!
- Write a poem "taking after" your favorite poet, meaning that you will try to use that poet's style in your poem. This is a great way to learn to write great poems. Use T. S. Eliot's phrase (and my favorite saying!): Good writers borrow; great writers steal.
- Write a "patchwork" poem made entirely of sentences and phrases from non-poem sources, such as magazines, textbooks, and how-to articles. This is a fun exercise and will relieve you of some of the anxiety of starting a poem—great for warming up.
- Write an *aubade,* a poem written at dawn, usually expressing the regret of two lovers parting. This means that you'll have to get up early!

The Least You Need to Know

- Always keep a writing utensil and a notebook handy so that you won't miss a moment of inspiration.
- Don't wait for the "Muse" to write—get started now!
- Read for inspiration. Reading other poets will fill you with ideas.
- Try to use all five senses in your poems. This will help the reader to feel what you are trying to convey.
- Enrolling in a poetry workshop is a great way to get feedback on your poetry.

Chapter 4

All Your Words Fit to Print (and Some That Aren't!): Keeping Journals

In This Chapter

- Why journaling is important
- Types of journals
- A short course in journaling
- How to get poems out of your journals
- Fun journaling exercises

Not every word you write is going to end up in a poem. That's simply the way writing works. If you treasure every word you write, you are in for a shock and are missing a large part of the act of writing. William Faulkner had this advice for writers: "Murder your darlings." By this, Faulkner meant that writers should be ruthless with their words, cutting and slashing and rewriting. Being a writer is a lot like being a butcher: You've got to know when and where to hack off the fat.

Journaling is about experimenting and writing without fear. Sometimes poets have a sense of dread when writing a poem; the inner critic emerges too early and begins to slash away at the poet's momentum. With journaling, you have no critic looking over your shoulder. You are simply writing happily away, without thinking about your words being "good." A journal is a safe place. Eventually you will be able to "murder your darlings" in your journal and extract the good stuff, the bits and pieces that will become poems. What about the abandoned words? They are just stepping-stones on your way toward becoming a better poet. Thank them and move on.

What Is Journaling?

Journaling is the act of regularly writing in a journal. The journal is a place to feel free in your writing, to doodle, to begin poems, to write down inspired lines and not-so-inspired verses. A journal is for pressing flowers and pasting images cut from magazines. You can do and be anything in your journal.

Most writers use journals. They record the day's events, noteworthy moments, memories, stray images, new words, inspirations, feelings, and anything else they need to get out of their heads and on to paper. Journals are great for letting go of the flotsam rattling around in your head. Writing in the journal makes way for new "flotsam," and that makes way for new poems.

The Importance of Journaling

The more you write, the better a poet you will become—that's a fact. Being a beginning writer is a lot like being a beginning pianist who must play the scales over and over: You have to learn where to place your fingers.

Writing in a journal also enables you to "trash" all the words in your head so that you can get down to the business of writing poems. Remember, in poetry, "less is more." If you don't have a way to release all of the garbage in your head, you may want to put it all in a poem, which is a bad idea, especially for beginning and novice poets.

Dodging Doggerel

Use only the best material out of your journals for your poems. Consider the rest "toss-away" junk. It's often difficult for beginning poets to throw anything away, but the less you hoard, the more room you'll have for better stuff.

Journaling also gives you something to do when you're not writing poems, and can offer you a wealth of material when you go back and look at your journal later. You may not see the poem in your journal entry at the moment, but later you may see it and write it.

Journal writing is a great way to "warm up" for writing. Say you have a great idea for a poem but you're just not "inspired." Work a bit in your journal and you might find the energy and inspiration to get to that poem.

The Difference Between a Journal and a Diary

A journal can be a lot like a diary, but it doesn't have to be. The word "diary" implies that you are going to be writing the most personal details of your life, and that can be scary, especially if there's the potential for someone else to read them. Instead, think of your journal as a place where you are doing the daily work of being a poet. That means recording images, ideas, and starting poems.

Touchstones

I went through a period once where I felt like I was dying. I wasn't writing any poetry, and I felt that if I couldn't write I would split. I was recording in my journal, but no poems came. I know now that this period was a transition in my life. The next year, I went back to my journal, and here were these incredible poems I could lift out of it ... These poems came right out of the journal. But I didn't see them as poems then.

—Audre Lorde

When to Write in Your Journal

Try to write in your journal every day at the same time. The actual time doesn't matter: It can be when you wake up, just before you go to bed, or sometime in the middle of the day. But do it regularly and make it a "date" that you can keep every day.

Perhaps you're a "jotter," someone who carries a journal around and jots in it all day long. That's great! You're not going to miss a thing this way. Your journal is probably going to be small and portable, and you're probably going to have a stack of them ready to start when you fill the one you're using.

Roses Are Red

Tie a pen to your journal (a spiral-bound notebook is useful here). That way you won't ever have to hunt for a pen while you forget the most inspired line poetry has ever seen!

Types of Journals

There are many types of journals aside from the "garden salad" journal into which you throw everything. You can keep various "theme" journals where you explore something specific.

Choose at least two or three of these types of journals and keep them regularly. When you don't want to write in one on a certain day, you can write in another. This leaves you with a lot of options—and you have no excuse for not writing!

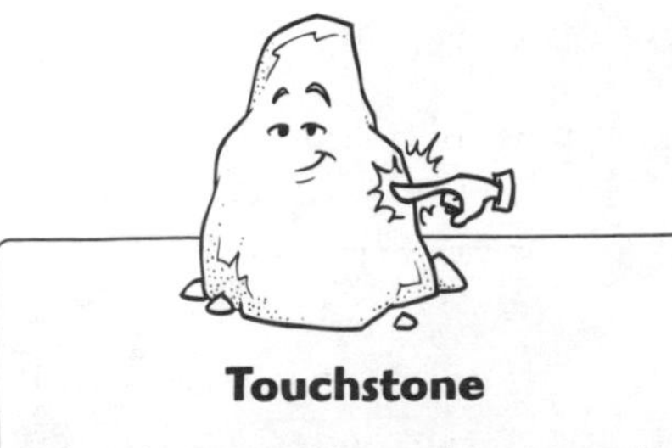

Touchstone

A writer uses a journal to try out the new step in front of the mirror.
—Mary Gordon

- **Daily log.** This is a diary, of sorts, about what you've done during the day. You can log everything from what you ate for breakfast to how you felt after a tough day at work. This is an easy one to keep, and you may find yourself starting to write about the day and ending up discovering something about yourself. This is a good way to "warm up" for writing.
- **Dream journal.** Excellent for tapping into the subconscious, which is a very important thing for a poet. Keep this journal by your bedside, and the second you wake up, before even running to the bathroom, record your dream. You will be surprised at the results.
- **Emotion journal.** Name a journal Fear, Jealousy, Anger, Rage, Loss, Happiness, Freedom, Inspiration (see where I'm going with this one?), etc., and just get all of it out on paper. Perhaps choose the emotion on which most of your poems are based. You're bound to get a lot of material from this one.
- **Memory journal.** Record your memories here—from your earliest memory to an hour before—just make them significant.
- **Urban journal.** Perfect for city folk. Keep a record of your interaction with the city.
- **Nature journal.** Keep a record of the natural happenings around you: the changing of the seasons, the movements of the planets, and the natural events happening to you as you grow up and grow older.
- **Love journal.** A life- and heart-affirming journal. Write about those you love, and about love in general. Might keep you going on those tough days. And think of the possibilities for your poems!
- **Letter journal.** When in doubt, write a letter. This is a great journal to keep when you have no intention of sending the letters, or when someone has passed on—what a terrific opportunity to express yourself. Hint: You can write letters to yourself from other people, too.
- **Wisdom journal.** Do you give great advice? Crummy advice? Doesn't matter. This journal will make you feel like Confucius, and you can say what you like without alienating your friends and family.
- **Relationship journal.** Everything about any relationship, which is perfect for poetry. Past, present, or future (!) relationships.
- **Confessional journal.** Diary exemplified. Let it all hang out. Spare nothing. But make sure it has a lock.

The Short Course in Journaling

Journaling seems like it would be easy, right? After all, you have no pressure for anything you write to be good, or even to turn into a poem. Well, for most of us, any type of writing can create anxiety, especially if there's a blank page involved. Here are some tips to get you started writing in your journals.

- Write each letter of the alphabet down the left side of the page and then, starting from the top, write a sentence starting with the appropriate letter. You'll invent a kind of poem to how you are feeling at the moment.
- Begin the journal with a string of sentences about what you aren't going to write about. For example: This entry is not about today when the bus was late. It's not about the time my dog ran away ... you get the idea. This will get you warmed up and writing.
- Write an abstract word on the top of the page, like love, hope, pain, hunger, and so on, and begin listing all of the associations you have with that word. You should come to a point where you begin writing about a memory or a feeling.
- Choose an object from your immediate surroundings. Describe that object in exquisite detail, leaving nothing out. Make sure to use metaphor and simile.
- Write with your journal turned the "wrong" way, i.e., horizontally instead of vertically, or begin writing in the middle or at the back of the journal. This might help to free you from the notion that everything must be done the "right" way.

Extracting Poems from Your Journals

Once you've got a fair amount of journal entries written, and you're going through a dry spell, you may want to go back to your journal to find the poems hidden there. Some may shout at you and be nearly finished, while others may take a while to find and will need a good bit of reworking.

Poet Richard Cecil used his journal doodlings to compose a sonnet—but he didn't know it was a sonnet when he began journaling.

Richard Cecil says of his poem:

> "I started with a big doodle pad and two lines of iambic pentameter that I've circled on the bottom of the first page—that was the first clump of language that I thought could grow into a poem. By the second typed page I realized I was going to write a sonnet because I had a (pretty lame) rhyme—say/way—and a meter that would lead to a sonnet if I could push it for 11 more lines. By the

next page I realized that if I reversed the first two lines I could open more strongly, switch from Shakespearean to Petrarchan form, and strengthen the rhyme—say/x-ray. At least that's the way it looks to me now, six months after writing this, though at the time I just plodded along from line to line, trying to make this poem go somewhere. When I came to the last page, final draft, I gave it the title for the first time, my standard procedure—I call everything 'Work in Progress' in order to prevent me from knowing where I'm going until I get there. I didn't much like the title I gave it, though, and then I remembered a purple flyer I'd gotten in the mail the week before calling for essays on the topic 'Essays about Poetry, Science, & Mathematics.' That's when it dawned on me that this sonnet was my essay—not that it would ever get published as one. So I crossed out 'Creative Writing's Place in the Pre-Med Program' and re-titled it 'On the Relationship Between Science and Poetry.'"

On the Relationship Between Science and Poetry

I'm sorry to inform you that you're doomed,"
your skull-faced doctor isn't going to say
while pointing out the black spot in your x-ray
as if he'd just been told to act out "gloom"
in tryouts for his small part in this play
called "The Death of X," where you portray
the lead reluctantly, though you've been groomed
your whole life to star in this tragedy.
No, Dr. Grim is going to sugarcoat
the poison pill death's ramming down your throat
with a thin layer of fictitious hope:
"With chemo many like you've learned to cope."
In other words, he's going to forget
his scientific training and turn poet.

—Richard Cecil

A Poem a Day

If you're feeling up to a challenge, start a "poem-a-day journal" and stick to it. Many poets get to the serious work of writing poems every day and wouldn't even think of keeping a journal.

Poet David Lehman wrote a book called *The Daily Mirror* in which he gave himself the exercise of writing a poem a day for an entire year. Try it for a month in your journal and see what happens. Don't worry so much about the poem being "great"; just get it written.

Here's an entry from Lehman's *Daily Mirror*. It has the feeling of a pantry list, but it uses politics (note the date: Pearl Harbor Day) and the self-consciousness of writing poetry to underlie the seemingly simple list of "don'ts." Try writing something like it yourself.

December 7

Rhyme *wave* with *leave*.
Postpone diet.
Do not do today what you can
as easily not do tomorrow.
Do not lend your car to a friend
of a friend. When you get it back,
you will need a new solenoid switch.
Mourn quietly. Drink lots of liquids.
Watch parts five and six of Dennis Potter's
Lipstick on Your Collar.
Read up in the Suez Crisis of 1956
and what it meant for "Little England."
Was the invasion really known
as "Operation Musketeer?"
Do not answer the phone.
Do not comply with alternate
side of the street parking regulations.
Do not remember Pearl Harbor.
Whatever you were going to do,
don't do it. No need for a handshake.
Just wave and leave.

Touchstones

One learns by doing the thing; for though you think you know it, you have no certainty until you try.

—Sophocles

Exercises

Here are some fun exercises that will help you to cull poems out of your journals:

- Flip to five unrelated pages in your journal(s). Pull out the best lines from these five places and make a poem from them.
- Take the last sentences from 10 of your journal entries and begin a 10-part poem with them.
- Write a letter to your future self: a month from now, a year, 10 years, 20.
- Find five objects from nature and describe them in your journal—leave nothing out.
- Find a map of the world, close your eyes, and point. Write in your journal about what you think it would be like to live in the place under your finger. Then write an entry in the persona of a person who lives in that place.

The Least You Need to Know

- Journaling is a great way to "warm up" for writing.
- A poet's journal isn't a diary, though you can use it as one if you'd like.
- Try to write in your journal every day at the same time—or at least every day!
- Choosing two or three specific types of journals enables you to focus your writing and gives you options.
- Writing journal entries during "dry spells" is a great way to create material for poems you'll write later.

Part 2

Opening the Stanza's Door: Entering Poetry

The crown of literature is poetry. It is its end aim. It is the sublimest activity of the human mind. It is the achievement of beauty and delicacy. The writer of prose can only step aside when the poet passes.

—W. Somerset Maugham

Poetry, like other arts, has a certain set of skills that a poet must practice to create his or her art. A painter knows when to use a certain size brush and how to use a blade for the proper effects; so, too, the poet must know when to use a metaphor and how to use rhyme well. This part will show you these skills and give you practical advice on how to use them. To engage in the "sublimest" of activities takes knowing the ins and outs of the pieces that make up a poem.

Chapter 5

Painting with Words: Imagery

In This Chapter

- "No ideas but in things."
- Show, don't tell
- Using the five senses
- Avoiding abstractions
- How to create an image

Imagery is like a tour guide the poet hires to help show the reader around his or her poem. This tour guide points out things along the journey, like the way something looks or sounds, and maybe even why it looks and sounds that way. The tour guide should have a lot to do, helping the reader to see the "Kodak moments" in the poem; if the tour guide is off drinking coffee and flirting with the tourists, you may have some work to do with imagery!

An image is a "picture" a poet creates for the reader. The "picture" is not always visual, but it should be sensory, meaning that a poet uses one or more of the five senses to create images that should, in turn, invoke a sensual response in the reader. Our only contact with the world beyond ourselves is through our senses; a poet using sensory images in a poem indeed wields a powerful tool.

No Ideas but in Things

Poet William Carlos Williams said that there are "No ideas but in things." Williams meant that the things of our world, nouns, should comprise a good part of a poem, not ideas. You can't see, touch, hear, smell, or taste an idea, can you? Can you touch, hear, or taste suffering, happiness, or love? These are concepts—ideas—that hold various associations for the reader. Why leave the associations to chance? Some readers might associate suffering with war, while others might associate it with running out of pistachio ice cream. Which of these do you mean? You lead the reader to your poem's intention by *showing* what you mean with images.

Show, Don't Tell

You may have heard the phrase "show, don't tell" if you've ever been in a writing workshop. Perhaps you've presented a poem to a workshop or a friend and they thought your poem was about fishing at high tide on Miami Beach, when you intended the poem to be about the mating rituals of Barn Owls. What went wrong? It's possible you didn't use any imagery at all or you weren't specific enough in your use of it. Imagery helps the reader understand your poem by remembering through their *senses*. For a good poet creating good images, a thing can equal an idea. After all, you are writing about something—probably an idea or concept. You will show it through images.

Telling (Idea/Concept)	Showing (Image)
You've got nice legs.	Your thighs are appletrees/whose blossoms touch the sky. —William Carlos Williams
When I was young I never thought of death.	I was a boy, I never knew cessation/Of the bright course of blood along the vein. —Allen Tate
The smell of anger is familiar.	His anger smells like dinner parties/like trays of frothy daiquiris. —Maxine Kumin
I snore loudly.	For I can snore like a bullhorn —Galway Kinnell

The more abstract your concept for the poem, the more precise your imagery should be. Here's a poem by Emily Dickinson that uses an abstraction, "hope," as the concept for the poem, but uses bird imagery to make "hope" concrete and tangible. "Hope" takes on the properties of a bird, and Dickinson has done her job—you will not mistake "hope" for anything else.

[Hope is the thing with feathers]

Hope is the thing with feathers
that perches in the soul
and sings the tune
without the words
and never stops at all.

And sweetest in the gale is heard;
And sore must be the storm
That could abash the little bird
That kept so many warm.

I've heard it in the chillest land,
And on the strangest sea;
Yet, never, in extremity,
It asked a crumb of me.

Touchstones

Poetry is the synthesis of hyacinths and biscuits.

—Carl Sandburg

Even if your poem relies heavily on ideas, you are obligated to help your reader understand your poem. You are not the maker of puzzles. If you want to confuse people, go to work for the government. If your reader is baffled, you've not done your job as a poet. One precise image is worth pages and pages of ideas.

Dodging Doggerel

Don't use too many abstractions unless you couple them with concrete images. For the lovers of abstraction: You can get away with using abstractions if your poem is laden with images—the more concrete imagery you use, the more abstractions you can use! You might write "I feel pain" but if you couple that abstract concept with "because I cut my thumb off chopping onions" the reader is more apt to understand the type of pain you're trying to write about.

Literal and Figurative Images

Literal images mean that the poet describes a thing itself, literally, as he or she perceives it. For example, "The granite boulder, half buried in the red clay soil" is a literal description of the stone and its locale.

Figurative images mean that the poet likens the thing he or she is describing to something else, usually using a metaphor or simile. For example, "The pigeon-colored boulder, buried like a gravestone in the ruddy earth." Here, the stone is compared loosely to a pigeon and to a gravestone, and the word "ruddy" implies "blood." A figurative image can often hold more associations than a literal image.

Touchstones

Poetry is fact given over to imagery.
—Rod McKuen

Abstract vs. Concrete

Abstractions are those words that have huge meanings that we can't easily perceive and sometimes can't even define: love, death, hope, anger, pain, sorrow, etc. Nothing is specifically sensory about these words—their meanings are large and leave a lot to interpretation.

Concrete words are things that we can perceive with our senses: beach ball, schnauzer, rain, light bulb, watermelon, thermometer. We can see, feel, hear, smell, and taste these things (please don't taste a schnauzer!).

Poetically Correct

An **abstraction** is a word that represents an idea rather than a thing, such as love, honesty, pain, hate, sorrow, hope, etc. A **concrete word** represents a specific condition, thing, or idea; referring to something particular and specific, not abstract.

Abstractions may be necessary in order for you to compose your poem. However, long strings of abstractions are tiresome, and do not serve your poem well. Because they mean so much, they are essentially meaningless in your poem; the reader will place his or her associations onto the abstraction and your intention may be lost. Poetry is about precision, and abstractions are anything but precise.

Try to use a variety of concrete images in your poems. A poem with a multitude of sensory images is a delight to read, while a poem relying heavily on abstractions is a bore.

The Five Senses

You probably learned in kindergarten about the five senses: sight, touch, taste, smell, and hearing. These are the tools you use to create your images. Beginning poets often choose one or two of the senses, while neglecting the others. Try to use all of them if you can (but not necessarily every one in each poem!).

Touchstones

An 'Image' is that which presents an intellectual and emotional complex in an instant of time.
—Ezra Pound

Let Me Count the Ways

Poet Frank O'Hara (1926–1966) worked at the Museum of Modern Art in New York City and was involved in the art world for much of his adult life. Many of his poems were written in the spare moments away from work, some at lunchtime, and as a result they are often short and highly imagistic, detailing the city and its events. O'Hara was also greatly influenced by the art he admired, and some of his poems address painting directly. He was run down by a dune buggy on Fire Island when he was just 40 years old, and many of his poems were published posthumously.

Visual Imagery

Since, for most of us, sight is the primary sense we use to navigate the world, it follows naturally that most poets use a lot of visual imagery in their poems. Visual imagery describes how something looks, and enables the reader to visualize the objects or actions in a poem. Here's a poem by William Carlos Williams that uses a solitary visual image as its primary strategy:

The Red Wheelbarrow

so much depends
upon

a red wheel
barrow

glazed with rain
water

beside the white
chickens

In this poem, Williams paints a word-portrait of the wheelbarrow for the reader. Can you imagine what the rest of the scene looks like? Could you draw a picture of it?

Auditory Imagery

Auditory imagery tries to capture a sound on paper, usually using a comparison to do so. The following poem by William Butler Yeats uses at least one auditory image or description in each of the stanzas, and ends the poem with a culmination of all of these sounds, which he imagines he "hears" in his heart. Isn't it lovely to be a poet?

The Lake Isle of Innisfree

I will arise and go now, and go to Innisfree,
And a small cabin build there, of clay and wattles made:
Nine bean-rows will I have there, a hive for the honeybee,
And live alone in the bee-loud glade.

And I shall have some peace there, for peace comes dropping slow,
Dropping from the veils of the morning to where the cricket sings;
There midnight's all a glimmer, and noon a purple glow,
And evening full of the linnet's wings.

I will arise and go now, for always night and day
I hear lake water lapping with low sounds by the shore;
While I stand on the roadway, or on the pavements grey,
I hear it in the deep heart's core.

—William Butler Yeats

Tactile Imagery

Tactile imagery describes how something, even something intangible, feels, either to touch or to experience with the whole body. Tactile imagery can also describe a spiritual experience. Using descriptive, tactile words like wet, cold, sweltering, and heavy, for instance, enables the reader to experience these things in your poems.

The rope I pull is stiff and cold,
 My straining ears detect no sound
 Except a sigh, as round and round
The wind rocks through the timbers old.

—Amy Lowell

This example from Walt Whitman also helps you to imagine how something feels through its descriptive language.

Or if you will, thrusting me beneath your clothing,
Where I may feel the throbs of your heart or rest upon your hip,
Carry me when you go forth over land or sea;
For thus merely touching you is enough, is best,
And thus touching you would I silently sleep and be carried eternally.

Olfactory Imagery

Olfactory images describe how something smells. It's easy to disregard this sense, so try to work it into your poems if you can. Use your imagination! If want to attach a smell to something intangible, or something you haven't smelled before, make it up! Here's how poet Catherine Bowman used this sense in her work:

This year's fragrance is a haunting scent,
embodying all the nuance of a war victim's last breath,
the subtle zest of gunchamber grease, a cherry-red sheath,
the bourbon and sweat of a melancholy vet.

Edgar Lee Masters' use of language conjures up the smell of death during war:

And there was the deadly water,
And the cruel heat,
And the sickening, putrid food;
And the smell of the trench just back of the tents
Where the soldiers went to empty themselves;

Roses Are Red

Try to use as many different senses as you can in your poetry. Making a conscious effort to use the senses will help the practice to become routine.

Here's another great example of olfactory imagery from Catherine Bowman:

... The drunks smell
like ripe watermelon ...

Taste Imagery

Taste is another often-overlooked sense you can try to work into your poems.

A woman bared her breasts and lifted her open mouth to
mine.
I kissed her.
The taste of her lips was like salt.
She left blood on my lips.

—Edgar Lee Masters

I am enamour'd of growing out-doors,
Of men that live among cattle or taste of the ocean or
woods

—Walt Whitman

And another by Elizabeth Barrett Browning shows yet another way to use the sense of taste ...

What I do/And what I dream include thee, as the wine
Must taste of its own grapes.

Synesthesia

Synesthesia combines two senses together, as in "a velvety voice," "sparkling silence," or being able to taste a color, as in "the sharp taste of yellow on my tongue."

Emily Dickinson wrote, "To the bugle every color is red." Poets like to use synesthesia because it adds "umph" to an image—synesthesia is imagery intensified. Here are a few examples:

I am hearing the shape of the rain
Take the shape of the tent ...

—James Dickey

Under hard yellow light, under glass ablaze

—David Wojahn

A hiss of gold
Blooming out of darkness

—Amy Lowell

Painting with Words: How to Create an Image

Beginning poets often have a difficult time with imagery because they think that their poems have to be complicated and mysterious; they feel that a poem easily understood is not a poem. Unfortunately, such a technique—however well-intentioned—tends to lead to some pretty bad poetry!

To create an image, begin with the central thing or idea itself. Say you want to describe an animal the way poet Elizabeth Bishop does in her poem, "The Fish." Bishop describes the skin of the fish as hanging in strips "like ancient wallpaper." What if

Bishop wrote, "the skin of the fish was kind of peeling"? Sure, that's visual, but it's not as precise as "ancient wallpaper."

Here's a poem by Walt Whitman that uses concrete imagery, nouns, the things of the world. Try to imagine this poem without them:

[I will take an egg out of a robin's nest]

I will take an egg out of a robin's nest in the orchard,
I will take a branch of gooseberries from the old bush in
the garden, and go and preach to the world;
You shall see I will not meet a single heretic or scorner,
You shall see how I stump clergymen, and confound them,
You shall see me showing a scarlet tomato, and a white
pebble from the beach.

Concrete imagery is precise imagery. Instead of "vegetable," Whitman writes "tomato"; instead of "egg," he writes "egg out of a robin's nest." If he simply wrote egg, one reader might think of a chicken's egg and another reader might think of an ostrich's egg. Whitman knew that the only way to make his reader understand *egg* was to name it precisely.

Say this word to yourself: fruit. What did you imagine? Some of you probably imagined bananas, while others imagined plums. The word "fruit" is imprecise. However, we can see, touch, taste, smell, and hear (the peeling of) "banana." That's how you want to create your images. Think: bananas. Or plums.

Exercises

Here are a few exercises to get you thinking about imagery:

- Write a poem featuring an object. Try to make the reader see, feel, smell, taste, or hear this object. Use metaphor and simile. Make sure that your comparisons are also images. It's better to compare one object to another, rather than compare your object to an abstraction. Use William Carlos Williams's "The Red Wheelbarrow" earlier in this chapter as an example.
- Make a list of abstractions such as love, hunger, pain, death, grief, and so on, create an image for them, and try to make your images as original as possible. In other words, don't have *love* = a red heart. Next, write a poem using as many of the images as you can. This is a flexible exercise; use only as many of the images as you need to make the poem work.
- Write a poem in which you focus on one of the five senses. Title the poem the name of the sense, i.e., "Touch," and use as many concrete nouns as you can.

- Visit a museum (or a place where paintings are hanging, like your local bank) and write a detailed description of a painting or other piece of art. Next, try to connect that description to something happening in your life at the moment. For example, if the painting is of a boat on a rough sea, try to find something in your life to compare that to—remember to use images and concrete language.
- Write a poem about your own hands.

The Least You Need to Know

- An image uses the senses to help the reader see, feel, hear, smell, or taste something in the poem.
- Showing in a poem is often better than telling for helping the reader understand the poet's intentions.
- Precision is the key to imagery; make your images as exact as possible.
- Synesthesia is the act of combining two of the senses together, and it gives an "umph" to an image.
- Concrete images are precise images. Think: bananas!

Chapter 6

Metaphorically Speaking

In This Chapter

- Living among metaphor (or, it was there all along!)
- Types of metaphor
- Avoiding the dreaded mixed metaphor
- How to create metaphor
- Exercises for the metaphorically impaired

Part of a poet's work is to make original comparisons. A poet may want the reader to experience things the way he or she experiences them, exactly, and there's no better way to accomplish that than using precise, fresh comparisons—we call these comparisons *metaphors*.

We live every day with metaphor all around us. You probably use metaphor all the time, without even noticing. Take these examples of flora and fauna:

- Spider Monkey
- Leopard Tortoise
- Umbrella Plant
- Ladybug
- Glass Lizard
- Swordbill Hummingbird
- Sunflower
- Christ Lizard

In each of these examples, the thing itself (monkey, flower, lizard) is compared to something else, which helps to make the understanding of the initial thing clearer. In the monkey's case, the comparison is to a spider. A Spider Monkey is not an experimental genetic cross between a spider and a monkey. The Spider Monkey is a long-armed, long-tailed monkey resembling a spider (at least in the estimation of the imaginative field scientist who named it). The Glass Lizard has a translucent body, the Ladybug is "wearing" a spotted dress, the Christ Lizard walks on water, and the Leopard Tortoise has spots like a leopard. These comparisons exist in the language of every field of study. Can you think of any metaphors in the computer and technology industry? How about "virus," "spider," and "bug"? Can you think of any geographical metaphors? Try "finger lakes," "mouth of the river," and "river's elbow."

To use a gruesome example, say you have to go to the emergency room because you have chest pain. The doctors will want to know what the pain in your chest feels like. Is the pain stabbing (like a knife), sharp (like a needle), or dull and persistent (like your mother-in-law's presence)? In using metaphor to describe your pain, the doctors will be better able to tell whether you are having a heart attack or indigestion (from your mother-in-law's green bean casserole!). Metaphor can save your life!

Metaphor

Metaphor is simply a comparison between two unlike things, though it's easier to define than to do well. Metaphor can be a powerful mode of expression in a poem, showing the reader something with a fresh, new perspective.

Touchstones

By far the most important thing to master is the use of the metaphor. This is the one thing that cannot be learnt from anyone else, and is the mark of a great natural ability, for the ability to use metaphor implies a perception of resemblances.

—Aristotle

Sobriety is a jewel
That I do much adore;

—William Butler Yeats

And all her face was honey to my mouth
And all her body pasture to mine eyes;

—Algernon Charles Swinburne

The night we drive in is a snake

—Catherine Bowman

Here's a poem by Ezra Pound that uses a single metaphor, a single image, to build the body of the entire poem:

In the Station of the Metro

The apparition of these faces in the crowd;
Petals on a wet, black bough.

In this poem, Pound takes the abstract notion of faces in a crowd and compares them to the very specific "petals on a wet, black bough." Can you see the faces?

Touchstones

Poetry begins in trivial metaphors, pretty metaphors, "grace" metaphors, and goes on to the profoundest thinking that we have. Poetry provides the one permissible way of saying one thing and meaning another. People say, 'Why don't you say what you mean?' We never do that, do we, being all of us too much poets. We like to talk in parables and in hints and in indirections—whether from diffidence or some other instinct.

—Robert Frost

The feelings we experience are generally abstractions: love, hate, pain, sorrow, hunger, and so on. These feelings are difficult to understand and to explain, though they are commonly felt, and are often expressed and explored in poems. Using metaphor makes these feelings more specific. Here's a poem by Sarah Teasdale that uses metaphor to explore lost love:

After Love

There is no magic any more,
We meet as other people do,
You work no miracle for me
Nor I for you.

You were the wind and I the sea —
There is no splendor any more,
I have grown listless as the pool
Beside the shore.

But though the pool is safe from storm
And from the tide has found surcease,
It grows more bitter than the sea,
For all its peace.

Poetically Correct

A **cliché** is a dead or over-used metaphor, phrase, or image, or a metaphor whose original meaning has been forgotten. A good rule of thumb (to use a cliché, since we don't measure anything using our thumbs anymore) is to eliminate phrases from your poem that seem familiar. If you've heard it before, take it out of your poem!

In the second and third stanzas, Teasdale uses a comparison of the wind and the sea to a dead relationship between two lovers, one lover representing the wind and the other representing the sea. What does the wind do to the sea? What is the "life" of a tide pool like?

These metaphors complicate the poem and lend it imagery and texture. Without this metaphor, Teasdale could have written "We're not together now and I'm pretty bothered about it, even though life is more peaceful now that you're gone." The metaphors Teasdale uses create the poetry: They give power and expression to the feelings in this poem. Without them, this would be a journal entry about a relationship ending.

As an exercise, try to write 10 good metaphors. Don't count the metaphors that you've heard before, such as "She was 'dog tired'" or "He is a 'hot-house flower.'" These are *clichés,* and should be avoided in your poems. Make your metaphors fresh and new.

Tenor and Vehicle

A metaphor has two parts: the *tenor,* or the main subject of the metaphor, and the *vehicle,* the thing that the tenor is being compared to, the object "carrying" the comparison. For example, in the metaphor "You are a shiny apple," the "you" is the tenor, and the "shiny apple" is the vehicle. "You" is being compared to the "apple."

In order to concoct a metaphor, the tenor and the vehicle must be dissimilar. A good metaphor does not compare an apple to a plum, but an apple to something wholly unlike the apple, like a person one loves. In Pound's poem "In the Station of the Metro," what is the tenor and what is the vehicle?

Simile

Simile is a metaphor that uses the words "like" or "as" between the tenor and the vehicle. Simile is not as powerful as metaphor, because the things being compared are only said to be like one another, not exactly the same, as in metaphor.

Even so, it's not practical to use straight metaphor all of the time. Instead, play around with metaphor and simile to see which one will work for a particular comparison. For example, "You are like a shiny apple" is not as powerful as "You are a shiny apple." Which would you like someone to say to you?

Here are some examples of simile:

> She walks in Beauty, like the night
>
> —George Gordon, Lord Byron

> I crawl like an ant in mourning
>
> —Sylvia Plath

> My feet are feathered like a bird
>
> —Edith Sitwell

> My heart is like a singing bird
>
> —Christina Rosetti

> The moon fell in the sky like a cultured pearl
> In a curvy bottle of Prell.
>
> —Catherine Bowman

Metonymy and Synecdoche

Metonymy is a type of metaphor that uses a closely associated object as a substitute for the original object, as in, "The White House spoke today with world leaders," meaning that the President spoke with the world leaders. (Only in poems can houses speak!)

- I'm reading Whitman. (I'm reading Whitman's poems. The actual person, Walt Whitman, is unreadable, besides being quite dead.)
- Put the Beatles in the CD player. (Put The Beatles' CD in the CD player. You can't put the actual Beatles in the CD player—that would hurt!)

Touchstones

Some objects are less susceptible to metaphor than others. The whole world is less susceptible to metaphor than a teacup is.
—Wallace Stevens

Synecdoche (*sin-EKK-toe-key*) is a type of metaphor that uses a part as a stand-in for the whole, as in "There were seven sails on the bay," meaning that there were seven ships on the bay.

- I'm going to get me some wheels and roll out of town. ("Wheels" standing in for "car.")
- Please give me a hand. (I need your help. "Hand" standing in for the whole person.)

Personification

Personification gives human (or animal) qualities to inanimate objects, and is a great way to make your metaphors fresh and new.

Here are three examples of the personification of *fog:*

The yellow fog that rubs its back upon the window-panes,
The yellow smoke that rubs its muzzle on the window-panes
Licked its tongue into the corners of the evening,
Lingered upon the pools that stand in drains,
Let fall upon its back the soot that falls from chimneys,
Slipped by the terrace, made a sudden leap,
And seeing that it was a soft October night,
Curled once about the house, and fell asleep.

—T. S. Eliot

The yellow fog came creeping down
The bridges, till the houses' walls
Seemed changed to shadows, and St. Paul's
Loomed like a bubble o'er the town.

—Oscar Wilde

The Fog

The fog comes
on little cat feet.

It sits looking
over harbor and city
on silent haunches
and then moves on.

—Carl Sandburg

What do these three examples of personification have in common?

In this poem, Emily Dickinson personifies death as a carriage driver:

[Because I could not stop for Death]

Because I could not stop for Death,
He kindly stopped for me;
The carriage held but just ourselves
And Immortality.

We slowly drove, he knew no haste,
And I had put away
My labor, and my leisure too,
For his civility.

We passed the school where children played,
Their lessons scarcely done;
We passed the fields of gazing grain,
We passed the setting sun.

We paused before a house that seemed
A swelling of the ground;
The roof was scarcely visible,
The cornice but a mound.

Since then 'tis centuries; but each
Feels shorter than the day
I first surmised the horses' heads
Were toward eternity.

Conceit

A *conceit* is a metaphor that extends throughout a portion of a poem, and in some cases, through the entire poem. Other metaphors often spring from the overriding metaphor to reinforce the initial comparison.

Here's a poem by Richard Blanco that uses the extended metaphor of shaving to write about the death of the speaker's father:

Poetically Correct

A **conceit** is a metaphor that extends throughout a large portion of a poem or throughout the entire poem.

Shaving

I'm not shaving, I'm writing about it.
and I conjure the most elaborate idea—
how my beard is a creation of silent labor
like ocean steam rising to form clouds,
or the bloom of spiderwebs each morning;
the discrete mystery of how whiskers grow,
like the drink roses take from the vase,
or the fall of fresh rain, becoming
a river, and then rain again, so silently.
I think of all these slow and silent forces
and how quietly my father's life passed us by.

I think of those mornings, when I *am* shaving
and remember him in a masquerade of foam, then,
as if it were his beard I took the blade to,
the memory of him in tiny snips of black whiskers
swirling in the drain—dead pieces of the self
from the face that never taught me how to shave.
His legacy of whiskers that grow like black seeds
Sown over my cheek and chin, my own flesh.

I am not shaving, but I will tell you about the mornings
with a full beard and the blade in my hand,
when my eyes don't recognize themselves
in a mirror echoed with a hundred faces
I have washed and shaved—it is in that split second,
when perhaps the roses drink and the clouds form,
and perhaps the spiders spin and rain transforms,
that I most understand the invisibility of life
and the intensity of vanishing, like steam
at the slick edges of the mirror, without a trace.

The overriding, or extended, metaphor in this poem is shaving/the death of the speaker's father; can you find other metaphors in this poem?

When Good Metaphors Go Bad: Mixed Metaphor

A mixed metaphor exists when one or more of the elements of a metaphor don't belong together. Writing a mixed metaphor is like hitting the wrong note in a symphony, and is as obvious to a keen reader of a poem as the wrong note is to the listener of the symphony.

- If you skate on thin ice you could end up in hot water.
- The bitter aftertaste of getting fired rang in my ears.

There's also the plain old "bad" mixed metaphor/simile combination:

> "The hammer striking the nail was a tapeworm eating Julia's intestines, repeating the blow like a kitten lazing in the sun."

This comparison simply doesn't make sense. Here are three distinct images that don't "play well" together. Can you think of better comparisons for these three images? (Note: Please avoid "kittens" in your poetry if you can; poetry editors worldwide will thank you.)

Touchstones

The cure for mixed metaphors, I have always found, is for the patient to be obliged to draw a picture of the result.

—Bernard Levin

How to Create a Metaphor

Creating a good metaphor is not as easy as you might think. If it were easy, everyone would be a poet! Start with a tenor, something you want to compare. Let's say that you want to describe "snow" in a line in your poem. What are the properties of snow? It's cold, wet, and white; it drifts, dusts, drops, sheets, sweeps, sparkles, blankets, covers, falls, freezes, avalanches, melts. That's a lot to work with. Try these:

- The snow drifts like ______________ in __________.
- White as ____________, the snow is cold as _________.
- Dropping like ____________, snow sheets the ____________ like ______________.
- The avalanche of snow sounded like ____________ when it covered the ____________ like a ______________.

Roses Are Red

When you're attempting to use an extended metaphor, look up both the vehicle and the tenor in the dictionary or encyclopedia. You might find some interesting words or phrases to keep the metaphor going. This will also help you to avoid mixing your metaphors by keeping your comparisons on the same subject matter.

- The melting snow is ____________ as a __________.
- The snow drifts like _____________ and tastes like ________ when you _________ it on your __________.

Remember: Make your metaphors original! Don't write that the snow is "as white as a dove" or "as white as the moon." Those are clichés. Realize that your reader knows that snow is white; that's a given.

Now it's your job as a poet to make the reader see "snow" differently, which you can do through metaphor.

Here, Robert Frost compares snow to a newspaper. Now that's an original comparison!

A Patch of Old Snow

There's a patch of old snow in a corner
  That I should have guessed
Was a blow-away paper the rain
  Had brought to rest.

It is speckled with grime as if
  Small print overspread it,
The news of a day I've forgotten—
  If I ever read it.

Exercises for the Metaphorically Impaired

Here are some exercises to get you started thinking about metaphor.

- The following poem contains several types of metaphor. Can you find them all? Remember, a metaphor is a comparison between two unlike things, for example, "My heart is but a mouse" or the personification of a snail "patching his house."

  The Flower of Mending

  (To Eudora, after I had had certain dire adventures.)

  When Dragon-fly would fix his wings,
  When Snail would patch his house,
  When moths have marred the overcoat
  Of tender Mister Mouse,

The pretty creatures go with haste
To the sunlit blue-grass hills
Where the Flower of Mending yields the wax
And webs to help their ills.

The hour the coats are waxed and webbed
They fall into a dream,
And when they wake the ragged robes
Are joined without a seam.

My heart is but a dragon-fly,
My heart is but a mouse,
My heart is but a haughty snail
In a little stony house.

Your hand was honey-comb to heal,
Your voice a web to bind.
You were a Mending Flower to me
To cure my heart and mind.

—Vachel Lindsay

- ➤ Write the name of an object on the top of a piece of paper—for example, "teacup." This object should be something you have around the house or can get to easily. Make the object simple. Now, write a list of metaphors about the object: "The teacup is ..." Be as wacky as you want. Write a poem using the three best metaphors in your list.
- ➤ Write several two-line poems (called a "mote"), like Pound's "In the Station of the Metro," in which the first line is the tenor and the second line is the vehicle.
- ➤ Write a poem that personifies weather: rain, snow, sleet, wind, hurricane, tornado, etc.
- ➤ Start a metaphor journal. Make it a tiny notebook that you can carry around in your pocket. Tie a pen to it so that you won't have to go searching for one when you need it. If you begin to consciously create metaphors out of much of what you see, hear, and experience, you will naturally begin to see metaphors wherever you look. I have a poet-friend who can't go two minutes without calling out a metaphor when we're together, usually when we're traveling. Later, I often see these metaphors in his poems.

The Least You Need to Know

- Metaphor is a comparison between two unlike things and is one of the fundamental parts of poetry.
- A metaphor has two parts: the tenor, or the main subject of the metaphor, and the vehicle, the thing that the tenor is being compared to, the object "carrying" the comparison.
- Personification is a kind of metaphor that gives human (or animal) qualities to inanimate objects.
- A conceit is a metaphor that extends throughout a portion of a poem, and in some cases, through an entire poem.
- A mixed metaphor happens when one or more of the elements of a metaphor don't belong together.

Chapter 7

Repetition, Repetition, Repetition

In This Chapter

- Why repetition is important
- Types of repetition and types of repetition
- Anaphora? What the heck is that?
- How *not* to repeat, and repeat
- Exercises, exercises, exercises!

Why do poets repeat themselves? Why do poets repeat themselves? Okay, I'll stop! Repetition is a commonly used element of poetry, and is one of the oldest poetic conventions. Most formal poetry involves repetition, and poetry would not be poetry without it. Poets pre-dating the Bible used repetition, and poets still use it today. Repetition is a powerful and memorable tool: Remember Martin Luther King's "I Have a Dream" speech? The rhetorical power in that speech comes from its repetitive devices; that's what makes it so memorable and so moving. Here's part of that famous speech:

> *I say to you today, my friends, that in spite of the difficulties and frustrations of the moment, I still have a dream. It is a dream deeply rooted in the American dream.*
>
> *I have a dream that one day this nation will rise up and live out the true meaning of its creed: "We hold these truths to be self-evident: that all men are created equal."*
>
> *I have a dream that one day on the red hills of Georgia the sons of former slaves and the sons of former slaveowners will be able to sit down together at a table of brotherhood.*

I have a dream that one day even the state of Mississippi, a desert state, sweltering with the heat of injustice and oppression, will be transformed into an oasis of freedom and justice.

I have a dream that my four children will one day live in a nation where they will not be judged by the color of their skin but by the content of their character.

I have a dream today.

I have a dream that one day the state of Alabama, whose governor's lips are presently dripping with the words of interposition and nullification, will be transformed into a situation where little black boys and black girls will be able to join hands with little white boys and white girls and walk together as sisters and brothers.

I have a dream today.

I have a dream that one day every valley shall be exalted, every hill and mountain shall be made low, the rough places will be made plain, and the crooked places will be made straight, and the glory of the Lord shall be revealed, and all flesh shall see it together. ...

Repetition is about returning: to a theme, a word, or a musical phrase. Repetition unifies a poem and, like this speech, sets up expectations for the reader or listener. Repetition intensifies the subject matter in a poem, and can be found in even the most free free-verse. Repetition emphasizes and points to the important elements in a poem. When an element is repeated in a poem, that's generally an element you want to pay attention to. Poets use repetition for a reason, not just for the sake of repeating themselves!

Repeating Words

Repeating single words in a poem calls attention to that word's meaning and sound, giving the word an intensity it might not have otherwise. Here's a poem whose word repetitions build upon one another like a chant, leaving the reader breathless by the last stanza.

Annabel Lee

It was many and many a year ago,
  In a kingdom by the sea,
That a maiden there lived whom you may know
  By the name of ANNABEL LEE;
And this maiden she lived with no other thought
  Than to love and be loved by me.

I was a child and she was a child,
In this kingdom by the sea;
But we loved with a love that was more than love—
I and my Annabel Lee;
With a love that the winged seraphs of heaven
Coveted her and me.

And this was the reason that, long ago,
In this kingdom by the sea,
A wind blew out of a cloud, chilling
My beautiful Annabel Lee;
So that her highborn kinsman came
And bore her away from me,
To shut her up in a sepulchre
In this kingdom by the sea.

Touchstones

Gertrude Stein, mistress of repetition, once said: "It takes a lot of time to be a genius, you have to sit around so much doing nothing, really doing nothing."

The angels, not half so happy in heaven,
Went envying her and me—
Yes!—that was the reason (as all men know,
In this kingdom by the sea)
That the wind came out of the cloud by night,
Chilling and killing my Annabel Lee.

But our love it was stronger by far than the love
Of those who were older than we—
Of many far wiser than we—
And neither the angels in heaven above,
Nor the demons down under the sea,
Can ever dissever my soul from the soul
Of the beautiful Annabel Lee.

For the moon never beams without bringing me dreams
Of the beautiful Annabel Lee;
And the stars never rise but I feel the bright eyes
Of the beautiful Annabel Lee;
And so, all the night-tide, I lie down by the side
Of my darling—my darling—my life and my bride,
In the sepulchre there by the sea,
In her tomb by the sounding sea.

—Edgar Allen Poe

Repeating Phrases and Refrains

A refrain is a repeated phrase throughout the poem, and can be one repeating line, a few lines, or whole stanzas that repeat. The poet may choose to vary the refrain so that it won't become tedious.

The Rainy Day

The day is cold, and dark, and dreary;
It rains, and the wind is never weary;
The vine still clings to the moldering wall,
But at every gust the dead leaves fall,
And the day is dark and dreary.

My life is cold, and dark, and dreary;
It rains, and the wind is never weary;
My thoughts still cling to the moldering Past,
But the hopes of youth fall thick in the blast
And the days are dark and dreary.

Be still, sad heart! and cease repining;
Behind the clouds is the sun still shining;
Thy fate is the common fate of all,
Into each life some rain must fall,
Some days must be dark and dreary.

—Henry Wadsworth Longfellow

Beginning and Ending Repetition

Beginning and ending a poem with the same line allows the poem to return fully to its origin. Even though the same line is repeated at the beginning and the end of the poem, the line may take on different properties in a different placement. In the poem "Smoke," for example, the beginning line seems matter-of-fact, while the same line on the end seems like self-accusation:

Smoke

I sit in a chair and read the newspapers.

Millions of men go to war, acres of them are buried, guns and ships broken, cities burned, villages sent up in smoke, and children where cows are killed off amid hoarse barbecues vanish like finger-rings of smoke in a north wind.

I sit in a chair and read the newspapers.

—Carl Sandburg

Anaphora

Anaphora is a fancy poetic term for when the beginning of each line in a poem repeats the same word or phrase. Read Genesis in the Bible and you'll find lots of anaphora there.

Here's a poem by Richard Blanco that deals with the subject of a Cuban refugee leaving his homeland via a homemade raft.

El Juan

Juan, meet with neighbors.
Juan, meet with strangers.
Juan, tie wire and truck tires.
Juan, take your oars and rosary.
Juan, leave the necklace of palms.
Juan, supplicant of the sea.
Juan, bastard of the sun.
Juan, of salt and blistered lip.
Juan, of bloated feet and fingers.
Juan, this is your sacrament.
Juan, fold your hands and pray:
in the name of your father, of your son,
and of your holy virgin of the sea.

Dodging Doggerel

Beware of the dangers of tedium in repetition. Repetition must be energetic and active, and should serve a purpose in the poem. Repetition for repetition's sake can be very boring!

The repetition of the refugee's name, Juan, at the beginning of each line, forces the reader to pay attention to Juan and his individual struggles. The repetition suggests obsession, and, certainly, obsession is part of Juan's journey. The variation in the end—the couplet that does not use the repetition—serves to emphasize the prayer and to break up the text visually.

Try writing three poems using the same technique—one using a friend's name, one an enemy's name, and one using the name of a famous person.

Beginners

HOW they are provided for upon the earth, (appearing
 at intervals;)
How dear and dreadful they are to the earth;
How they inure to themselves as much as to any—What a paradox
 appears their age;
How people respond to them, yet know them not;

How there is something relentless in their fate, all times;
How all times mischoose the objects of their adulation and reward,
And how the same inexorable price must still be paid for the same
great purchase.

—Walt Whitman

Image and Symbol Repetition

Poets often repeat images or symbols in their poems, which allows the images and symbols to accumulate intensity and take on deeper and larger meanings. Imagistic and symbolic repetition also lends unity to the poem.

Here's a Pill

The night is a knife standing on end—
there's a bird outside
in the darkness, singing, alone—
if you don't like yourself, here's a pill.
It's yellow, like the flowers
planted outside a home
you might want to sell.
There may be something left of your heart,
that crazy midnight bird
plotting against its cage—
the night will be still, the trees will hang
like treasonous soldiers.
You can preserve the knife and let the bird
exhaust the tree
outside your window at 3 A.M., the astonished
night like a dark pill in your empty gullet,
or you can let your shrunken body
free in the song, though half an inch
from your skin, on the inside,
your real self waits to be born.

*

There's a bird outside in the darkness singing alone
beside your yellow flowers
and nobody came to buy the house today.
The pill you want
to sell hangs in the bird's gullet like 3 A.M.—

if your heart is a knife, then the song is a shrunken
body towing you through the night
like that crazy bird carrying your sleep
in its hard-cleft mouth—
nothing will be left
of the house, the cage conspiring
against its bird, though half an inch
from the house another bird waits to be born.
If the flowers won't hawk the house, here's a pill.
Wooden, like a door, still and open
You can enter the house
and shut out the bird,
or exit and loose the bird free in the night,
though the new owners will want to know what self
whimpers there like something awaiting execution.

*

Outside the name
you want to sell, flowers perch like yellow gizzards.
The yellow pill sings in the night, alone
as the darkening house
you call your body at 3 A.M.
when the bird's mouth is a difficult shell
and the house your only
sharpened tool.
If you can't find the bird, here's a pill—
a knife standing on end in the only house you recognize—
the new owners will want to know
why the pill sings and the bird doesn't, or
they will want
to keep the bird inside the pill
though you think the pill has shrunken the bird
inside your gullet
where it contrives to keep sleep
at the knife's edge,
the flowers in a porcelain bowl,
and your name like the night ebbing into the bird's
beak, waiting for the pill to sustain it.

—Nikki Moustaki

See Wallace Stevens's poem, "Thirteen Ways of Looking at a Blackbird" for image and symbol repetition.

Syntactical Repetition

Syntactical repetition is when a poet repeats a certain sentence structure to emphasize a certain part of speech, which in turn may emphasize the poet's intention in the poem. In Martin Luther King's famous "I Have a Dream" speech, Dr. King uses the phrase "I have a dream" before each of his proposals. The listener comes to expect, even wait anxiously for, the words that come after the phrase "I have a dream."

Touchstones

Poetry is an extravagance you hope to get away with.

—Robert Frost

Poetically Correct

Syntax is the arrangement of and relationships among words, phrases, and clauses forming sentences. **Syntactical repetition** is when a poet repeats a specific arrangement of parts of speech.

The poem "The Road to Acuna" uses syntactical repetition to unify and create movement in the poem. Read this poem aloud:

The Road to Acuna

The night we drive in is a snake.
The snake at the edge of the schoolyard.
The ditch encircled by children.
The legend dug deep to the devil.
The place we discuss our childhood.
The place where we hum in the desert.
The ice melts away in the bucket.
The white lace of the hotel bed.
The smile that covers two lovers.
The lovers on their way to the Acuña.
The glare on the rabbits, the rocks.
The headlights that blaze on the roadside.
The signs that all point to Acuña.
The panting road to Acuña.
The pot-bellied road to the border.
The spiraling storm to the city.

—Catherine Bowman

What is the subject matter of this poem? How does the syntactical repetition work with the content? This poem also has the added repetition of having three beats per line—we'll learn more about counting beats and meter in Chapter 9, "You've Got Rhythm: Metrical Poetry."

Metrical Repetition

Metrical repetition is one of the oldest types of repetition in poetry. We'll look more closely at meter later, but for now, read this poem out loud and try to hear the cadences, the music. Listen for each line's measurement. Note that this poem also uses repetition in rhyme, words, and phrases as well:

Spring and Fall

MÀRGARÉT, àre you gríeving
Over Goldengrove unleaving?
Leàves, líke the things of man, you
With your fresh thoughts care for, can you?
Àh! às the heart grows older
It will come to such sights colder
By and by, nor spare a sigh
Though worlds of wanwood leafmeal lie;
And yet you wíll weep and know why.
Now no matter, child, the name:
Sórrow's spríngs àre the same.
Nor mouth had, no nor mind, expressed
What heart heard of, ghost guessed:
It ís the blight man was born for,
It is Margaret you mourn for.

—Gerard Manley Hopkins

Roses Are Red

You can blend many different types of repetition together to create wonderful textures in your poems. For example, you can write a poem in meter where you use rhyme and alliteration (repetition of sounds), syntactical repetition, image repetition, refrains, and word repetition. Since each of these types of repetition are different, or at least will seem different to your reader, you can "get away with" overloading your poem with repetition. This is a fun challenge to give yourself: Try to write a poem using as many different types of repetition as you can without the poem becoming overly repetitive. Can it be done?

Sonic Repetition

Sonic repetition is the repetition of sounds in a poem. Poet Gerard Manley Hopkins is the master of sonic repetition. Read this poem aloud and you'll hear the repetitive sonic quality of this poem. Can you name the poetic devices Hopkins uses to create these repetitions?

Strike, churl; hurl, cheerless wind, then; heltering hail

Strike, churl; hurl, cheerless wind, then; heltering hail
May's beauty massacre and wispèd wild clouds
Out on the giant air; tell Summer No,
Bid joy back, have at the harvest, keep Hope pale.

—Gerard Manley Hopkins

Exercises

Here are some exercises to get you repeating yourself!

- Write a poem using four-line stanzas in which you repeat the same line in each stanza. It doesn't matter where the line occurs in the stanza. Try for 5 to 10 stanzas or more.
- Write a poem about an incident in your childhood that seems particularly obsessive to you. Find a word associated with that memory and use it to begin or end almost every line.
- Read "Thirteen Ways of Looking at a Blackbird" by Wallace Stevens and write your own 13-part poem using one repeating image or symbol.
- Write a string of end-stopped lines in which you use the same syntax, for example, a list of questions or a list of commands.

The Least You Need to Know

- Repetition is a commonly used element of poetry, and is one of the oldest poetic conventions.
- Repetition lends intensity and emphasis to a poem.
- Repetition unifies a poem and sets up expectations for the reader.
- Repetition comes in many forms: word, line, phrase, refrain, metrical, syntactical, imagistic, symbolic, and sonic.
- Beware of becoming tedious in your repetition. Be sure you are repeating something for a reason.

Chapter 8

The Sound of Music

In This Chapter

- How sound works in poetry
- Rhyme and reason
- Alliteration, assonance, and consonance
- Onomatopoeia
- Understanding tone and diction

Sipsop's Song

Hang your serious songs, said Sipsop & he sung as follows

Fa ra so bo ro
    Fa ra bo ra
Sa ba ra ra ba rare roro
Sa ra ra ra bo ro ro or
Radara
Sarapodo no flo ro

—William Blake

Poetry was once a musical art, accompanied by a lyre or other instrument (most recently bongos, but let's try to forget that era, shall we?). Because of its musical roots, poetry still has musical elements. These elements make up the way a poem sounds. That's what we'll talk about in this chapter.

The Music of Poetry

Poets often say that a person's breath is the instrument though which a poem is played. For this reason, a poet may choose certain words that "play" off one another in a particular way to lend a certain "sonic" quality to the poem. A poet, by making very specific word choices, can determine how his or her poem is read aloud by another person. Musical elements also help to unify a poem, to give the reader expectations and a way to read and understand the poem better.

Most poets concern themselves with sound to some degree. Using musical elements is part of a poetic tradition that has been around since poetry began. Musical elements help to make the poem more memorable, something that the earliest of poets knew was important for the life of their poems. Since poems were traditionally spoken, a poem had to "stick" in the mind or be lost forever.

Touchstones

Don't imagine that the art of poetry is any simpler than the art of music, or that you can please the expert before you have spent at least as much effort on the art of verse as the average piano teacher spends on the art of music.

—Ezra Pound

Can you think of any poems from which you remember at least a few lines? Why do you remember those lines and not others? How about nursery rhymes? Can you remember any of those? When you're in the car listening to the radio, how many of the songs can you sing along with? Probably a lot of them. Have you ever wondered why we have the capacity to remember thousands of song lyrics but we can't remember what we had for breakfast? We remember lyrics and poetry because our brains are programmed to respond to rhythms and regularity. The gift of being remembered is what musical elements offer to a poem.

Musical elements often mirror their subject matter. A serious poem may have a very different type of sound than, say, a light nursery rhyme. Even if you had no recognizable words, you'd be able to tell, just from the music of the lines, whether the subject matter of the poem was light or serious.

Poets take musical elements into consideration when they're writing poems. Indeed, subject matter and sound should coincide. Imagine writing a poem about the death of a loved one in a silly, sing-songy tone. That would be a little ridiculous, not to mention disrespectful!

Read the following poem aloud:

Jabberwocky

'Twas brillig, and the slithy toves
Did gyre and gimble in the wabe:
All mimsy were the borogoves,
And the mome raths outgrabe.

"Beware the Jabberwock, my son!
The jaws that bite, the claws that catch!
Beware the Jubjub bird, and shun
The frumious Bandersnatch!"

He took his vorpal sword in hand:
Long time the manxome foe he sought —
So rested he by the Tumtum tree,
And stood awhile in thought.

And, as in uffish thought he stood,
The Jabberwock, with eyes of flame,
Came whiffling through the tulgey wood,
And burbled as it came!

One two! One two! And through and through
The vorpal blade went snicker-snack!
He left it dead, and with its head
He went galumphing back.

"And hast thou slain the Jabberwock?
Come to my arms, my beamish boy!
Oh frabjous day! Callooh! Callay!"
He chortled in his joy.

'Twas brillig, and the slithy toves
Did gyre and gimble in the wabe:
All mimsy were the borogoves,
And the mome raths outgrabe.

The poet, Lewis Carroll, makes up his own words for this poem. Nevertheless, we understand what these words mean. How is that so? Through the word's sound. What if the sword was "mimsy" instead of "vorpal," or the "manxome foe" was the "frabjous foe"? Would that change the meaning of the poem? Why? Remember, words often carry meaning in their sound. Think of emotion words: angry, happy, sorrowful, frustrated, etc. Don't the sounds of these words match their meanings?

Rhyme

Rhyme is an important musical element often misused by beginning poets. Because rhyme is so entrenched in our idea of what poetry should be, beginning poets often force rhyme into their poems with disastrous effects.

Forced rhyme often distorts regular, natural syntax and takes the poem off in directions it shouldn't go, all in search of the perfect rhyming word. So, I'll dispel the myth for you. You heard it here: Poems don't have to rhyme.

That being said, you might want to try to rhyme anyway. You might be good at it and your work may benefit from the musical qualities that rhyme can lend to your poems. Certain fixed forms even require rhyme. If you're going to rhyme, simply learn to do it well. You'll find some tips on how to rhyme well in a moment—keep reading.

Straight Rhyme

No, straight rhyme isn't rhyme looking for a date of the opposite sex. Straight rhymes are words that rhyme exactly.

Good Hours

I had for my winter evening walk—
No one at all with whom to talk,
But I had the cottages in a row
Up to their shining eyes in snow.
And I thought I had the folk within:
I had the sound of a violin;
I had a glimpse through curtain laces
Of youthful forms and youthful faces.
I had such company outward bound.
I went till there were no cottages found.
I turned and repented, but coming back
I saw no window but that was black.
Over the snow my creaking feet
Disturbed the slumbering village street
Like profanation, by your leave,
At ten o'clock of a winter eve.

—Robert Frost

Straight rhyme can often lead to the deadly moon/June type rhyme. If you're going to use straight rhyme, try to avoid overused rhymes: rose/knows, knees/bees, love/dove. Straight rhyme should be as original and unobtrusive as possible. Rhyme should not stand out more than the content of your poem.

Slant Rhyme

Slant rhyme occurs when two words sound alike, but don't rhyme exactly.

I reason, earth is short,
And anguish absolute,
And many hurt;
But what of that?

I reason, we could die:
The best vitality
Cannot excel decay;
But what of that?

I reason that in heaven
Somehow, it will be even,
Some new equation given;
But what of that?

—Emily Dickinson

Can you hear the slant rhymes in short/hurt/that and heaven/even/given? Slant rhyme is considered more sophisticated than straight rhyme; it's less obtrusive and lends a nice musical texture to a poem without being in the way of the poem's meaning.

You can get very silly with slant rhyme if you want—here's a fun example:

Impromptu

If I were a cassowary
  On the plains of Timbuctoo
I would eat a missionary,
  Cassock, bands and hymn-book too.

—Samuel Wilberforce

Dodging Doggerel

You never want any element of your poem to stand out so much that it becomes more important than what you are trying to convey—unless, of course, you are writing a poem whose *point* is to be musical. In that case, go ahead!

Internal Rhyme

Internal rhyme happens when the poet places rhyming words inside the poem, rather than at the end of the line. Internal rhymes intensify the sound of the poem and can deepen its meaning as well. Here's an example from a part of a sonnet by Shakespeare:

From fairest creatures we desire increase,
That thereby beauty's rose might never die,
But as the riper should by time decease,
His tender heir might bear his memory:
But thou contracted to thine own bright eyes,
Feed'st thy light's flame with self-substantial fuel …

Linked rhymes occur when the last word or syllable in a line rhymes with the first word or syllable in the next line.

The Bereaved Swan

Wan
Swan
On the lake
Like a cake
Of soap
Why is the swan
Wan
On the lake?
He has abandoned hope.
    Wan
    Swan
    On the lake afloat
    Bows his head:
    O would that I were dead
    For her sake that lies
    Wrapped from my eyes
    In a mantle of death,
    The swan saith.

—Stevie Smith

Identical Rhyme

With identical rhyme, a poet uses the exact same word as a rhyme of itself. This is really a form of repetition, but you can see here how Edgar Allen Poe uses identical rhyme and straight rhyme together to create emphasis in this stanza:

For the moon never beams without bringing me dreams
Of the beautiful Annabel Lee;
And the stars never rise but I feel the bright eyes
Of the beautiful Annabel Lee;
And so, all the night-tide, I lie down by the side
Of my darling— my darling— my life and my bride,
In the sepulchre there by the sea,
In her tomb by the sounding sea.

Touchstones

Do I deliberately utilize devices of rhyme, rhythm, and word-formation in my writing— I must, of course, answer with an immediate Yes. I am a painstaking, conscientious, involved, and devious craftsman in words, however unsuccessful the result so often appears, and to whatever wrong uses I may apply my technical paraphernalia. ... Poets have got to enjoy themselves sometimes, and the twisting and convolutions of words, the inventions and contrivances, are all part of the joy that is part of the painful, voluntary work.

—Dylan Thomas

Here's a silly one by the most famous poet of them all, Anonymous, that uses identical rhyme and internal rhyme:

I saw Esau sawing wood,
And Esau saw I saw him;
Though Esau saw I saw him saw,
Still Esau went on sawing.

Other Types of Rhyme

There are several other types of rhyme to choose from—here are a few:

- **Eye rhymes** are words that look like they should be straight rhymes but are really pronounced quite differently: mood/wood, laughter/slaughter, prove/love, over/hover.

- **Homonyms** are the opposite of eye rhymes. Homonyms look dissimilar but sound exactly the same: pear/pare, through/threw, meet/meat, grate/great.
- **Rising rhyme** is when the rhyming word has only one syllable or, in the case of words with more than one syllable, the rhyme ends with the accented last syllable, as in knows/rose (one syllable per word) or refer/defer (stress on the last syllable).
- **Falling rhyme** is when a rhyme ends with an unaccented final syllable, as in under/thunder and writing/fighting.
- **Apocopated rhyme** (*a-POCK-oh-pated*) is when only the first syllable of a word is used in creating the rhyme, as in meeting/feet, meaner/clean, rotten/got.

Rhyme Scheme

The rhyme scheme is the general pattern that the rhymes follow in a poem. For example, a poem might rhyme abba baab, cddc, dccd, meaning that "a" rhymes with "a," and "b" rhymes with "b," and so on. You have no limit to the patterns you can create!

- **Rhyming couplet.** Two lines with end rhymes; this often occurs at the end of a poem, such as a sonnet.
- **Terza rima.** A complicated rhyme scheme invented by Dante Alegheri for *The Divine Comedy;* this rhyme scheme resembles a braid: aba bcb cdc ded efe and so on.
- **Rhyme royal.** A seven-line stanza rhyming ababbcc; it is called "rhyme royal" because King James I used it, though Chaucer is the first to claim invention of this rhyme scheme.

Alliteration, Assonance, and Consonance

Alliteration is the repetition of initial consonant sounds (*b*rown *b*ears *b*eat *b*oats) and consonance is the repetition of consonant sounds within words (be*tt*er le*tt*ers li*tt*er ligh*t*er). Assonance is the repetition of similar vowel sounds in successive or proximate words: "High in the sky shines a field as wide as the world" (Vachel Lindsay).

Here's a fun poem that uses a lot of alliteration:

One Old Ox

One old Oxford ox opening oysters;
Two tee-totums totally tired of trying to trot to Tadbury;
Three tall tigers tippling tenpenny tea;
Four fat friars fanning fainting flies;
Five frippy Frenchmen foolishly fishing for flies;
Six sportsmen shooting snipes;
Seven Severn salmons swallowing shrimps;
Eight Englishmen eagerly examining Europe;
Nine nimble noblemen nibbling nonparels;
Ten tinkers tinkling upon ten tin tinder-boxes with
 ten tenpenny tacks;
Eleven elephants elegantly equipt;
Twelve typographical topographers typically translating
 types.

—Anonymous

Read the following poem and see if you can find examples of these three musical elements:

Pied Beauty

Glory be to God for dappled things—
 For skies of couple-colour as a brinded cow;
 For rose-moles all in stipple upon trout that swim;

Fresh-firecoal chestnut-falls; finches' wings;
 Landscape plotted and pieced—fold, fallow, and plough;
 And áll trádes, their gear and tackle and trim.

All things counter, original, spare, strange;
 Whatever is fickle, freckled (who knows how?)
 With swift, slow; sweet, sour; adazzle, dim;
He fathers-forth whose beauty is past change:
 Praise him.

—Gerard Manley Hopkins

Hopkins was a little "musically happy" but he wrote well musically; as for your own poems, use these elements sparingly—alliteration is like garlic—a little goes a long way!

Touchstones

Apt alliteration's artful aid.
—Charles Churchill

Onomatopoeia

Onomatopoetic words sound similar to their meaning, such as plop, hiss, fizz, skid, buzz, whirr, sizzle, bang, roar, and squeak, to name just a few.

Here's a particularly onomatopoetic stanza from Poe's poem, "The Bells." Read this section out loud:

> Hear the sledges with the bells—
> Silver bells!
> What a world of merriment their melody foretells!
> How they tinkle, tinkle, tinkle,
> In the icy air of night!
> While the stars that oversprinkle
> All the heavens, seem to twinkle
> With a crystalline delight;
> Keeping time, time, time,
> In a sort of Runic rhyme,
> To the tintinnabulation that so musically wells
> From the bells, bells, bells, bells,
> Bells, bells, bells—
> From the jingling and the tinkling of the bells.

Can you hear Poe's bells in this stanza? I can!

Touchstones

Granted no one but a humanist much cares how sound a poem is if it is only a sound. The sound is the gold in the ore. Then we will have the sound out alone and dispense with the inessential. We do till we make the discovery that the object in writing poetry is to make all poems sound as different as possible from each other, and the resources for that of vowels, consonants, punctuation, syntax, words, sentences, meter are not enough. We need the help of context-meaning-subject matter. That is the greatest help towards variety. All that can be done with words is soon told. So also with meters—particularly in our language where there are virtually but two, strict iambic and loose iambic. ... The possibilities for tune from the dramatic tones of meaning struck across the rigidity of a limited meter are endless.

—Robert Frost

Euphony and Cacophony

Euphony is when a group of words, or a poem, has a smooth, pleasing sound, and *cacophony* is when a group of words or a poem has a harsh, grating sound.

Compare this euphonic line from Tennyson: "The murmuring of innumerable bees," and this line from Poe: "And the silken sad uncertain rustling of each purple curtain," to the cacophonous line by Hopkins: "The blood-gush blade-gash." It's difficult even to say Hopkins's line aloud.

Poets tend to make their sounds match their subject matter. If your subject matter were about something harsh and difficult, you may want your words to clang against one another. If you're writing a love poem, you may want your words to flow, depending on what kind of love poem you're writing!

Poetically Correct

A **euphony** is a pleasant combination of agreeable sounds in words. A **cacophony** is a combination of words used to create a harsh, dissonant sound.

Tone, Voice, and Diction

Tone is most easily understood when compared to the term "tone of voice." When someone wins a million dollars, they might say "Wonderful!" and so might someone who has just dropped a glass full of red wine on their white carpeting. The word "wonderful" would sound different depending on which of these two people uttered it, wouldn't it? Tone helps the reader understand the emotion of the poem and helps to set a mood in the poem.

The voice in a poem is similar to the way you hear a person speak; it's kind of like the poem's accent. For example, if you were to write a poem in the voice of a coal miner, the poem would have a different voice than if you were to write it in the voice of a three-year-old child. Voice is different from tone in that tone indicates feeling or intensity; both the coal miner and the three-year-old child can speak in a poem (voice) but the reader will discover how either speaker is feeling through the tone of voice.

Read the following poems out loud. Do you hear a voice in them? Do they sound different when you read them? What's the tone?

How Doth the Little Crocodile ...

How doth the little crocodile
Improve his shining tail,
And pour the waters of the Nile
On every golden scale!

How cheerfully he seems to grin
How neatly spreads his claws,
And welcomes little fishes in,
With gently smiling jaws!

—Lewis Carroll

The Fish

Although you hide in the ebb and flow
Of the pale tide when the moon has set,
The people of coming days will know
About the casting out of my net,
And how you have leaped times out of mind
Over the little silver cords,
And think that you were hard and unkind,
And blame you with many bitter words.

—W. B. Yeats

Both poems have eight lines, both use animals in their subject matter, and both rhyme abab cdcd. Why do they sound so different, have a different tone? Carroll uses a much more regular rhythm than Yeats does here, he uses parts of speech that Yeats doesn't (adverbs), and he drops words to force the rhythm, giving the poem a sing-songy quality. All of these things affect tone and voice.

The "poetic voice" is something that many beginning poets worry needlessly about. Your poetic voice is made up of all the choices you make, on a continuous basis, for your poems. Once you "develop" your voice, readers should be able to tell that you were the poet responsible for a particular poem, just like we are able to tell a Monet painting from a Picasso. Unfortunately, there's no way to develop your voice beyond simply practicing and experimenting. Don't worry about voice for now. Just write—your "voice" will show up eventually.

Diction is how all of the words in a poem sound once they are placed against one another. Poets choose words that compliment or argue with each other; every word is meaningful, and how words sound together in a poem is as meaningful as their definitions. If you read many poems by a single poet, you will begin to hear the particular diction belonging to that poet. Diction is like a fingerprint that a poet leaves on the poem. A poet may choose to use a "high" diction for a poem of a certain subject matter, using more formal or elevated words, while another poem will require a more "plain" diction. For example, the preceding poems, "How Doth the Little Crocodile" and "The Fish" sound differently because of the poets' word choice—diction. The words in "The Fish" are more complex than the words in "Crocodile," and the idea is more complex as well, whereas both the idea and the word choice in "Crocodile" are simpler.

Meter

Meter is one of the most commonly used musical elements in poetry and involves the placing of words together in such a way as to create certain rhythms out of their stresses. Why are words stressed? you might ask. They are concerned with complexities of modern life, as we all are. You'll discover more than you ever wanted to know about meter in Chapter 9, "You've Got Rhythm: Metrical Poetry."

Exercises

Try these exercises to get your words singing.

- Lewis Carroll's famous poem, "Jabberwocky," uses a lot of musical elements. Carroll even makes up his own nonsense words to add to the musicality of the poem. Try to pick out all of the musical elements discussed in this chapter. Next, make up 10 fun, musical words, and use them in a poem.
- Here's a fun poem by Vachel Lindsay that uses a lot of musical elements: repetition, several types of rhyme, consonance, and onomatopoeia. Read it and then write your own poem about two animal species communicating, and use these same types of musical elements. What would your poetic animals say to one another?

Two Old Crows

Two old crows sat on a fence rail,
Two old crows sat on a fence rail,
Thinking of effect and cause,
Of weeds and flowers,
And nature's laws.
One of them muttered, one of them stuttered,
One of them stuttered, one of them muttered.
Each of them thought far more than he uttered.
One crow asked the other crow a riddle.
One crow asked the other crow a riddle:
The muttering crow
Asked the stuttering crow,
"Why does a bee have a sword to his fiddle?
Why does a bee have a sword to his fiddle?"
"Bee-cause," said the other crow,
"Bee-cause,
B B B B B B B B B B B B B B B B-cause."

Just then a bee flew close to their rail: —
"Buzzzzzzzzzzzzzzzzzzz zzzzzzzzz zzzzzzzzzzzzzzzz ZZZZZZZZ."
And those two black crows
Turned pale,
And away those crows did sail.
Why?
B B B B B B B B B B B B B B B B-cause.
B B B B B B B B B B B B B B B B-cause.
"Buzzzzzzzzzzzzzzzzz zzzzzzzzzz zzzzzzzzzzzzzzz ZZZZZZZ."

- ➤ Write a poem of at least 10 stanzas using the rhyme scheme terza rima.
- ➤ Write a poem in rhyme royal using only slant rhyme.

The Least You Need to Know

- ➤ Musical elements in a poem can mirror the poem's content.
- ➤ Use musical elements sparingly or else risk "overwriting."
- ➤ Using euphony or cacophony will help to enforce your poem's meaning.
- ➤ A little alliteration, assonance, and consonance go a long way!
- ➤ Don't worry right now about your "poetic voice." Just keep on writing and it will emerge naturally through practice.

Chapter 9

You've Got Rhythm: Metrical Poetry

In This Chapter

- Why poets use meter
- The short-course in scansion
- Blank verse
- Accentual meter
- Syllabics

When beginning poets first encounter the idea of writing in meter, they often feel daunted and overwhelmed, or they discount the practice at first mention. I'm here to tell you that writing in meter is not only challenging, it's also fun. It will help you to pay close attention to your word choices and your lines, and even help you to become a better reader of poems. When you can begin noticing how other poets put together their own poems, you'll start to let those poems inform your own work. Don't let meter daunt you. It's a big part of using language carefully—like a poet!

You probably already know what meter is—most nursery rhymes use meter, as do many songs. Meter is a great mnemonic device, allowing you to remember something more easily. Do you remember the words to any poems by Mother Goose? I'd bet you do—and those are poems you probably first heard long ago, in childhood; yet they still remain with you. Many fixed forms you may want to try are traditionally written in meter as well, including the sonnet. Meter has a very long history and contains a lot of details—far more than will fit into any one chapter. This chapter gives you the short-course in meter and will show you how using it can help your work.

Why Poets Use Meter

People have a natural tendency to try to order the universe. Take a look at a farmer's fields; plants in nature do not grow in neat, furrowed lines. Metrical poetry is like that field, and meter is the plow that neatens and orders the earth. Sure, the farmer could just toss seeds on the field and hope they grow, but that would make reaping the crop messy and difficult. Meter orders. We, as humans, like order.

Natural rhythms occur around us all the time: our heartbeat, the rising and setting of the sun and the moon (or, more accurately, the rotating of the earth), the changing of the seasons, and so on. We're used to such things, so much so that we don't really even notice them anymore.

Dodging Doggerel

Don't skip meter because it seems difficult or complicated. The act of writing in meter isn't nearly as difficult as remembering all the jargon that goes with it! Give meter a try—you might really like it! You certainly don't have to use meter, but it's a fun convention to try. When you use meter, you're participating in a tradition that goes back many hundreds of years.

Try to remember back to the last time you noticed your heartbeat; perhaps you were frightened for a moment, or you were working a little too hard shoveling snow. What did noticing your thumping heart feel like, emotionally? Did it prompt you to pay attention, even if for just a moment? Using meter in a poem is a little like forcing the reader to notice his or her own heartbeat; it brings a heightened awareness to the reader, who must be attentive to how the poem is meant to be read in order to understand it.

How can meter lend understanding to a poem? The poet working in meter knows how a poem sounds and where the emphasis is. For example, a variation in meter will stick out in a poem that doesn't have a lot of metrical variation. It's a place of emphasis that may mirror the subject matter. The poet knows that the reader will notice the variation (it's hard to miss it, especially in a very regularly metered poem), and can force a reader's eye and ear to that place. Meter can be used to manipulate a reader (in a good way, of course) to see what the poet wants the reader to see. It's a powerful tool.

What Is Meter?

Meter is an ordering and unifying element in poetry that mimics and heightens the rhythms of our speech and the rhythms of the natural world around us. Certainly, you can use other ways to organize poems: repetition, stanza forms, other musical elements, and syntactical structure. However, meter is closer to us as human beings; it's available inside our language, inside the words we use to create poems, and is one of the most fundamental tools poets have to "make sense" of their verse.

Sound complicated? It isn't. Meter, put very simply, is a musical element that involves the stresses of words and the placement of those words next to one another to create a metrical pattern. You will hear the word "stress" referred to as beat or accent as well; these are interchangeable terms. You probably speak in regular meter all the time and don't even know it. Even if you write in the most free free-verse, your poems will probably have some metrical moments.

Words, when put together with other words, take on a certain sound. Say this word aloud: *the*. The word "the" has weight of its own. Now say: *the camel*. Which word is weightier? Did you say: the "CAMel" or "THE camel"? The word "camel" has a stress on the first syllable: CAMel. We don't say "camEL," do we? When the word "the" is placed in front of the word "camel," it loses some of its weight. It takes a back seat to the stressed syllable in "CAMel." Words with two or more syllables will naturally have a stress in a set place, like CAMel does. If you've understood how this example works, you're beginning to understand meter.

Let's take a look at some words that have built-in stresses according to their syllables and how we say them:

PARakeet	NONsense	CANdle	disCREtion
INcome	PORtrait	POem	creAtive

Do you agree with the stresses in these words (the letters in capitals)? Or do you say "poEM" and "canDLE." I didn't think so. There's generally an accepted way to place the stresses in words. However, when we place words in context, their traditional stresses can potentially lose their weight to a stronger stress, just as "the" lost its weight to "camel," above.

So, we see that words themselves have certain stresses, but how do these stresses affect one another when they're put together? Read these lines aloud:

> I do not eat green eggs and ham
> I do not eat them Sam-I-Am.

How do *you* read these lines? I read them like this:

> i DO not EAT green EGGS and HAM
> i DO not EAT them SAM-i-AM.

Touchstones

A beautiful line of verse has twelve feet and two wings.

—Jules Renard

Why not: "I do NOT eat GREEN eggs AND ham?" Stressing it this way makes the sentence mean something else entirely—potentially that the "I" only eats the eggs (not green ones) without the ham. We know from the story (assuming you know Dr. Seuss's *Green Eggs and Ham*) that the character saying these lines will NOT eat those green eggs and ham (not even in a boat or with a goat). We also know that the entire book is written in a particular rhythm that tells us how to read the story and where to place the stresses. Reading the stresses in a different place changes the story. It works the same for poetry. Meter and meaning are often inseparable.

The Short Course in Counting: Scansion

The method that poets use to measure metrical patterns is called scansion. Scansion helps us to identify certain elements of meter and the places of emphasis in a poem. This is the part of learning to write in meter that's filled with lots of poetic jargon—don't worry so much about memorizing all of these terms as getting the basic idea down so that you can apply it to your poems.

We measure meter in what we call "feet." Yes, that's actual poetry terminology. A metrical foot is a unit of measure that measures the stresses in a line of poetry. Here are the names and measurements of the most common feet (the U represents an unstressed syllable and the / represents a stressed syllable):

Iamb: U /	as AN | unPER | fect ACT | or ON | the STAGE
Trochee: / U	AFter | SOLid | SINKing
Anapest: U U /	and the SONG, | interLUDE
Dactyl: / U U	JACqueline | KENnedy
Spondee: / /	NOTEBOOK | RIFRAF | BOXCAR
Pyrrhic: U U	when THE | inter | TWINED ROPE (Here, "inter" is the Pyrrhic foot)

Please note that the above could be scanned a number of ways; scansion is not an exact science. When these feet are placed together in lines, they create another kind of measurement, one in which the line itself is measured by the number of feet it contains. Lines of meter are measured as follows (these are the most common line measurements):

- Monometer: 1 foot
- Dimeter: 2 feet
- Trimeter: 3 feet
- Tetrameter: 4 feet
- Pentameter: 5 feet
- Hexameter: 6 feet
- Heptameter: 7 feet
- Octameter: 8 feet
- Nonameter: 9 feet

When we "scan" a poem using this method, we're counting the types and number of feet in the individual lines of a poem. Here's what a scanned line looks like:

U / U / U / U /
Whose woods | these are | I think | I know

You can see that this line is "iambic," meaning that all of the feet in the line are iambs. Further, we see that it has four feet in the line, so this line is called "iambic tetrameter." There! You've just learned how to scan a line of poetry! This line should remind you of our earlier line:

U / U / U / U /
I do | not eat | green eggs | and ham.

Part of scanning a poem for its metrical elements is being able to hear where the stresses are. You should read a poem aloud to tune your ear to the patterns a poet creates with meter. This is a good way to begin to write your own poems in meter.

Again, scansion is not an exact science. Each individual will hear a poem a little bit differently. We all bring our own ear to a poem. Where a person is from can have a great impact on how they scan a line—regional dialect can change the scansion of a line significantly. Take, for example, the city *New Orleans*. I'd scan it *NEW orLEANS;* someone else might scan it *new ORleans,* while a third person might scan it *new orLEans*.

You may occasionally see other less-used poetic feet. They include these:

Tribrach: U U U

Cretic: / U /

Bacchius: U / /

Ionic a minore: U U / /

Epitrite: U / / /

Mollossos: / / /

Amphibrach: U / U

Antibacchius: / / U

Ionic a majore: / / U U

Choriamb: / U U /

Here's a poem in a fun form called the "double-dactyl"—it will help you to develop an ear for this foot (pardon the mixed metaphor, please). Can you see (or hear) why it's called "double-dactyl"? Scan this poem:

Bouncity-Flouncity
Pamela Anderson
Flirting, with silicon
Under her top.

Diving for volleyballs
Hyper-frenetically.
Flashing a breast to a
Day-player cop.

—M. M. De Voe

Metrical Variation

Most poets know that varying the primary strategy of a poem—such as tweaking a fixed form or mixing straight and slant rhyme—can lead to new and interesting poetic moments, and helps keep the reader's attention. This variation in regular meter is sometimes called *counterpoint*.

Read these lines aloud and hear how the strict meter of these lines makes it singsongy as well as forces the poet to distort syntax. I've placed the stresses in capital letters for you:

> the WELL was DRY beSIDE the DOOR,
> and SO we WENT with PAIL and CAN
> aCROSS the FIELDS beHIND the HOUSE
> to SEEK the BROOK if STILL it RAN;

Here's a sonnet by Elizabeth Barrett Browning that uses a lot of metrical variation in this primarily iambic pentameter poem. The stresses here are mine. You may disagree with me, but this is how I hear the poem:

> YES, CALL me BY my PET-name! LET me HEAR
> the NAME i USED to RUN at, WHEN a CHILD,
> from INnocent PLAY, and LEAVE the COWslips PLIED,
> To GLANCE UP in some FACE that PROVED me DEAR
> with the LOOK of its EYES. i MISS the CLEAR
> FOND VOIces WHICH, BEing DRAWN and REconciled
> inTO the MUsic of HEAven's undeFILED,
> CALL ME no LONGer. SIlence on the BIER,
> while I call GOD—CALL GOD!—so LET thy MOUTH
> be HEIR to THOSE who are NOW exANImate.
> GAther the NORTH FLOWers to comPLETE the SOUTH,
> and CATCH the EARLy LOVE up IN the LATE.
> YES, CALL me BY that NAME,—and I, in TRUTH,
> with the SAME HEART, will ANswer and not WAIT.

By beginning with an emphatic foot, the spondee (//), the poet tells the reader how to hear that imperative "Yes" in the beginning of the poem. Look for yourself at the variations in this sonnet and see how they affect the poem.

Dodging Doggerel

Try not to stick to a metrical pattern that employs no variation; you risk boring your reader, or, in some cases, you make your poem sound silly. Toss some variation into your meter. If your poem is largely iambic, throw some trochees in with the iambs. However, be careful of *too* much variation—wild and wacky feet can result in a poem that doesn't resemble a metrical poem at all, which is fine, but not if your intention is to write in meter.

Blank Verse

Iambic pentameter (five feet, all iambs: U /) is the most-used metrical pattern in poetry written in English. Many forms, such as the sonnet, use iambic pentameter as a springboard. Blank verse is not secret poetry code; it's simply unrhymed iambic pentameter. Many poets used (and still use) blank verse, including Shakespeare. Try scanning his plays and you'll find that they are in iambic pentameter (though he often has some rhyming going on, too).

Blank verse relies on the subtlety of iambic pentameter. In fact, we often speak in iambs because they come naturally to us. In English, some stresses are stronger than others, and that lends a nice texture to the meter. Here's the opening of a Robert Frost poem, "Mending Wall"; read it aloud:

> Something there is that doesn't love a wall,
> That sends the frozen-ground-swell under it,
> And spills the upper boulders in the sun;
> And makes gaps even two can pass abreast.

If you read this section in your own voice, without looking at the stresses, you can barely tell that it's in meter. Here I've added the stresses for you:

> SOMETHING | there IS | that DOES | n't LOVE | a WALL,
> that SENDS | the FRO | zen-GROUND | -swell UN | der IT,
> and SPILLS | the UP | per BOULD | ers IN | the SUN;
> and MAKES | gaps EV | en TWO | can PASS | aBREAST.

Here are the next few lines of the poem—scan them and see what you come up with:

> The work of hunters is another thing:
> I have come after them and made repair
> Where they have left not one stone on a stone,
> But they would have the rabbit out of hiding,
> To please the yelping dogs. The gaps I mean,
> No one has seen them made or heard them made,
> But at spring mending-time we find them there.

Poetically Correct

Sprung rhythm is a form of metrical measurement, invented by poet Gerard Manley Hopkins, which uses a scheme of over-stressing different from accentual-syllabic meter (which uses a scheme of alternating stresses with unstressed syllables).

Poetically Correct

Caesura is from the Latin word for "to cut" and is a pause in the middle of a metrical line, having to do with tempo; it can be syntactic, grammatical, formed by punctuation, or even a bit of white space on the page.

Did you find any variations? I found an anapest in the beginning of the second line, a possible trochee in the beginning of the sixth line, and another possible anapest in the last line. However, I can also read these variations right out of the lines and see the whole section as iambic pentameter. Remember: Scanning is all about how you hear the poem.

Sprung Rhythm

In *sprung rhythm,* even one syllable can make a foot, so long as it is stressed, and can be butted against another "foot" consisting of two stressed syllables. Look at this line, for example:

```
 /      /     /       /   U     /      /     / U U  /
Strike, churl; hurl, cheerless wind, then; heltering hail
```

Hopkins himself said that sprung rhythm could not be counterpointed; there's no room for variation.

Accentual and Syllabic Meter

The type of meter we've been discussing relies on stresses (accents) and the number of syllables used—it's sometimes called accentual-syllabic meter. Two options break this type of meter into its components—accentual and syllabic.

Accentual verse is a very early poetic form that relies only on the number of accents (or stresses) in a line, and doesn't count where they fall in the line. The early Anglo-Saxon poets used this form, counting four beats (stresses) per line. They also used alliteration to unite the stressed syllables and commonly used a *caesura,* or a natural pause falling within a metrical line. You can use the traditional four stresses, or you can choose an arbitrary number and challenge yourself to maintain it.

Here's an example of a part of a metrical poem, by Robert Frost, having several caesuras:

> Out walking in the frozen swamp one grey day
> I paused and said, "I will turn back from here.
> No, I will go on farther—and we shall see."
> The hard snow held me, save where now and then
> One foot went down. The view was all in lines
> Straight up and down of tall slim trees
> Too much alike to mark or name a place by
> So as to say for certain I was here
> Or somewhere else: I was just far from home.

Look again at lines two, three, four, five, and nine. See where there's a pause in the middle of the line? Now read lines six and seven aloud. I hear a metrical pause in those lines, too, though it's subtler than the pauses in the other lines. I'll mark the caesuras for you here with a ():

> Out walking in the frozen swamp one grey day
> I paused and said, () "I will turn back from here.
> No, I will go on farther—() and we shall see."
> The hard snow held me, () save where now and then
> One foot went down. () The view was all in lines
> Straight up and down () of tall slim trees
> Too much alike to mark () or name a place by
> So as to say for certain I was here
> Or somewhere else: () I was just far from home.

Poets writing in syllabic meter only need count the syllables in each line, not worrying at all about the stresses—isn't that nice? You can make a decision about your syllable count before you write your poem. For example, you can challenge yourself to write a poem with nine syllables in each line. Or you can make a syllable pattern: a poem consisting of four stanzas or four lines each, each having five syllables in the first line, 10 syllables in the second, three syllables in the third, and 12 syllables in the last. Use your imagination and you can come up with thousands of combinations.

Touchestones

Blank verse, n. Unrhymed iambic pentameter—the most difficult kind of English verse to write acceptably; a kind, therefore, much affected by those who cannot acceptably write any kind.

—Ambrose Bierce

Exercises

Try these exercises to get you warmed up to writing in meter—trust me, it's fun!

- Scan the following Shakespearian sonnet (by The Bard himself) to find its metrical pattern:

  Not from the stars do I my judgement pluck;
  And yet methinks I have astronomy,
  But not to tell of good or evil luck,
  Of plagues, of dearths, or seasons' quality;
  Nor can I fortune to brief minutes tell,
  Pointing to each his thunder, rain and wind,
  Or say with princes if it shall go well
  By oft predict that I in heaven find:
  But from thine eyes my knowledge I derive,
  And constant stars in them I read such art
  As 'Truth and beauty shall together thrive,
  If from thyself, to store thou wouldst convert';
  Or else of thee this I prognosticate:
  'Thy end is truth's and beauty's doom and date.'

- Try to write a 20-line poem in blank verse—use at least five metrical variations on the iambic pentameter.
- Write a poem in accentual verse, which is four beats per line if you want to write Anglo-Saxon accentual verse. Use alliteration in each line and try for a caesura in some of the lines if you can.
- Write 10 syllabic poems; poem one will have one syllable in each line, poem two will have two, poem three will have three, and so on. For fun, write them on the same subject—you can make this a 10-part poem if you'd like.

Roses Are Red

Here's a tip: If you want to write in a certain meter, such as iambic pentameter or trochaic tetrameter, begin your lines with your chosen foot—say, an iamb—and then just count syllables from there. Chances are that you'll achieve the desired effect, with a lot of variations. However, you have a 50-percent shot that you'll just end up with a syllabic poem that's way off the meter you were trying for. But that's okay, too, as long as the poem's good!

The Least You Need to Know

- Meter is one way of unifying and ordering the language in poetry.
- Meter involves the stresses of words and how we place those words next to one another to create a metrical pattern.
- The method that poets use to measure metrical patterns is called scansion.
- Iambic pentameter (five feet, all iambs: U /) is the most-used metrical pattern in poetry written in English.
- Variation in regular meter is sometimes called counterpoint. This variation helps prevent a metrical poem from becoming monotonous or silly.

Part 3

Popular Types of Poems and How to Write Them

Poetry is simply the most beautiful, impressive, and widely effective mode of saying things.

—Matthew Arnold

Part 3 will verse you in the art of "saying things." You'll discover a variety of ways to write poems, from the love poem to the sonnet. You will get a crash course on popular fixed forms, as well as tips and hints on writing other types of conventional poems. There are thousands of ways to write a poem—here are a few.

Chapter 10

Tell Me a Story: Narrative Poetry

In This Chapter

- The narrative poem
- Who's speaking?
- Point of view
- Dialogue
- The ballad form

A narrative poem is simply a poem that tells a story. The narrative poem has been around since poetry began and has a long history in the written form. The epic poem is traditionally a narrative, as are some established fixed forms such as the ballad.

Poets are natural storytellers. Often the urge to write poetry is the urge to tell what has happened to us and how those events have affected our lives. The narrative is a powerful means of expression in poetry. The difference between a narrative poem and a short story is in the poem's ability to "cut to the chase," to include only what's necessary, and, in many cases, to enable the reader to reach his or her own conclusions. In this chapter, you'll discover the elements you need to render your tale into verse.

Cause and Effect

To understand the narrative poem, you first have to understand the basic elements of a story. The word "story" implies causal events: Something happened, and as a result something else happened. Think about a movie you love—say, *The Wizard of Oz*. Because of the tornado, Dorothy ends up lost in Oz and has to find her way home. Although this is obviously a simplification of a complicated tale, you get the idea, I hope. Let's look at an example of the concept of cause and effect in a poem:

Deacon Taylor

I belonged to the church,
And to the party of prohibition;
And the villagers thought I died of eating watermelon.
In truth I had cirrhosis of the liver,
For every noon for thirty years,
I slipped behind the prescription partition
In Trainor's drug store
And poured a generous drink
From the bottle marked "Spiritus frumenti."

—Edgar Lee Masters

So, Deacon Taylor, the speaker in the poem (we know this from the title), drank too much booze and died as a result, though the villagers thought he died from eating watermelon. This was a simple case of cause and effect: Because the deacon drank booze every day for 30 years, he died of cirrhosis of the liver. Add the complication of the villagers bamboozled into thinking that the deacon died of eating watermelon, and you have a poem. The idea of dying of eating watermelon is humorous, to say the least; it becomes even more so when we learn that the deacon was nipping his stash at the local drug store, and it becomes ironic when we look back at line two and see that he was a member of the party of prohibition. This seemingly simple poem actually has a lot going on in it: irony, humor, confession, and a story that encompasses a whole life in just a few lines.

Who's the Speaker?

You've probably heard a lot about the famous poetic "speaker." The speaker in a poem does not necessarily have to be the poet. Indeed, the voice could be distinctly different from the poet's voice, especially if the narrative is told from another point of view, like that of an animal (see Chapter 12, "The Three Faces of Eve: Persona Poems and Letter Poems," for a discussion of persona poetry). In the preceding Masters poem, the speaker is Deacon Taylor. We know that because he's the one telling the story (and because of the title of the poem). I can guarantee you that Edgar Lee Masters wasn't a dead deacon at the time he wrote this poem.

Dodging Doggerel

Many beginning poets feel that everything they write must be true. Many beginners feel that it's not poetry if the facts have been changed. Well, think about some of the most famous narrative poems in history, such as Dante's *Inferno*. The *Inferno* is an epic poem that recounts the story of Dante himself traipsing through Hell with Virgil, a poet who died 18 years before Christ was born—and Dante wrote the Inferno in the 1300s. Does that sound like a recounting of factual events to you? Don't worry so much about "truth" as it happened. Instead, focus on getting to "a truth," which is far more important than whether a poet toured Hell or not. The *Inferno* is a detailed study of sin, human behavior, politics, religion, and the afterlife, and Dante comes to more truths through his fictional tale than he might have if he had been chained to the reality of our world, where few living souls sightsee through Hell and then write brilliantly about it.

Narrative poems generally have a speaker, a distinctive voice, and you can often tell easily to whom that voice belongs, depending on the poem's point of view (we'll get to that in a minute). When you write your own narrative poems, you'll have to decide who's going to tell the story. Do you want to tell it in your own voice or have someone else tell the story? In the Deacon Taylor poem, Masters chose to have the deacon tell his own story. He could have rendered it this way if he had chosen:

> Deacon Taylor belonged to the church,
> And to the party of prohibition;
> And the villagers thought he died of eating
>   watermelon.
> In truth he had cirrhosis of the liver,
> For every noon for thirty years,
> he slipped behind the prescription partition
> In Trainor's drug store
> And poured a generous drink
> From the bottle marked "Spiritus frumenti."

Touchstones

While many things are too strange to be believed, nothing is too strange to have happened.

—Thomas Hardy

Telling the story this way indicts the deacon and makes him less likable. This version removes the "closeness" the reader feels toward the deacon, and the poem isn't quite as funny. It also makes the deacon "more dead"; he doesn't have a voice in this version of the poem. Having him speak for himself was the right choice. You can see how changing the *point of view* in this poem changed the way you experienced it.

Point of View

Once you've decided on a speaker, you have to decide how your speaker is going to tell the story; this is called "point of view." Although this term is used primarily in fiction, the narrative poet should also take the time to consider the best way to tell the story. Some points of view draw readers into the poem, while others can distance them. You'll have to tinker with point of view to see what works for your individual poems. Here are a few common points of view to get you started.

Poetically Correct

Point of view refers to the viewpoint from which a story (or poem) is narrated.

Roses Are Red

If your poem isn't working just as you'd like, change the point of view and see if that helps. Changing the point of view changes how the reader interprets and experiences the poem, and you might find some nice effects if you play with different points of view.

First Person: The "I"

The first person is commonly used in poetry because it's personal and immediate, and speaks directly to the reader. We're used to speaking in the first person, so this point of view comes naturally to most of us. Here's an example of a poem I wrote:

Night Plumber

My neighbor comes at one A.M. in her night
clothes to say my toilet's screaming in the pipes
through her walls, and before I can turn her
away or tell her to joggle the handle she's got it
disassembled, got her hands wet, and now I
hear the water too, wanting away in our old
shared pipes, trying to spin some long mystery,
filling and refilling the basin, writing with rust
in perfect lines, wasting while the whole town
sleeps, water incognito; my neighbor yanks
the chain, bobs the rubber stopper, the water
rests at last, my neighbor drags her damp socks
back to bed. This embryonic Tuesday flutters
in its darkness around me like a new moth;
crickets; an ambulance; my steam heat ticking
its own old pipes with some other ancient code—
I try to decipher sleep again, hearing the very air
above my bed scratch its legs against the ceiling,
realizing I was smothered a little every night

by my toilet, of all the ridiculous things,
renegade water, or some tired bit of rubber
permitting the innocent water through, the
hushing music, like a friend saying *don't be
lonely,* or *I'm lonely too.*

It was natural for me to write this poem in the first person because this actually happened to me and I wanted to tell it in my own voice. The artifice in this poem—the place where the story of what actually happened turns to poetry—is the description of what the water was doing to the pipes, how the silence felt once the water stopped, and what the noise of the water ultimately meant to the speaker/poet.

Roses Are Red

You have three basic choices of tense in your poems: present (this is happening), past (this happened), and future (this will happen). The past tense is how we are used to hearing narratives told, and it's unobtrusive as a result. Present tense is more immediate than past tense, and the future tense will add tension to the narrative.

Second Person: The "You"

The second person, the "you" voice, lends immediacy to the narrative. The poet is essentially telling you that *you're* in the poem, experiencing the events of the poem as they occur. We know, as readers, that we're not really part of the poem, but if the poet is convincing enough, we feel as if we are. Here's an example:

The Year of Minimum Wage

You are a cashier without a green card, ringing up
chicken wings Buffalo style
complimentary celery and bleu cheese.
Your boss rents you the ground floor studio in the back
where your neutered Siamese dreams
of scaling the crisp airshaft's bricks.
You watch snow peak on majestic garbage bags.
Your boss calls you again from the bar next door. "I mean,
where's the money going?" he says,
"the more supplies I buy the less money comes in."
He asks you to keep an eye on the cook.
"You guys don't care. I'm gonna have cameras
aimed at the register, I'm gonna have spotters
watching from the sidewalk!"
You remember the gun in his basement office.
"Soon I'll fry somebody's hands — It's been done before."

> The only customer is David, snoring in his chair.
> The frankfurters he ate remind you of his bare toes
> you saw last summer
> when helping unload lard from the delivery van.
> Today he used his Social Security
> check to pay for his food instead of
> *Papi mira mira give me someting por favor.*
> Your boss walks in wearing no jacket, his stomach,
> a third trimester pregnancy. He stands next to the slumped man
> whose chin is covered with mucus.
> He slaps David once. A beat. A slap. David does not wake up.
> The cook keeps chopping fleshy things. Another slap.
> Two red faces. Your boss stops and glares
> at you, as if saying "This is how you do it!" Then he storms out,
> back into the snow. You hide behind the loaner register
> with "taxable items" handwritten on one of the keys
> you always misread as "taxable dreams."
>
> —Guillermo Castro

As the reader, you know that you're not a cashier without a green card (well, at least I'm assuming you're not), but this poet has chosen to place you in this character's shoes, forcing you to see what it's like in the world of fast food and minimum wage. Beware, however: The "you" can sometimes seem artificial and doesn't always work. Look at this, for example:

> You belonged to the church,
> And to the party of prohibition;
> And the villagers thought you died of eating watermelon.
> In truth you had cirrhosis of the liver,
> For every noon for thirty years,
> you slipped behind the prescription partition
> In Trainor's drug store
> And poured a generous drink
> From the bottle marked "Spiritus frumenti."

Know what I say to this? *I did not!* The second-person point of view doesn't ring true in this poem. Use it sparingly.

Third Person: "He" and "She" and "It"

The third-person point of view (using he, she, and it) is how we are used to hearing stories told. It has a distancing effect on the narrative, more so than the first or second person, because it can often seem more "story-like," more fictive, than the other choices. Here's an example:

Portrait of a Boy

After the whipping, he crawled into bed;
Accepting the harsh fact with no great weeping.
How funny uncle's hat had looked striped red!
He chuckled silently. The moon came, sweeping
A black frayed rag of tattered cloud before
In scorning; very pure and pale she seemed,
Flooding his bed with radiance. On the floor
Fat motes danced. He sobbed; closed his eyes and dreamed.

Warm sand flowed round him. Blurts of crimson light
Splashed the white grains like blood. Past the cave's mouth
Shone with a large fierce splendor, wildly bright,
The crooked constellations of the South;
Here the Cross swung; and there, affronting Mars,
The Centaur stormed aside a froth of stars.
Within, great casks like wattled aldermen
Sighed of enormous feasts, and cloth of gold
Glowed on the walls like hot desire. Again,
Beside webbed purples from some galleon's hold,
A black chest bore the skull and bones in white
Above a scrawled "Gunpowder!" By the flames,
Decked out in crimson, gemmed with syenite,
Hailing their fellows by outrageous names
The pirates sat and diced. Their eyes were moons.
"Doubloons!" they said. The words crashed gold. "Doubloons!"

—Stephen Vincent Benét

Imagine this poem is written in the first person:

After the whipping, I crawled into bed;
Accepting the harsh fact with no great weeping.
How funny uncle's hat had looked striped red!
I chuckled silently. The moon came, sweeping
A black frayed rag of tattered cloud before
In scorning; very pure and pale she seemed,
Flooding my bed with radiance. On the floor
Fat motes danced. I sobbed; closed my eyes and dreamed.

No one point of view is any more successful than the others; the one you use depends on what you want to achieve with your poem. Your best bet is to try a variety of points of view to see what works.

The Collective: "We"

The collective "we" is another option for the narrative. This point of view functions much like the first person: It draws the reader close to the narrative and can represent two or more individuals. Often it's obvious that the narrator in a poem using this voice isn't really embodying the "we" but is really an individual recounting an experience that the "we" had or is having. Here's an example:

Loon

We went out upon the lake,
quietly. In a canoe,
we went out. Not very far,
as it was getting dark,
but we went out
and crept along the shore.
Slowly and without talking,
we went out.
And without lifting the paddle
from the water,
so that there would not be
even the sound of dripping
when we went out.
And there was nothing in that silence
but itself.
Invisible twitters
in the underbrush,
plus whatever sound it is
the air makes
rubbing against itself.
Maybe there will be a loon tonight, we said.
There wasn't,
but we went out anyway
into a sort of inhabited silence,
at dusk, with pink light fading
and one bird
perched in the top limb of a dead tree.

It flew, and the sky
was several colors of dark blue slate,
and the lily pads
from which the lilies
recently had fallen,
rested on the water.
We had been in that tiny bay
a year before, also at dusk.
The sky had been dramatic then, impending,
streaked vermilion and blue.
Now it was slate blue and gray,
but changing, changing fast.
This year is like the last, we said,
but different.
We were as we were, as well,
though changed.
It was dusk and the end of summer
and the lake was probably dying,
though you could not tell it,
and we paddled back to the dock
as though we heard a call,
as though before we would even see it,
whatever it might be
would dive and disappear.

—Roger Mitchell

You can see here that this poem isn't just about two people having an experience; the collective point of view suggests that the two people are having the *exact same* experience.

Dodging Doggerel

Not all poetic narratives have to be huge stories like Dante's *Inferno*. You can write a poem about a very brief event. Don't get stuck just because your story isn't "grand" enough. Just write.

Dialogue

A dialogue is an exchange of words between two or more speakers, and poets often use dialogue in their poems. Dialogue can be important to a narrative poem, as you can see in "The Year of Minimum Wage" earlier in this chapter.

Here's a poem that uses a dialogue between the soul and body to reveal a sort of narrative about what each one does to the other—and reveals a larger message about life in general:

A Dialogue between the Soul and Body

Soul:
O Who shall, from this Dungeon, raise
A Soul inslav'd so many wayes?
With bolts of Bones, that fetter'd stands
In Feet; and manacled in Hands.
Here blinded with an Eye; and there
Deaf with the drumming of an Ear.
A Soul hung up, as 'twere, in Chains
Of Nerves, and Arteries, and Veins.
Tortur'd, besides each other part,
In a vain Head, and double Heart.

Body:
O who shall me deliver whole,
From bonds of this Tyrannic Soul?
Which, stretcht upright, impales me so,
That mine own Precipice I go;
And warms and moves this needless Frame:
(A Fever could but do the same.)
And, wanting where its spight to try,
Has made me live to let me dye.
A Body that could never rest,
Since this ill Spirit it possest.

Soul:
What Magic could me thus confine
Within another's Grief to pine?
Where whatsoever it complain,
I feel, that cannot feel, the pain.
And all my Care its self employs,
That to preserve, which me destroys:
Constrain'd not only to endure
Diseases, but, whats worse, the Cure:
And ready oft the Port to gain,
Am Shipwrackt into Health again.

Body:
But Physick yet could never reach
The Maladies Thou me dost teach;
Whom first the Cramp of Hope does Tear:
And then the Palsie Shakes of Fear.

The Pestilence of Love does heat:
Or Hatred's hidden Ulcer eat.
Joy's chearful Madness does perplex:
Or Sorrow's other Madness vex.
Which Knowledge forces me to know;
And Memory will not foregoe.
What but a Soul could have the wit
To build me up for Sin so fit?
So Architects do square and hew,
Green Trees that in the Forest grew.

—Andrew Marvell

Write a modern dialogue between the soul and the body, or between some other internal forces that seem to be in conflict, like the head and the heart, love and hate, and so on. Use a lot of concrete images in your poem, and try to avoid clichés, which can creep into a poem written in this way.

Here's a prose poem I wrote that's almost a verbatim conversation I had with a man sitting in a mall outside a hair salon as I was waiting to get my hair cut. I believed he was there to get his hair cut as well, and we started talking:

Scissors

Think of it, he says, *how many hairstyles there must be, in this town alone. Think about all the people getting their hair cut today. In all the world. Think about all the styles on all those people. Think about all the hairdressers knowing how to cut all those styles.* Yeah, I say, think of all that hair swept from hair salon floors around the world. *Must be tons of it,* he says. *There's a salon where they have a computer that takes your picture and tries out hairstyles on you.* Fancy, I say. *Not really,* he says, *There's one across town.* High tech, I say. *Yeah, it's great how you can try on different hairstyles on the computer. And it's free. Imagine all the hairstyles you can try on.* Yeah, I say, a lot of hairstyles. *I have to get my hair cut all the time, he says. But I shouldn't complain, at least I have hair. Some people don't, you know.* Yeah, I say, you're lucky. *Are you getting your hair cut today*? he says. Yeah, I say, are you? *No, I just like the scissors.*

The Ballad

The ballad is a traditional fixed form that tells a story, usually a thrilling and tragic tale ending with the death of a lover, family member, or so on. Ballads also often have a supernatural flair. They begin, almost always, at the moment of crisis, when the tragic ending is inevitable, and they often use little effort to describe things—the emphasis is on the narrative, and the characters often speak, making dialogue the bulk of the poem. The point of view of the ballad is generally the collective or third person—rarely does a first-person narrator speak.

Let Me Count the Ways

The ballad is a short narrative form that was transmitted orally between illiterate or semi-literate peoples. It was originally a folk song and sung as a means of passing it down through the generations. Ballads relied heavily on plot above all other elements, and didn't have much character development—the person hearing the ballad had to remember the key points of the plot, and not spend time considering why the things were happening in the first place.

The fixed form of the ballad consists of quatrains (four-line stanzas) where lines one and three have four beats (stressed syllable), and lines two and four have three beats and rhyme as well. When you read a traditional ballad out loud you can hear these beats—clap your hands along with the poem's stressed syllables to hear where the beats fall.

John Barleycorn: A Ballad

There was three kings unto the east,
Three kings both great and high,
And they hae sworn a solemn oath
John Barleycorn should die.

They took a plough and plough'd him down,
Put clods upon his head,
And they hae sworn a solemn oath
John Barleycorn was dead.

But the cheerful Spring came kindly on,
And show'rs began to fall;
John Barleycorn got up again,
And sore surpris'd them all.

The sultry suns of Summer came,
And he grew thick and strong;
His head weel arm'd wi' pointed spears,
That no one should him wrong.

Touchstones

I have no fancy ideas about poetry. It doesn't come to you on the wings of a dove. It's something you work hard at.

—Louise Bogan

The sober Autumn enter'd mild,
When he grew wan and pale;
His bending joints and drooping head
Show'd he bagan to fail.

His colour sicken'd more and more,
He faded into age;
And then his enemies began
To show their deadly rage.

They've taen a weapon, long and sharp,
And cut him by the knee;
Then tied him fast upon a cart,
Like a rogue for forgerie.

They laid him down upon his back,
And cudgell'd him full sore;
They hung him up before the storm,
And turn'd him o'er and o'cr.

They filled up a darksome pit
With water to the brim;
They heaved in John Barleycorn,
There let him sink or swim.

They laid him out upon the floor,
To work him further woe;
And still, as signs of life appear'd,
They toss'd him to and fro.

They wasted, o'er a scorching flame,
The marrow of his bones;
But a miller us'd him worst of all,
For he crush'd him between two stones.

And they hae taen his very heart's blood,
And drank it round and round;
And still the more and more they drank,
Their joy did more abound.

John Barleycorn was a hero bold,
Of noble enterprise;
For if you do but taste his blood,
'Twill make your courage rise.

'Twill make a man forget his woe;
'Twill heighten all his joy;
'Twill make the widow's heart to sing,
Tho' the tear were in her eye.

Then let us toast John Barleycorn,
Each man a glass in hand;
And may his great posterity
Ne'er fail in old Scotland!

—Robert Burns

Exercises

Here are some exercises to get you started writing narrative poems.

- Take a poem you've already written and change the point of view as many times as you can. Read the versions aloud. Did any of the changes make the poem better?
- Type one of your favorite poems (written by another poet) into your computer and change the point of view. What does that do to the poem?
- Write a dialogue between two people who could never meet, like Einstein and Madonna, for example.
- Write a ballad about a modern-day tragedy.

The Least You Need to Know

- A narrative poem is one that tells a story.
- Not everything you write has to be true or exactly as it happened.
- The speaker is the *voice* in the poem.
- You can use several points of view in a narrative poem, including first person (I), second person (you), and third person (he, she, it).
- The ballad is a traditional fixed form that tells a tragic tale.

Chapter 11

Love and the Great Beyond

In This Chapter

- Wooing 101: the love poem
- Desire poems
- Writing the erotic
- Elegies
- Writing about your own death—yikes!

The subjects of love and death are more frequently wrought into verse than any other, and, as a result, more bad poems are written about love and death than in any other subject!

It's natural to want to write about the things that produce strong feelings. Feelings are a natural consequence of the events in our lives, while poetry is artificial. Beginning poets often think that this excess of emotion is what poetry requires. On the contrary, poetry requires restraint, especially when love and death are the subjects.

Overwriting is common when emotions are high. Using concrete language—the things of the world—and finding a fresh way to express the feelings surrounding love and death will help to avoid falling into the "bad-poetry pit" common in novice poems using these two heavily loaded topics.

In this chapter, I've chosen sample poems that are unusual in some way—poems that didn't take the ordinary route. These should help you to see that you can fashion "good" poems out of the most commonplace subjects.

Wooing 101: Love Poems

Sonnet CXXX

My mistress' eyes are nothing like the sun;
Coral is far more red, than her lips red:
If snow be white, why then her breasts are dun;
If hairs be wires, black wires grow on her head.
I have seen roses damask'd, red and white,
But no such roses see I in her cheeks;
And in some perfumes is there more delight
Than in the breath that from my mistress reeks.
I love to hear her speak, yet well I know
That music hath a far more pleasing sound:
I grant I never saw a goddess go,—
My mistress, when she walks, treads on the ground:
  And yet by heaven, I think my love as rare,
  As any she belied with false compare.

—William Shakespeare

Touchstones

If it were not for poetry, few men would fall in love.

—La Rochefoucauld

Shakespeare is arguably the master of the love poem in the English language. He is the King of hyperbole, making everything—especially the love object of his poems—especially grand. Here, in "Sonnet CXXX," he uses an ironic twist on the love poem: The speaker seems to "insult" the lover, saying that, basically, she's not "all that." But, in the last couplet of the poem, the speaker reveals that his love is more rare than these false comparisons. The comparisons used in this sonnet are not terribly fresh or startling—a rose, coral, snow—but they work precisely because the mistress does not compare well to these things and, finally, we realize that this poem is no more an insult than if it had been written the opposite.

We often think of love poems as being written to the object of romantic desire, though poetry has a long tradition of love poems written to family members. This poem uses bridges as a metaphor for the relationship between father and son.

Papá's Bridge

I drive west every morning, away from the sun
inching up in the rear-view mirror as I climb up
slabs of reinforced concrete bent into a bridge
arcing with all its parabolic X^2 and Y^2 splendor.

I rise to meet the shimmering faces of buildings,
above tree tops meshed into a calico of greens,
forgetting the river below runs, insists on running,
and scouring the earth, moving it grain by grain.

And if only for a few inclined seconds I am again
your son, remembering a morning I was twelve,
from the 10th floor window of your hospital room
watching this same bridge like a mammoth bone
aching with the gravity of its own dense weight.
The glass dosed with a tepid light ushering through
the waking city as I read your sleep, wondering
what you might dream of in such dreamless white—

were you falling or flying? Who was I underneath
your eyes fluttering left and right like the dark shapes
of birds darting in the distance, amid stars fading
above rooftops, the cars streaming through avenues
like the tiny blood cells through your needled vein,
the I.V. spiraling down like a string of clear licorice
feeding your forearm bruised pearl-gray and lavender—
colors of the morning haze, the pills on your tongue.

Your ulcers healed, the room remained numbed
by the usual, ethereal silence between us, between
servings of water or juice in wilting paper cups,
the filling of menu cards stamped *Bland Diet,*
the flipping through of muted daytime channels,
the constant tucking of rubbery, scentless pillows,
and adjusting of the bed and your body into an S
shape mortared in place by layers of stiff percale.

You were ordered to walk, so I took your hand.
In your hospital, you rose as regal and feeble
as the city we surveyed before us in the window:
Someday you'll learn how to build bridges like that.
And so I have. And so I drive west, through a world
of what I've built and unbuilt, said and unsaid,
everyday: the city, the bridge, and the unbridgeable—
a father and son holding hands, secretly in love.

—Richard Blanco

Dodging Doggerel

When we are in love or have just experienced the loss associated with death, we tend to be overwhelmed with emotion. These emotions can take the form of abstractions in our poems. If you sense that your poem is becoming overrun with abstractions, try for some metaphors and concrete imagery—that should help.

Sometimes love poems surprise us. When you're writing about an emotion that can be described so easily with worn and clichéd language as love can, you may want to drop a bombshell on the reader. Here's a poem that uses a violent image to convey the intensity of love. This poem also offers advice on how to maintain love:

The Warning

For love—I would
split open your head and put
a candle in
behind the eyes.

Love is dead in us
if we forget
the virtues of an amulet
and quick surprise.

—Robert Creeley

Desire …

Verse wrought from desire … powerful indeed! The desire poem is one in which the speaker hasn't yet won the object of his or her affections, and is writing to win them, understand them, or lament them.

Touchstones

Love poems must be bounced back off a moon.

—Robert Graves

Here's a poem about the aftermath of desire—the object of the speaker's affections was not quite as she had hoped!

The Kiss

I hoped that he would love me,
 And he has kissed my mouth,
But I am like a stricken bird
 That cannot reach the south.

For though I know he loves me,
 To-night my heart is sad;
His kiss was not so wonderful
 As all the dreams I had.

—Sarah Teasdale

This next poem illustrates what love can do to us, which is make us crazy! The speaker in this poem, the bricklayer, loves a woman who doesn't love him, but says he has gotten to the point of not caring as much anymore. Or does he?

Bricklayer Love

I thought of killing myself because I am only a bricklayer and you a woman who loves the man who runs a drug store.

I don't care like I used to; I lay bricks straighter than I used to and I sing slower handling the trowel afternoons.

When the sun is in my eyes and the ladders are shaky and the mortar boards go wrong, I think of you.

—Carl Sandburg

Let Me Count the Ways

Chilean poet Pablo Neruda wrote 101 love poems for his new bride and presented her with one each day for the first 101 days they were married. You can find these poems collected in the book, *101 Love Poems*. Imagine day 102: "Pablo, where's my poem today?" "What poem? I was only going to write you 101. Sorry. Bring me a beer, will you?"

Writing the Erotic

Erotic poems don't have to be sexy, porn-style verses full of elaborate and meticulous "action" scenes. Sometimes careful attention to detail can suggest the erotic, like in the following poem:

From **I Sing the Body Electric**

This is the female form,
A divine nimbus exhales from it from head to foot,
It attracts with fierce undeniable attraction,
I am drawn by its breath as if I were no more than a
    helpless vapor, all falls aside but myself and it,
Books, art, religion, time, the visible and solid earth,
    and what was expected of heaven or fear'd of hell,
    are now consumed,
Mad filaments, ungovernable shoots play out of it, the
    response likewise ungovernable,

Hair, bosom, hips, bend of legs, negligent falling hands
  all diffused, mine too diffused,
Ebb stung by the flow and flow stung by the ebb, love-
  flesh swelling and deliciously aching,
Limitless limpid jets of love hot and enormous, quivering
  jelly of love, white-blow and delirious nice,
Bridegroom night of love working surely and softly into
  the prostrate dawn,
Undulating into the willing and yielding day,
Lost in the cleave of the clasping and sweet-flesh'd day.
This the nucleus—after the child is born of woman, man
  is born of woman,
This the bath of birth, this the merge of small and large, and the outlet again.

—Walt Whitman

Here's a poem about a common vegetable that suggests the erotic through the poet's carefully chosen language:

Bell Pepper

Bell —
the word buds at my lips,
smalls into seeing:

A bird's curved neck —
the stem ends
in a plunge of hollow,
a place to cull rain or shadows.

If I were a fat droplet
welling there, I'd spill
into green, waxy grooves,
rest as residue,
be
ephemeral ornament
dense as light.

But suppose I'm a knife —
I know that outside
is not the all of knowing
and so I'd desire
cleave,
would carve
a door.

Inside yawns a cave —
a mouth.
Uvula stalactite.
Membrane yields
below my steps,

for I'm no longer knife
but pilgrim, come from far
to this mouth of all
we can never know.
Its growl, its hum,
its prickly cat tongue.

—Dean Kostos

Roses Are Red

When you're writing about such complex subjects as love and death, you want to focus your poems on precise details, rather than try to toss everything you're feeling in the poem at once—remember, you can always write several poems on your subject—you don't have to put everything in one poem.

What's left out (understatement) often can be more powerful than what a poet includes. In this next poem, the poet doesn't have to film the back-story for the reader; it's all there.

Another Love Affair/Another Poem

it was afterwards
when we were in the shower
that she said

"you're gonna write a poem about this"

"about what?" i asked

—E. Ethelbert Miller

Death and Grieving

Poems about death and grieving have to use the same restraint as love poems do. The feelings are often so powerful that it's difficult to use them well in a poem unless you use the tools of poetry well. A poem that pays homage to a person who has died is called an *elegy*. Here's an elegy about a loved one who has passed on:

David Lemieux

My first boyfriend is dead of AIDS. The one
who bought me a terrarium with a cactus
I watered until it became soft. The one

who took me to his junior high prom where I was shy
about dancing in public. The one who was mistaken
for a girl by a clerk when he wanted to try on a suit.

In seventh grade my first boyfriend and I looked a lot alike:
chubby arms, curly hair, our noses touching
when we tried our first kiss. My first boyfriend

was the only one who met my grandmother
before she died. Though, as a rule, she didn't like boys,
I think she liked my first boyfriend.

My first boyfriend and I sat in the back seat
of my mother's car, and on the ledge behind us
was a ceramic ballerina with a missing arm.

We were driving somewhere to have her repaired
or maybe to buy the right kind of glue.
My first boyfriend was rich and had horses

and airplanes he could fly by remote control.
My first boyfriend died on a mattress
thrown on the back of a pick-up

because the ambulance wouldn't come.
There was a garden in my first boyfriend's yard.
One day his mother said to us,

"Pick out some nice things for lunch."
My first boyfriend and I pulled at the carrot tops,
but all we came up with were little orange balls

that looked like kumquats without the bumps.
My first boyfriend and I heard ripping through the soil
that sounded close to our scalps, like a hair brush

through tangles. We were the ones who pushed
the tiny carrots back down, hoping they were able
to reconnect to the ground. We were the ones.

—Denise Duhamel

In writing an elegy, you will want to consider the details about the person who has passed on, rather than try to "sum up" a life. As you can see in the preceding poem, the speaker uses specific memories about the deceased, and the reader can see, through these details, how his death, and his life, has affected her own life.

Poetically Correct

An **epitaph** is an inscription written on a tomb or a gravestone. Poets often use the form liberally to create poems.

An *epitaph* is a short, usually witty inscription meant to be written on a gravestone. Poets like this form and use it liberally to create poems. Here's an example:

Epitaph
(On a commonplace person who died in bed)

This is the end of him, here he lies:
The dust in his throat, the worm in his eyes,
The mould in his mouth, the turf on his breast;
This is the end of him, this is best.
He will never lie on his couch awake,
Wide-eyed, tearless, till dim daybreak.
Never again will he smile and smile
When his heart is breaking all the while.
He will never stretch out his hands in vain
Groping and groping—never again.
Never ask for bread, get a stone instead,
Never pretend that the stone is bread;
Nor sway and sway 'twixt the false and true,
Weighing and noting the long hours through.
Never ache and ache with the choked-up sighs;
This is the end of him, here he lies.

—Amy Levy

Poets are fond of the "comic" epitaph as well. Here is an example:

It was a cough that carried her off,
It was a coffin they carried her off in.

—Anonymous

Poems have a magic that enables the dead to speak. Poet Edgar Lee Masters wrote a book of poems entitled *The Spoon River Anthology* in which each poem is in the voice of someone buried in a cemetery on a hill. The voices tell stories, lament, and impugn one another for their deaths. Here's a sampling:

Robert Fulton Tanner

If a man could bite the giant hand
That catches and destroys him,
As I was bitten by a rat
While demonstrating my patent trap,
In my hardware store that day.
But a man can never avenge himself
On the monstrous ogre Life.
You enter the room that's being born;
And then you must live work out your soul,
Of the cross-current in life
Which Bring honor to the dead, who lived in shame.

Minerva Jones

I am Minerva, the village poetess,
Hooted at, jeered at by the Yahoos of the street
For my heavy body, cock-eye, and rolling walk,
And all the more when "Butch" Weldy
Captured me after a brutal hunt.
He left me to my fate with Doctor Meyers;
And I sank into death, growing numb from the feet up,
Like one stepping deeper and deeper into a stream of ice.
Will some one go to the village newspaper,
And gather into a book the verses I wrote?—
I thirsted so for love
I hungered so for life!

—Edgar Lee Masters

Here's one I wrote for a class from an assignment by poet David Wojahn. He passed around photocopies of crime-scene photos, each of which contained the image of someone who was murdered. My idea was to give the girl I selected some dignity because the police, by the way they stood over her, had robbed her of it.

Skirt

The bed neatly made, satin bedspread tucked
beneath the wooden footboard, and the girl,
posed across it, crinoline neatly pressed oblong
and flooded around her knees, that muscle tracing
a valley down her calf to new saddle shoes
and ruffle-edged socks, legs we would call *shapely*

if she weren't dead—and the uniforms standing above her,
guessing about her thighs cooling beneath all that skirt—
two years before 1960, when she might
have switched to a tight midi, something less
mysterious, ten years before she would have
batiked a new sarong, or gone skirtless completely;

and who can say she isn't the object of desire,
here in 1958, as the police photographer captures
her dead legs, her skirt now well out of date,
herself a capsule poised on the brink of a new age?
The policemen's bodies obscuring her face in the photo,
and what isn't more inspiring than a secret?
Even the sheer crinoline gives up its mystery:
each plastic fiber wound to form the thread,
thread woven tight into sheets, patterned into a bunch
over a girl's hips, men dreaming the swish
and whip of those silky legs beneath the veil of skirt.
And what about the girl within the skirt?

Faceless, nameless, photo captioned: *Victim in Family*
Slaying. And whose family doesn't have a *Victim*,
so pretty from the bottom down, someone whispered
about like the rustling of skirts if she licks
her fingers at the dinner table, or isn't asked
to the prom, someone whose ankles fall limp
from the bed's edge, someone who dies with shoes on?
Victim, how do we make things right for you,
years later, when even the planets have changed?
Even the moon, with its own dark skirt, its bright
and hopeful face tread upon by a budding technology.
Were you to see the moon again, *Victim,* you wouldn't
think of rockets and Neil Armstrong. Only, perhaps:

I left my school books in my locker and I have
quizzes Monday: Physics, Astronomy, Byzantium.

Do you ever think about your own death? I suppose that poets must wonder about their own deaths far more than other people. Or maybe that's just me. Anyway, poetry has a tradition of poets writing about their own deaths. Here's one by The Bard himself:

The Triumph of Death

No longer mourn for me when I am dead
Than you shall hear the surly sullen bell
Give warning to the world that I am fled
From this vile world, with vilest worms to dwell.

Nay, if you read this line, remember not
The hand that writ it; for I love you so,
That I in your sweet thoughts would be forgot
If thinking on me then should make you woe.

O if, I say, you look upon this verse
When I perhaps compounded am with clay,
Do not so much as my poor name rehearse,
But let your love even with my life decay;

Lest the wise world should look into your moan,
And mock you with me after I am gone.

—William Shakespeare

This next poem uses the metaphor of apple-picking to "disguise" it as a death poem. Read this poem through a few times and you'll see the metaphor at work.

After Apple-Picking

My long two-pointed ladder's sticking through a tree
Toward heaven still.
And there's a barrel that I didn't fill
Beside it, and there may be two or three
Apples I didn't pick upon some bough.
But I am done with apple-picking now.
Essence of winter sleep is on the night,
The scent of apples; I am drowsing off.
I cannot shake the shimmer from my sight
I got from looking through a pane of glass
I skimmed this morning from the water-trough,
And held against the world of hoary grass.
It melted, and I let it fall and break.
But I was well
Upon my way to sleep before it fell,
And I could tell
What form my dreaming was about to take.
Magnified apples appear and reappear,
Stem end and blossom end,

And every fleck of russet showing clear.
My instep arch not only keeps the ache,
It keeps the pressure of a ladder-round.
And I keep hearing from the cellar-bin
That rumbling sound
Of load on load of apples coming in.
For I have had too much
Of apple-picking; I am overtired
Of the great harvest I myself desired.
There were ten thousand thousand fruit to touch,
Cherish in hand, lift down, and not let fall,
For all
That struck the earth,
No matter if not bruised, or spiked with stubble,
Went surely to the cider-apple heap
As of no worth.
One can see what will trouble
This sleep of mine, whatever sleep it is.
Were he not gone,
The woodchuck could say whether it's like his
Long sleep, as I describe its coming on,
Or just some human sleep.

—Robert Frost

Writing about death doesn't have to be all that serious. Here's a poem about a defining moment in childhood that most of us probably had to face:

The Death of Santa Claus

He's had chest pains for weeks,
but doctors don't make house
calls to the North Pole,

he's let his Blue Cross lapse,
blood tests make him faint,
hospital gowns always flap

open, waiting rooms upset
his stomach, and it's only
indigestion anyway, he thinks,

until, feeding the reindeer,
he feels as if a monster fist
has grabbed his heart and won't

stop squeezing. He can't
breathe, and the beautiful white
world he loves goes black,

and he drops on his jelly belly
in the snow and Mrs. Claus
tears out of the toy factory

wailing, and the elves wring
their little hands, and Rudolph's
nose blinks like a sad ambulance

light, and in a tract house
in Houston, Texas, I'm 8,
telling my mom that stupid

kids at school say Santa's a big
fake, and she sits with me
on our purple-flowered couch,

and takes my hand, tears
in her throat, the terrible
news rising in her eyes.

—Charles Harper Webb

Exercises

Writing well about love and death isn't as easy as it seems—but a good poet will make it look easy. Here are some exercises to get you started.

Touchstones

Love is a state which has to be blinding to make things right.
—Robert Frost

- Write a poem in which you insult a loved one, then take it all back in the end such that you never meant the insults at all.
- Write a love poem to a family member.
- Write a desire poem in the voice of an animal or an inanimate object.
- Write an erotic poem using understatement.
- Write an elegy for someone you knew well. Then, write an elegy for someone you didn't know at all. What's the difference between your two poems?

- Write a poem in the voice of someone famous and long dead.
- Write a poem about the moment of your own death.

The Least You Need to Know

- Love and death poems need a "light touch."
- When you're writing about love and death, try to stay with the concrete.
- Abstractions are the death of a good love poem—and readers won't love them in your death poems, either.
- When writing about the "big" themes, try to pay attention to the "little" things.

Chapter 12

The Three Faces of Eve: Persona Poems and Letter Poems

In This Chapter

- The persona poem
- Negative capability
- The dramatic monologue
- How to write a letter
- Postcards from the edge

One of the most entertaining and diverse types of poetry you can write is the persona poem. In the persona poem, you wear another identity and speak through the mouth of another person, animal, inanimate object, or any other thing you can imagine. This approach gives you a lot of freedom and creativity; you can be anything you want, live any fantasy, and explore historical and fictional events. You can learn a lot about yourself and your poems writing in a persona.

Dear reader: The epistle poem, or letter poem, is also a flexible form with a long history in poetry. Letter poems frequently use a persona, which is why I put these two forms together here. In this chapter, you'll learn how to change your poetic identity and how letter-writing works in verse. Sincerely yours, your humble author.

Persona Poems

As I mentioned earlier, the persona poem is one that enables the writer to take on another identity, to write as someone or something else. If you write in your own identity (with your own experience, opinions, and values) often enough, you'll notice that your poems have a similar sound, a similar voice. This is because you have your own individual way of placing words next to one another so that the end product is distinct from the body of work of another poet. Sure, you pick up influences along the way—other poets whose voices creep into your work—but you probably don't write *exactly* like them. When you practice enough and gain a certain level of skill, your poetic voice emerges.

The persona poem forces you to write in another voice, to experiment with tone and diction. The persona in your poem should not sound much like *you*. For example, suppose you write two poems, one in the persona of Abraham Lincoln and one in the persona of Marilyn Monroe; do you suppose that the voices will sound the same? Probably not. Will the voices sound like the voice in all of your other poems? Maybe a little. But your poem should try to be true to the voice of these figures, as much as you can make it.

The persona enables you to write things you normally wouldn't. After all, you're not *you* in the poem, so you're not responsible, ultimately, for the feelings, opinions, and actions of your persona, which can be very freeing for a poet, especially one who is concerned with truth to the point of it becoming constricting.

Let Me Count the Ways

Poet John Keats wrote about the artist's "power of sympathy and freedom of self-consciousness," and called it negative capability. The concept of negative capability, very simply paraphrased, embodies the poet's ability to empty the self so that one could truly imagine being another (that's not all negative capability is about, but that's all we need at this moment). So, it's not so much that the persona poem is a gimmick but a real attempt to understand the persona and to render the attempt truthfully into verse.

Here are three interrelated persona poems from *The Spoon River Anthology,* by Edgar Lee Masters. The entire book is made of persona poems of dead people buried together in a cemetery. The titles are their names. Often, their stories overlap, as these do:

Aner Clute

Over and over they used to ask me,
While buying the wine or the beer,
In Peoria first, and later in Chicago,
Denver, Frisco, New York, wherever I lived
How I happened to lead the life,
And what was the start of it.
Well, I told them a silk dress,
And a promise of marriage from a rich man—
(It was Lucius Atherton).
But that was not really it at all.
Suppose a boy steals an apple
From the tray at the grocery store,
And they all begin to call him a thief,
The editor, minister, judge, and all the people—
"A thief," "a thief," "a thief," wherever he goes
And he can't get work, and he can't get bread
Without stealing it, why the boy will steal.
It's the way the people regard the theft of the apple
That makes the boy what he is.

Lucius Atherton

When my moustache curled,
And my hair was black,
And I wore tight trousers
And a diamond stud,
I was an excellent knave of hearts and took many a trick.
But when the gray hairs began to appear—
Lo! a new generation of girls
Laughed at me, not fearing me,
And I had no more exciting adventures
Wherein I was all but shot for a heartless devil,
But only drabby affairs, warmed-over affairs
Of other days and other men.
And time went on until I lived at
Mayer's restaurant,
Partaking of short-orders, a gray, untidy,
Toothless, discarded, rural Don Juan. ...
There is a mighty shade here who sings
Of one named Beatrice;

And I see now that the force that made him great
Drove me to the dregs of life.

Homer Clapp

Often Aner Clute at the gate
Refused me the parting kiss,
Saying we should be engaged before that;
And just with a distant clasp of the hand
She bade me good-night, as I brought her home
From the skating rink or the revival.
No sooner did my departing footsteps die away
Than Lucius Atherton,
(So I learned when Aner went to Peoria)
Stole in at her window, or took her riding
Behind his spanking team of bays
Into the country.
The shock of it made me settle down
And I put all the money I got from my father's estate
Into the canning factory, to get the job
Of head accountant, and lost it all.
And then I knew I was one of Life's fools,
Whom only death would treat as the equal
Of other men, making me feel like a man.

I can assure you that Masters wasn't dead when he wrote these—he was imagining what the stories of these dead people would sound like, and he gave them voices of their own.

Dodging Doggerel

When you write in a persona, don't mock your persona or make the character seem silly just because it's not your own voice. Instead, try to be true to that voice. Give the persona the dignity of its own personality—if that personality is silly, then so be it. You will find, if you are true to the voice, that your poem will be better for your effort to take the task seriously.

Here's a persona poem where the poet takes on the persona of a new butterfly:

From the Chrysalis

My cocoon tightens, colors tease,
I'm feeling for the air;
A dim capacity for wings
Degrades the dress I wear.

A power of butterfly must be
The aptitude to fly,
Meadows of majesty concedes
And easy sweeps of sky.

So I must baffle at the hint
And cipher at the sign,
And make much blunder, if at last
I take the clew divine.

—Emily Dickinson

Roses Are Red

Feel free to write in any form you want when you tackle a persona poem. Use a sonnet or a sestina, or blend the persona poem with another type of poem, like *ars poetica* or an acrostic (see Chapters 14, "Some Fun Fixed Forms," and 15, "More Fun Forms," on poetic forms for ideas).

You can see the effort here to really capture what the first moments of a butterfly's new life must be like in the first stanza. Then, in the next stanza, we realize that the persona is really a metaphor for something in the speaker's life, a new beginning, perhaps. The word "clew" in the last stanza has several meanings: It's a nautical term that has to do with sailing and wind; clew also alludes to the string that Theseus used to guide him out of the labyrinth; it's also an archaic spelling of "clue." Any (or all) of these interpretations works for the poem.

Here's a little persona poem that I wrote after having a conversation with a rather callous veterinarian at a party:

The Veterinary Student

He was the nicest steer, licking my boots mornings
when I fed the herd. Wasn't he a beautiful surprise
that morning we found him beneath his mother,
all spidery legs, quiet, knowing nothing yet of milk?

Sure, he never thought of himself as meat, trotting
the fence in his marbled fat. We knew him as Booger.
I'm not sure who got his steak at the graduation
bar-b-que, so much bloody meat; God, we ate like pigs.

When I wrote this I was trying to understand how the veterinary students could raise cows and steer, nurture and care for them, and then eat them at their graduation

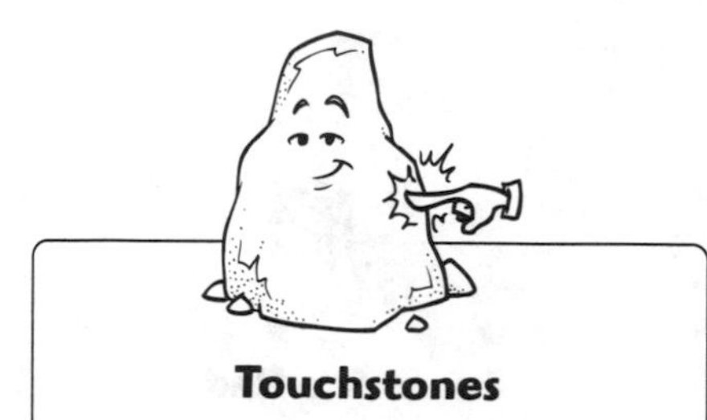

Touchstones

You can't blame a writer for what the characters say.

—Truman Capote

party. I tried to capture the student's voice here—I don't generally write poems with phrases beginning with "sure," or use words like "Booger"; but that's how I imagined the student would speak.

Try writing poems in one or more of the following personas: a famous person who is now dead, a politician, an animal on the way to be butchered, an emotion, the moon, a crab, a bird in a cage, a weather condition (snow storm, rain cloud, etc.), a writing utensil, a form of food (apple, steak, peas, and so on), a time of day, and your current neighbor. How are you going to make the voice in each of these poems sound different? Would the voice of the bird in a cage sound different from the voice of a snowstorm?

The Dramatic Monologue

The dramatic monologue, or dramatic lyric, is kind of a cross between the persona poem and the epistle poem (which is why it's sandwiched between them here). The dramatic monologue is written in the voice of one speaker, usually telling a story of some kind, and usually a persona. The assumption with this kind of poem is that the speaker is alone, speaking alone, usually aloud. The dramatic monologue is used in dramatic verse—here's an example from Shakespeare's *Romeo and Juliet:*

What if it be a poison which the friar
Subtilly hath minist'red to have me dead,
Lest in this marriage he should be dishonour'd
Because he married me before to Romeo?
I fear it is; and yet methinks it should not,
For he hath still been tried a holy man.
I will not entertain so bad a thought.
How if, when I am laid into the tomb,
I wake before the time that Romeo
Come to redeem me? There's a fearful point!
Shall I not then be stifled in the vault,
To whose foul mouth no healthsome air breathes in,
And there die strangled ere my Romeo comes?
Or, if I live, is it not very like
The horrible conceit of death and night,
Together with the terror of the place—
As in a vault, an ancient receptacle
Where for this many hundred years the bones
Of all my buried ancestors are pack'd;

Where bloody Tybalt, yet but green in earth,
Lies fest'ring in his shroud; where, as they say,
At some hours in the night spirits resort—
Alack, alack, is it not like that I,
So early waking—what with loathsome smells,
And shrieks like mandrakes torn out of the earth,
That living mortals, hearing them, run mad—
O, if I wake, shall I not be distraught,
Environed with all these hideous fears,
And madly play with my forefathers' joints,
And pluck the mangled Tybalt from his shroud,
And, in this rage, with some great kinsman's bone
As with a club dash out my desp'rate brains?
O, look! methinks I see my cousin's ghost
Seeking out Romeo, that did spit his body
Upon a rapier's point. Stay, Tybalt, stay!
Romeo, I come! this do I drink to thee.

This is obviously a passage spoken by Juliet, wondering aloud about the poison that the friar has given her. No consideration of audience is here on the part of the speaker; Juliet believes she's alone. The speaker is unaware of the watcher (reader), though the writer isn't.

Touchstones

The true artist declares himself by leaving out a lot. The artist alone sees spirits. But after he has told of their appearing to him, everybody sees them.

—Goethe

The Epistle Poem

The *epistle* poem, or letter poem, dates as far back as the ancient Romans and the Bible. Subject matter for the traditional epistle poem was love, religion, and philosophical matters. Today, the main characteristic of the letter poem is that it's addressed to a certain someone (or something) from a certain someone (or something) and is "talky," or less formal than the epistles you'd find in the Bible. Letter poems today include gossip, advice, desires, and anything else one person would want to share with another.

Poetically Correct

Epistle comes from the Latin, *epistula,* meaning "letter."

The letter poem is frequently written in a persona and to an imagined recipient, which allows for a lot of creativity and invention, making the form a fun one to try. Letter poems are great for expressing yourself; you get to write a letter that you don't have to send (though if you publish it the intended recipient might read it anyway!).

Poetically Correct

Apostrophe is to address a person or thing that isn't there, such as a dead person, a thing, or a concept, as if it is present.

When you're writing your letter poems, think about the person (or thing) you're writing to; this will help inform the tone of the letter. Is it a formal, business-type letter or a casual letter to a friend?

Try writing a letter poem to a person or thing as if the person or thing was present, even if that's not the situation, as in the case of someone who is dead. This is called *apostrophe,* and is an interesting way to address the recipient of a poem, especially if you make it clear to the reader (perhaps in the title) that the person or thing is not actually able to receive the "letter."

Because letter poems have no fixed form, you can use any of the poetic skills or forms you've learned. Here's one of my favorite letter poems—it takes on the persona of a young girl:

The River Merchant's Wife: A Letter

While my hair was still cut straight across my forehead
I played about the front gate, pulling flowers
You came by on bamboo stilts, playing horse,
You walked about my seat, playing with blue plums
And we went on living in the village of Chokan:
Two small people, without dislike or suspicion.
At fourteen I married My Lord you.
I never laughed, being bashful.
Lowering my head, I looked at the wall.
Called to, a thousand times, I never looked back.
At fifteen I stopped scowling,
I desired my dust to be mingled with yours
Forever and forever, and forever.
Why should I climb the look out?
At sixteen you departed,
You went into far Ku-to-Yen, by the river of swirling eddies,
And you have been gone five months.
The monkeys make sorrowful noise overhead.
You dragged your feet when you went out.
By the gate now, the moss is grown, the different mosses,
Too deep to clear them away!
The leaves fall early this autumn, in wind.
The paired butterflies are already yellow with August
Over the grass in the West garden,

They hurt me.
I grow older,
If you are coming down through the narrows of the river Kiang,
Please let me know beforehand,
And I will come out to meet you,
As far as Cho-fu-Sa.

—*By Rihaku.* Translated, Ezra Pound

Letter poems don't have to take the standard letter form. You can write one as an e-mail, a telegram, or even a postcard, like this next poem:

Postcard to W. C. Williams from Cienfuegos

On the other side of these words
are the tender green cane fields—
my sugar, my alcohol, my rum—
the chartreuse just after the rain.

This is my green wheelbarrow,
beauty, compelled by verdure,
even the white roses in head
burn jealous in a candle flicker—

petals turn and coil in the flame,
blacken to a foil of happy ash
that scatters among the palms.

—Richard Blanco

Here's an ambitious letter poem addressed to a wide audience:

[This is my letter to the world]

This is my letter to the world,
 That never wrote to me,—
The simple news that Nature told,
 With tender majesty.

Her message is committed
 To hands I cannot see;
For love of her, sweet countrymen,
 Judge tenderly of me!

—Emily Dickinson

To whom you address your letter makes a vast difference in the tone of the letter. A letter written in the persona of George Washington to his wife, Martha, will have a distinctly different tone than a letter to one of his generals. You probably will know without thinking too hard about it what tone to use, especially if you write a lot of letters or e-mails to the various people in your life.

Roses Are Red

When you write a letter poem, it's obvious that you have one voice speaking in the poem, but you have to consider the recipient as well. It's interesting for the reader to know whom the letter is addressed to. Consider putting an indication of the recipient in the title of the poem—anywhere near the poem's opening will do.

Exercises

Here are some fun exercises to get you started writing persona poems and letter poems.

- Write in the persona of a utilitarian inanimate object that you use on a daily basis, e.g., a cooking pan, the bathtub, or a light fixture.
- Write a dramatic monologue of a space alien explaining how he got to earth and why he wants to go home.
- Write a letter in the persona of a tree writing to the soil, of a cloud writing to the sky, or of a car writing to gasoline. Then write a response letter.
- Write a very short poem in the form of a postcard or a telegram. You can choose a short form like the haiku, tanka, or triolet if you like (see Chapter 14 on fixed forms for ideas).

The Least You Need to Know

- The persona poem is one that enables the writer to take on another identity, to write as someone or something else.
- The ability of the poet to take on another's persona is sometimes called negative capability.
- The dramatic monologue is written in the voice of one speaker, usually telling a story of some kind, and usually a persona.
- The epistle poem, or letter poem, dates as far back as the ancient Romans and the Bible.
- Letter poems have no fixed form, so you can use any of the skills or forms you've learned.

Chapter 13

Spellbinding!: List Poems and Rituals

In This Chapter

- The catalogue poem
- The power of prayer poems
- Invocations
- Charms and incantations
- Recipe poems

Poetry grew up holding hands with its sibling, Ritual, and as a result the combined pair make a kind of lasting, powerful magic. We often perform rituals, like prayer or charms, to try to make something happen. In poetry, we can use ritual much the same way—to compel the reader to remember something important, or to call down a muse to help us think of an inventive metaphor.

Sometimes, poems use ritual as a poetic form to express content that has little to do with the ritual, to play with words, or to parody the ritual. Many rituals are quite ancient, and it's fun to take an old ritual and make it "new." This chapter illustrates a few fun rituals and will break down the elements of these rituals so that you can write them yourself.

Starting with a List ...

Some of the oldest poems use the form of the list, or catalogue. The list functions as a mnemonic device, and enables the poet to furnish the maximum of information in a small space. A list can take the form of a chant, a prayer, or any other type of ritual where many things follow one after the other.

The list can be one of the most straightforward types of poems to write, and it has a long poetic history. Here's a bit from the Homer's *Iliad* (around 1100 B.C.E.):

> Peneleos, Leitus, Arcesilaus, Prothoenor, and Clonius were captains of the Boeotians. These were they that dwelt in Hyria and rocky Aulis, and who held Schoenus, Scolus, and the highlands of Eteonus, with Thespeia, Graia, and the fair city of Mycalessus. They also held Harma, Eilesium, and Erythrae; and they had Eleon, Hyle, and Peteon; Ocalea and the strong fortress of Medeon; Copae, Eutresis, and Thisbe the haunt of doves; Coronea, and the pastures of Haliartus; Plataea and Glisas; the fortress of Thebes the less; holy Onchestus with its famous grove of Neptune; Arne rich in vineyards; Midea, sacred Nisa, and Anthedon upon the sea. From these there came fifty ships, and in each there were a hundred and twenty young men of the Boeotians. ...

This list of who attended the big battle and in how many ships goes on for pages. If you read it aloud, you'll find that it begins to have an almost hypnotic, chant-like effect. Here's a bit from the Old Testament that has the same effect:

> These are the generations of the sons of Noah, Shem, Ham, and Japheth; sons were born to them after the flood. The sons of Japheth: Gomer, Magog, Madai, Javan, Tubal, Meshech, and Tiras. The sons of Gomer: Ash'kenaz, Riphath, and Togar'mah. The sons of Javan: Eli'shah, Tarshish, Kittim, and Do'danim. From these the coastland peoples spread. These are the sons of Japheth in their lands, each with his own language, by their families, in their nations. The sons of Ham: Cush, Egypt, Put, and Canaan. The sons of Cush: Seba, Hav'ilah, Sabtah, Ra'amah, and Sab'teca. The sons of Ra'amah: Sheba and Dedan. Cush became the father of Nimrod ...

You can see how using the list allows for the cramming of information; both lists convey the importance of the relationships between the items listed. These lists are simple catalogs that eventually add up to a larger story.

Try writing a short "family tree" list poem and include lots of names and places. Remember, you only have to write a list. The larger story of how you came into being should emerge naturally from the list.

Roses Are Red

A good way a getting "unstuck" when you're looking for something to write about is to begin with a list. Begin listing all the people you went to high school with, all the neighbors surrounding the house you grew up in, the stuff in your medicine cabinet, things you've found on a beach, all the flowers you can remember, etc. Making a list will often help to generate ideas.

Here's a contemporary poem that uses a list of ordinary objects to convey the nature of a specific relationship:

Things My Father Sends Me Via the U.S. Mail

A box of assorted baklava, a stuffed ghost, a black and white photo of Grandmother Josephine in Baton Rouge, a food processor with a bird drawn on a yellow sticky note inside looking suspiciously like the notes in my lunchbox in second grade, his set of Edward Gorey books, a fairy with stained glass wings held up by fishing wire, a green jacket to keep me dry in the rain, a chapter from his new spy novel, a square jar of apricot marmalade, Christmas presents in July, tiny French soaps with Verbena printed on their backsides, newspaper clippings of the latest Washington scandals, sheets of bubble wrap to pop between my fingers and toes when bored, lotion samples, pear and apple, an annotated edition of Ulysses, photo of me, framed, when I was 5 years old selling tomatoes in our front yard, promises to one day live in Acapulco smoking cigars and eating bon bons on the beach.

—Laura Howard

This prose poem functions like the above sections from Homer and the Bible, and does so with concrete, average things that the speaker's father sent through the U.S. mail. Through this simple list (and the title), the reader can gather a lot of information: The father and the speaker are far apart, probably overseas. The speaker is an adult, though the father is still sending items suited for a child. The father and the speaker are emotionally close, but not close enough for the promises of living in Acapulco to be more than promises at the moment. The plurality of "promises" suggests that the speaker has been waiting for the reality of Acapulco, or something like it, for a long time—waiting, really, for the father to appear.

Make a list of things someone has sent you or given you over the years. The list should suggest your relationship. You'll find that it may do that naturally, without having to force it.

Let Me Count the Ways

The list poem is a favorite assignment for a beginning poetry class. The list is an easy poem to generate, but it's just as difficult to make sense out of it if the poet has not tried for some larger meaning. It's fun to combine the list format with another form, such as a sonnet, sestina, ars poetica, etc. This way the poem does double duty, and the poem has more aspects for the reader to appreciate.

Walt Whitman is famous for the catalogue poem. In this next poem section, Whitman considers the human body:

From **I Sing the Body Electric**

O my body! I dare not desert the likes of you in other
    men and women, nor the likes of the parts of you,
I believe the likes of you are to stand or fall with the
    likes of the soul, (and that they are the soul),
I believe the likes of you shall stand or fall with my
    poems, and that they are my poems,
Man's, woman's, child, youth's, wife's, husband's,
    mother's, father's, young man's, young woman's poems,
Head, neck, hair, ears, drop and tympan of the ears,
Eyes, eye-fringes, iris of the eye, eyebrows, and the
    waking or sleeping of the lids,
Mouth, tongue, lips, teeth, roof of the mouth, jaws, and
    the jaw-hinges,

Nose, nostrils of the nose, and the partition,
Cheeks, temples, forehead, chin, throat, back of the neck,
    neck-slue,
Strong shoulders, manly beard, scapula, hind-shoulders,
    and the ample side-round of the chest,
Upper-arm, armpit, elbow-socket, lower-arm, arm-sinews,
    arm-bones,
Wrist and wrist-joints, hand, palm, knuckles, thumb,
    forefinger, finger-joints, finger-nails,
Broad breast-front, curling hair of the breast, breast-
    bone, breast-side,
Ribs, belly, backbone, joints of the backbone,
Hips, hip-sockets, hip-strength, inward and outward
    round, man-balls, man-root,
Strong set of thighs, well carrying the trunk above,
Leg-fibres, knee, knee-pan, upper-leg, under-leg,
Ankles, instep, foot-ball, toes, toe-joints, the heel;
All attitudes, all the shapeliness, all the belongings of
    my or your body or of any one's body, male or female …

—Walt Whitman

The list poem generally consists of things that have something in common, as you can see from this example. This list's power is in Whitman's careful, detailed examination of his subject. The words he uses are simple in themselves but gain power and momentum when they are placed next to one another. Another way the items in your list poems can gain power is through *auxesis,* placing the items in ascending or climactic order.

Poetically Correct

Auxesis is a rhetorical strategy that places items in ascending or climactic order.

To try something similar to the Whitman poem, study a photo of an exotic animal and write a list of its body parts as you see them; use metaphor if you'd like.

Touchstones

A poet dares to be just so clear and no clearer; he approaches lucid ground warily, like a mariner who is determined not to scrape bottom on anything solid. A poet's pleasure is to withhold a little of his meaning, to intensify by mystification. He unzips the veil from beauty, but does not remove it. A poet utterly clear is a trifle glaring.

—E. B. White

Not all lists have to be composed of concrete things, nouns. This next famous list is a catalogue of actions by the speaker's cat:

From **Jubilate Agno**

For I will consider my Cat Jeoffry.
For he is the servant of the Living God duly and daily
  serving him.
For at the first glance of the glory of God in the East
  he worships in his way.
For this is done by wreathing his body seven times round
  with elegant quickness.
For then he leaps up to catch the musk, which is the
  blessing of
God upon his prayer.
For he rolls upon prank to work it in.
For having done duty and received blessing he begins to
  consider himself.
For this he performs in ten degrees.
For first he looks upon his forepaws to see if they are
  clean.
For secondly he kicks up behind to clear away there.
For thirdly he works it upon stretch with the forepaws
  extended.

For fourthly he sharpens his paws by wood.
For fifthly he washes himself.
For sixthly he rolls upon wash.
For seventhly he fleas himself, that he may not be
interrupted upon the beat.
For eighthly he rubs himself against a post.
For ninthly he looks up for his instructions.
For tenthly he goes in quest of food.
For having consider'd God and himself he will consider
his neighbour.
For if he meets another cat he will kiss her in kindness.
For when he takes his prey he plays with it to give it a
chance.
For one mouse in seven escapes by his dallying.
For when his day's work is done his business more
properly begins. ...

—Christopher Smart

As an exercise, write a list of things that your pet (or a former pet) does on a daily basis. See David Lehman's poem, "For I Will Consider Your Dog Molly" from his book, *Operation Memory,* for a poem written in the style of Smart's cat poem.

Touchstones

Poetry is the opening and closing of a door, leaving those who look through to guess about what was seen during a moment.
—Carl Sandburg

Part of writing a good list poem is playing with the order of the things listed. If someone gave you a group of random words, you could probably find some way to fit them together to get the most out of their music. That's what you want to do with your list. A poet tries to make his or her words work double and triple duty. When you're working on a list poem, read it aloud to yourself over and over; you should be able to hear the places where the music soars and where it needs a little help.

The next poem, "Chicago," uses a kind of dialogue between the speaker, the citizens of Chicago, and Chicago itself to form its list. This is a musically charged poem; by that I mean that Sandburg places words upon one another to form certain sounds that mirror his meaning—read it aloud.

Chicago

Hog Butcher for the World,
Tool Maker, Stacker of Wheat
Player with Railroads and the Nation's Freight Handler;
Stormy, husky, brawling,
City of the Big Shoulders:

They tell me you are wicked and I believe them, for I
have seen your painted women under the gas lamps
luring the farm boys.
And they tell me you are crooked and I answer: Yes, it is
true I have seen the gunman kill and go free to
kill again.
And they tell me you are brutal and my reply is: On the
faces of women and children I have seen the marks
of wanton hunger.
And having answered so I turn once more to those who sneer
at this my city, and I give them back the sneer and say to them:
Come and show me another city with lifted head singing so
proud to be alive and coarse and strong and
cunning.
Flinging magnetic curses amid the toil of piling job on
job, here is a tall bold slugger set vivid
against the little soft cities;
Fierce as a dog with tongue lapping for action, cunning
as a savage pitted against the wilderness,
Bareheaded,
Shoveling,
Wrecking,
Planning,
Building, breaking, rebuilding,
Under the smoke, dust all over his mouth, laughing with
white teeth,
Under the terrible burden of destiny laughing as a young
man laughs,
Laughing even as an ignorant fighter laughs who has never
lost a battle,
Bragging and laughing that under his wrist is the pulse
and under his ribs the heart of the people,
Laughing!

Laughing the stormy, husky, brawling laughter of Youth,
half-naked, sweating, proud to be Hog Butcher,
Tool Maker, Stacker of Wheat, Player with
Railroads and Freight Handler to the Nation.

—Carl Sandburg

Hear the clashing, brawny sounds in this poem? It has a lot of stacked K sounds throughout, even in words beginning with C. Go back and read it aloud again and hear how the sounds here mimic the content of the list.

Note all the things that the personified Chicago is and does. This poem has a lot of verbs, lots of action. Write a poem about your own town that uses the same strategy. If you live in Chicago, do you see something about the city that Sandburg didn't?

Dodging Doggerel

Your list poems shouldn't be just a list of things in a category, though you can begin with that. The poem should have some sort of logic to it, something larger that the poem is reaching for. Let's suppose you make a list of book titles; think about how those book titles work together to *say* something bigger than just the titles of the books. For example, the titles may link to form a narrative, or may show how you've progressed from Mother Goose to Shakespeare.

This next poem uses another type of catalogue—a list of directives:

Directions for a Thursday Afternoon:
How to Keep Me Whole and Unbroken

Crack an egg directly onto the cigarette
burn in the linoleum, think

only of burnt squash casseroles and how
I've forgotten all my mother's cures
for insomnia. Sleep

with just one pillow, leave the other
beside you

to hold the memory of me in your bed.

Drink out of wineglasses stolen from your neighbor,
left for months on your shared balcony, remember how

I saw his lover kissing another man.

Forget what temporary means,
forget you

always leaving me always leaving you.

Put life back into order, potholder
on top of potholder,

second drawer from bottom. Lay no claim
on objects left behind.

Catch months of rainwater
and algae in the cupped hands

of a homeless woman in Buenos Aires
who talks only to birds.

Sob out loud while doing the dishes,
being extra careful

with your great aunt's antique blue teacup,
then drink out of it the strongest maté you can find,

afterwards, write my name on a piece of paper

smaller than a cat's eye marble.

Study paintings from Europe,
begin with Vermeer's Girl with a Pearl Earring, notice

not the brushstrokes or angle of light on her face but
how much she looks like me, upper lip over teeth,

making sound
come from your oboe,

keeping all the reeds you make for it
whole
and unbroken.

—Laura Howard

This list gives directives from a specific "I" to a specific "you," and we, the readers, are given a glimpse into their private lives through the list. The directives here aren't meant literally as directions; they are meant to expose the nature of the relationship between these two lovers.

Write a list of directives to someone emotionally close to you who's far away in terms of physical distance.

Rituals

Public rituals come in many forms, and we'll look at just a few of them here. You probably have some private rituals that you may be able to use in your poems as well.

Ritual implies a certain set of rules or conventions undertaken, such that the end is granted by the means. For example, we all know what *prayer* is: a kind of wish that we ask of a higher power, whatever that higher power might be. Poets like to fashion poems from prayers; here's a sweet prayer rendered into verse:

Grandma's Prayer

I pray that, risen from the dead,
  I may in glory stand—
A crown, perhaps, upon my head,
  But a needle in my hand.

I've never learned to sing or play,
  So let no harp be mine;
From birth unto my dying day,
  Plain sewing's been my line.

Therefore, accustomed to the end
  To plying useful stitches,
I'll be content if asked to mend
  The little angels' breeches.

—Eugene Field

Write a prayer using this rhyme scheme, but write the prayer in the voice of someone famous; for example, "Santa's Prayer," or "The President's Prayer."

An invocation is a kind of prayer as well, generally to a muse or one of the gods, and it tries to *invoke,* or call forth, the aid of the one being requested. Invocations were common in the poetry of the Ancient Greeks and Romans, the folks who *really* believed in the muses. Dante uses invocations several times during tough spots in his *Inferno*. Homer's Odyssey begins with an invocation:

> *Tell me, O muse, of that ingenious hero who traveled far and wide after he had sacked the famous town of Troy. Many cities did he visit, and many were the nations with whose manners and customs he was acquainted; moreover he suffered much by sea while trying to save his own life and bring his men safely home; but do what he might he could not save his men, for they perished through their own sheer folly in eating the*

> *cattle of the Sun-god Hyperion; so the god prevented them from ever reaching home. Tell me, too, about all these things, O daughter of Jove, from whatsoever source you may know them.*

When you get stuck on a poem, or you're having a dry spell, try an invocation. Choose your favorite muse (see Chapter 2, "Exposing Poetry's Bones: What Poetry Is Made Of") and write a poem invoking her—or write one invoking your favorite saint, dead loved one, or even someone or something you invent.

Here's a modern invocation/prayer-type poem by poet Ezra Pound:

The Lake Isle

O God, O Venus, O Mercury, patron of thieves,
Give me in due time, I beseech you, a little
tobacco-shop,
With the little bright boxes
piled up neatly upon the shelves
And the loose fragrent cavendish
and the shag,
And the bright Virginia
loose under the bright glass cases,
And a pair of scales
not too greasy,
And the *votailles* dropping in for a word or two in a
passing,
For a flip word, and to tidy their hair a bit.
O God, O Venus, O Mercury, patron of thieves,
Lend me a little tobacco-shop,
or install me in any profession
Save this damn'd profession of writing,
where one needs one's brains all the time.

—Ezra Pound

Part of the irony in this poem is that Pound uses an invocation to help him do something *other* than write, when the form is traditionally used for the poet in need of writing assistance.

Write an invocation, like this one, where you call on the muses or the gods to help you change one aspect of your life.

Charms and incantations are similar to invocations, but they don't necessarily use traditional deities and figures as their focus. A charm or incantation can take the form of the directions for making a love potion or some other type of magic "spell." They can also take the form of a *chant,* which is a repetitive form that's part song and part speech. A charm is generally a set of directives—a "do this, do that" poem that will lead to a specific result. Charms are similar to recipe poems. Look in any recipe book for ideas on formatting. Here's the first stanza of a poem by poet T. H. White called *The Which's Work Song:*

Poetically Correct

Chant is a form of oral poetry composed generally, but not necessarily, to be communally performed; it is something between a speech and a song.

Two spoons of sherry
Three oz. of yeast,
Half a pound of unicorn,
And God bless the feast.
Shake them in the colander,
Bang them to a chop,
Simmer slightly, snip up nicely,
Jump, skip, hop.
Knit one, knot one, purl two together,
Pip one and pop one and pluck the secret feather.

An invitation poem is exactly what it sounds like—a request for the reader (or a character in the poem) to do something:

The Pasture

I'm going out to clean the pasture spring;
I'll only stop to rake the leaves away
(And wait to watch the water clear, I may):
I sha'n't be gone long.—You come too.
I'm going out to fetch the little calf
That's standing by the mother. It's so young,
It totters when she licks it with her tongue.
I sha'n't be gone long.—You come too.

—Robert Frost

This poem calls the reader to follow the speaker into the "poetic" pasture of the poem. We, as readers, are drawn in through the invitation and can't help but to follow—the poet usually takes us there if we keep reading. This particular poem also opens one of Frost's books of poems, so it is also an invitation to enter the entire book.

Write an "impossible" invitation poem to your reader; assume that your reader cannot do what you ask, e.g., fly, eat a mountain, sit inside a whale, etc.

Exercises

Here are some fun exercises to get you started with lists and rituals. These are loose forms, so you can feel free to experiment with them as wildly as you want.

- Write a three-part list poem. In the first section, list all of the places you'd like to visit in the world—you might have to drag out a map. In the second part, choose a place and list the reasons why you want to go there. In the third part, imagine that you're in that place and list all of the fascinating things you do and see. You can keep the poem as is, or you can use it as a springboard for other poems.
- Write an invocation to your chosen muse. What is the one thing about your poems that you'd like to do better? Ask for help with that.
- Try a prayer poem asking for something for someone else.
- Look in a cookbook and find a complicated recipe. Using the format, write a recipe for an abstraction: hope, love, fear, rage, justice, etc.
- Write an invitation poem to another poet.

The Least You Need to Know

- The list poem is an ancient form and is effective in getting a lot of information into a small space.
- When using the list form, think about how the music of the words can help the meaning of the poem.
- A list doesn't have to be just nouns; it can be a dialogue, directives, questions, or anything else you can think to list.
- An invocation poem is an ancient form used to call the aid of the muses, and it is still a popular form.
- You can use charms, incantations, and recipes as poetic forms.

Chapter 14

Some Fun Fixed Forms

In This Chapter

- Move over, Shakespeare: sonnets
- Pantoums (no, that's not a dirty word)
- A ghazal isn't a kind of elk ... it's a poem!
- Haiku, you ku, we all ku
- Poems to dance by

By now you know that poems come in a variety of forms. Many formal poems have fixed elements that a poet uses to create poems; these elements are things you've learned in earlier chapters—repetition, meter, rhyme, counting syllables, and so on—except that fixed forms have a pattern to how these elements are used.

Why use fixed forms? Because they're fun and challenging, and because many of the forms have a long history, making them especially appealing—poets like to take the old and make it new.

In this chapter, you'll discover the inner workings of a few popular fixed forms. You'll find that they're easier and more fun than you may have thought!

Sonnets

The sonnet is one of the most popular poetic forms in the Western Tradition. It was created around the thirteenth century in Italy, and its name means "little song." The sonnet is traditionally a 14-line poem with a set rhyme and metrical scheme, though modern sonnets often abandon the latter. The subject matter for a sonnet is usually simple on the surface, but the development of thought in a sonnet can be complicated. A good sonnet explores its concept, sometimes an argument or a quandary, and, by the end, has developed an answer. Here we'll discuss three commonly written fixed sonnets.

Also called the Elizabethan sonnet or the English sonnet, the Shakespearean sonnet is the most commonly written type of sonnet. The main distinction between this type of sonnet and its counterparts is its rhyme scheme: ababcdcdefefgg. Here's an example from Shakespeare:

CXLIII

Lo, as a careful housewife runs to catch a
One of her feather'd creatures broke away, b
Sets down her babe, and makes all swift dispatch a
In pursuit of the thing she would have stay; b
Whilst her neglected child holds her in chase, c
Cries to catch her whose busy care is bent d
To follow that which flies before her face, c
Not prizing her poor infant's discontent; d
So runn'st thou after that which flies from thee, e
Whilst I thy babe chase thee afar behind; f
But if thou catch thy hope, turn back to me, e
And play the mother's part, kiss me, be kind; f
 So will I pray that thou mayst have thy 'Will,' g
 If thou turn back and my loud crying still. g

Roses Are Red

Here's a tip for the beginning sonneteer: Instead of getting caught up in trying for perfect meter, count 10 syllables per line—the English language is naturally iambic, and chances are that some of your lines will be iambic without your even trying.

Note that the last two lines are a "rhyming couplet." This is the place where the poet "closes" the poem, where the idea, or argument, of the poem is "solved." We'll take another look at this concept in a moment. Shakespeare sets his couplet off by indenting it a little bit, but you don't have to do that unless you want to.

Attributed to the Roman poet Petrarch, the Petrarchan sonnet consists of an octave (eight-line stanza), rhyming abbaabba, and a sestet (six-line stanza), rhyming cdcdcd, though there are accepted rhyming variations in the sestet; the Spencerian sonnet, attributed to Edmund Spencer and less widely used than the previous two, rhymes abab bcbc cdcd ee.

Sonnets are traditionally written in meter, primarily iambic pentameter. Many modern sonnets abandon meter altogether, and you may want to as well, though trying for some meter and line regularity will make your sonnet more "sonnety" than if you write wild lines and give no attempt at rhythm or meter at all. See Chapter 9, "You've Got Rhythm: Metrical Poetry," to brush up on your metrical skills.

The Volta

The volta is the fancy term for the "turn" in the idea, quandary, or argument in the sonnet; it's the place where the poet begins to close the poem or to tell what the poem is really about, or begins to solve the poem's dilemma. The volta can happen as early as the eighth line in the sonnet and as late as the couplet. In the above Shakespearian sonnet, the volta begins around line nine, when the speaker reveals the metaphor of the poem—he is the "babe" chasing after the object of his affection. Without this turn, and the couplet tying up the ending, this poem would look and sound like a sonnet, but it wouldn't contain the essence of a sonnet. The Petrarchan sonnet has a built-in place to begin the volta, which is right after the initial octave, around line nine.

The couplet at the end often serves as a natural volta for the sonnet, though it comes late in the poem; the two lines can be set off from the rest of the poem to tie up the story or the argument that is set up in the previous 12 lines.

Variations in and on the Sonnet

As with any poetic form, there's no hard and fast rule to how the form is executed. The sonnet, possibly because of its age and popularity, comes in various incarnations. Here's one by Robert Frost that plays with the traditional rhyme scheme:

The Oven Bird

There is a singer everyone has heard,	a
Loud, a mid-summer and a mid-wood bird,	a
Who makes the solid tree trunks sound again.	b
He says that leaves are old and that for flowers	c
Mid-summer is to spring as one to ten.	b
He says the early petal-fall is past	d
When pear and cherry bloom went down in showers	c
On sunny days a moment overcast;	d
And comes that other fall we name the fall.	e
He says the highway dust is over all.	e
The bird would cease and be as other birds	f
But that he knows in singing not to sing.	g
The question that he frames in all but words	f
Is what to make of a diminished thing.	g

—Robert Frost

You can see that this poem has 14 lines and is written in pretty regular iambic pentameter (though line two has a variation, which begins with a trochee for emphasis). So how is this a sonnet if it doesn't conform to any of the recognized sonnet rhyme schemes? Well, it's a variation on a sonnet, and as valid as the sonnets Shakespeare wrote. Not only does this poem use many of the conventions of a sonnet, it has a volta around line nine and a couplet, although not rhyming (it holds together as a couplet grammatically), which ties the whole concept of the poem together. Here's another sonnet by Frost that varies the traditional sonnet form:

Into My Own

One of my wishes is that those dark trees,	a
So old and firm they scarcely show the breeze,	a
Were not, as 'twere, the merest mask of gloom,	b
But stretched away unto the edge of doom.	b
I should not be withheld but that some day	c
Into their vastness I should steal away,	c
Fearless of ever finding open land,	d
Or highway where the slow wheel pours the sand.	d
I do not see why I should e'er turn back,	e
Or those should not set forth upon my track	e
To overtake me, who should miss me here	f
And long to know if still I held them dear.	f
They would not find me changed from him they knew—	g
Only more sure of all I thought was true.	g

—Robert Frost

Poetically Correct

A **curtail sonnet** is a shortened version of the sonnet, usually around 10 lines. A **caudate sonnet** is a lengthened sonnet containing a "coda," usually a couplet, at the end. A **sonnet sequence** is a string of sonnets containing related or similar subject matter.

This sonnet uses rhyming couplets throughout, but still has 14 lines, a volta beginning around line nine, and a couplet tying up the end. You can see how modern poets can change fixed forms but still have them resemble their ancestors. There are even "fixed" variations on the sonnet that you can try: the *curtail sonnet* (having only about 10 lines), the *caudate sonnet* (having the addition of another couplet at the end), and the *sonnet sequence* (a group of sonnets having related subject matter). You can reverse the rhyme scheme and write a *reverse sonnet* (opening with the rhyming couplet, for example), or you can attempt a *crown of sonnets,* consisting of seven sonnets, each one beginning with the last line of the preceding sonnet, with the first line and the last line of the crown being identical.

The modern sonnet is almost an "anything goes" proposition, as long as some of the components of the sonnet are recognizable. Here's a modern sonnet sequence that takes liberties with line length, meter, and rhyme scheme:

Elk Island

A forest outside Moscow

I.

Below the canopy — a
of sky-shouldering trees, — b

we kept seeing old people — a
down on their knees. — b

You said—in words — c
like the clamor of birds— — c

they're searching for mushrooms. — d
Under birch and pine, blooms — d

bent orange-starred in ground. — e
I chased your words around — e

each turn, unscrolling this maze — f
to a hidden field, days — f

we could keep finding — g
ourselves utterly lost in. — g

II.

Like temple ruins, the pillared aisles — a
of birch and pine betrayed human order. — b
Even at the forest's core, signs each mile — a
marked the distance to Moscow's border. — b
You explained: *once, the woods were called islands,* — c
between the fields and towns. Each tree steepled — d
a sky we thought holy. When the Germans — c
threatened, Red Army tanks—our own people — d

tore through, destroyed what they could not save. — e
Limbs, trunks, green leaves like raised hands, fell. — f
Moscow held. Later, we scooped small graves — e
in the blasted ground, planted seeds in lines, — f
so each tree could breathe. So, in time, the mass — g
of roots would raise the heavens back into place. — g

III.	
The train's pleated tracks, our own crooked wake	-
behind us, we pull each shin through blank drifts	-
of blued snow, so deep only tanks could tread	a
and forget. Across the frozen plain,	-
Elk Island lies, the birches like bleached ribs bared	a
to air. We're stopped. A net of branches snags	-
the moon, spilling itself out in the shroud	b
of dark. Wind bristles. Above, pines clatter	c
like elk locking horns. With every sway,	d
the churned and frozen sea shatters	c
into uncountably faceted light:	-
before us, the field we'd found, the sky	d
flaking down. No, it's another field,	b
in the slow and broken amnesia of snow.	-

—Philip Metres

Poetically Correct

A **reversed sonnet** is a sonnet that uses one of the traditional rhyme schemes backward. A **crown of sonnets** consists of seven sonnets, the last line of each sonnet beginning the first line of the one following it; the last line of the crown is a repetition of the first line of the opening sonnet, also called a **corona.**

The first sonnet in this sequence has an almost Shakespearian rhyme scheme, and although it doesn't work metrically, it is still considered a sonnet. The second poem in the sequence uses the Shakespearian rhyme scheme and has some metrical moments: Line three, for example, is iambic. Note that many of the rhyming words are loose slant rhymes. The third sonnet in the sequence abandons the rhyme scheme but contains 14 lines, some metrical moments, and is the last in a sequence of sonnets. So, is it a sonnet, too? Yes, it's a variation on the form.

Villanelle

A villanelle is a sixteenth-century French form that means "rustic song" or "dance." Its roots are in Italy, but the French poets made it what it is today: five stanzas of three lines each, with a sixth four-line stanza. The first line and the third line of the first stanza are repeated in a pattern throughout the poem and it has a specific rhyme scheme consisting of two rhyme sounds. Confused? Take a look at the following poem:

Theocritus

O SINGER of Persephone!	A1
In the dim meadows desolate	b
Dost thou remember Sicily?	A2
Still through the ivy flits the bee	a
Where Amaryllis lies in state;	b
O Singer of Persephone!	A1
Simætha calls on Hecate	a
And hears the wild dogs at the gate;	b
Dost thou remember Sicily?	A2
Still by the light and laughing sea	a
Poor Polypheme bemoans his fate:	b
O Singer of Persephone!	A1
And still in boyish rivalry	a
Young Daphnis challenges his mate:	b
Dost thou remember Sicily?	A2
Slim Lacon keeps a goat for thee,	a
For thee the jocund shepherds wait,	b
O Singer of Persephone!	A1
Dost thou remember Sicily?	A2

—Oscar Wilde

You can see that all of the "a" words rhyme and all of the "b" words rhyme, and that refrains one and two repeat in a particular pattern. This is a tough form to do well, though it's fun to try. Choose your repeating refrains so that they are flexible in both content and structure. For example, you can choose a refrain that can be broken into two parts such that the one line forms two "sentences," both from the previous line and when it's carried over onto the next line.

Though Wilde doesn't vary his refrain lines, you can feel free to replace words and even shift words around. You can ditch the rhyme scheme as well if you'd like.

Poetically Correct

An **envoi** is a short, concluding stanza, mainly found in French poetic forms.

Sestina

The sestina, invented around 1190, is an unrhymed form used by the troubadours and made popular by the German poets in the seventeenth century and the French and the English in the nineteenth century. It made a revival in English poetry in the nineteenth century and is today a favorite form of poets of all levels and skill.

The sestina consists of six stanzas and an envoi, which is a short concluding stanza. The sestina used to have a certain meter and specific number of syllables, though today's sestinas have far less strict standards. Each of the first six stanzas contains six lines, each line of which ends in the same set pattern of words, with a three-line envoi containing all six words. Confused? The word pattern goes as follows:

Stanza 1: abcdef
Stanza 2: faebdc
Stanza 3: cfdabe
Stanza 4: ecbfad
Stanza 5: deacfb
Stanza 6: bdfeca
Envoi: bd, dc, fa

Here's an example of a modern sestina; the key to this form is in the repeating end words—note the repetition:

My Confessional Sestina

Let me confess. I'm sick of these sestinas
written by youngsters in poetry workshops
for the delectation of their fellow students,
and then published in little magazines
that no one reads, not even the contributors
who at least in this omission show some taste.

Is this merely a matter of personal taste?
I don't think so. Most sestinas
are such dull affairs. Just ask the contributors
the last time they finished one outside of a workshop,
even the poignant one on herpes in that new little magazine
edited by their most brilliant fellow student.

Let's be honest. It has become a form for students,
an exercise to build technique rather than taste
and the official entry blank into the little magazines—
because despite its reputation, a passable sestina
isn't very hard to write, even for kids in workshops
who care less about being poets than contributors.

Granted nowadays everyone is a contributor.
My barber is currently a student
in a rigorous correspondence school workshop.
At lesson six he can already taste
success having just placed his own sestina
in a national tonsorial magazine.

Who really cares about most little magazines?
Eventually not even their own contributors
who having published a few preliminary sestinas
send their work East to prove they're no longer students.
They need to be recognized as the new arbiters of taste
so they can teach their own graduate workshops.

Where will it end? This grim cycle of workshops
churning out poems for little magazines
no one honestly finds to their taste?
This ever-lengthening column of contributors
scavenging the land for more students
teaching them to write their boot-camp sestinas?

Perhaps there is an afterlife where all contributors
have two workshops, a tasteful little magazine, and sexy
students
who worshipfully memorize their every sestina.

—Dana Gioia

Canzone

The canzone is an Italian form that I like to think of as a sestina on some serious speed. It was made popular by poet Dante Alegheri, though the form in English bears little resemblance to his canzones of the fourteenth century.

The canzone, like the sestina, uses repeating end words. The form consists of five 12-line stanzas and a 6-line envoi. This form has variations on how the end words repeat, but you can use the following pattern as a guideline:

Stanza 1: abaacaaddaee
Stanza 2: eaeebeeccedd
Stanza 3: deddaddbbdcc
Stanza 4: cdcceeeaacbb
Stanza 5: bcbbdbbeebaa
Envoi: abcde

The canzone is one of my favorite forms. I'll give you a hint on how to choose your end words—this goes for the sestina as well. Try to choose words that can be used in various parts of speech. For example, in Catherine Bowman's canzone, *The Lights of Marfa,* she uses the word *eye* as one of the end words, and turns "eye" into "eyes," "wild-eyed," "islands," "ionized," "eye-witness," and "I." In a canzone that I wrote, I used the word "yellow," and I used "Yell. Oh," at the end of the line and then went to the next—it worked.

As an exercise, go through your dictionary and find versatile words for a sestina and a canzone. The more you can manipulate the words you choose, the better.

Pantoum

The pantoum is an old Malayan verse form (originally, pantoun) invented around the fifteenth century. It uses both repetition and rhyme woven into a sort of braid. It once used a fixed number of lines and stanzas, but the Malay form mutated over the years, with the French and English becoming fond if it in the nineteenth century.

Today, the pantoum is a poem of indeterminate length (it can consist of just a few stanzas or go on forever) using four-line stanzas and repetition and braiding, similar to how the villanelle works. The pantoum's pattern is as follows:

Line one
Line two
Line three
Line four

Line two repeated (five)
Line six
Line four repeated (seven)
Line eight

Line six repeated (nine)
Line ten
Line eight repeated (eleven)
Line twelve

And so on indefinitely (or until the poem comes to a natural end). Here's an example of a modern pantoum:

Mi Rosa y Mi Sal

to S.B.

Some December years ago I took four rose petals
set them on a mat board, sprinkled them with salt,

and framed them behind glass. This was my gift
to you—*mi rosa y mi sal*—my rose and my salt.

Those petals—edge-torn, flattened, salt-sprinkled—
that still hang as mementos on your studio wall
with my inscription—*aqui mi rosa y mi sal—12/96.*
I remember that time, how it was all about beauty,

those moments suspended inside your studio walls
spent on the art of smoky talk about our lives, *la vida,*
you always said, is all about the beauty, I remember,
and how I believed, or wanted to believe that idea.

Those smoky years spent on the art of our lives—
the salted petals on the wall silently browning
as we discussed wanting and believing over
our daily lives of modest dinners and hearty music.

For years, four petals on the wall slowly browning
with the irony of salt that stings yet preserves flesh;
and after all the shared meals and music, I've learned
to live not so much on beauty, but on its echoes

and on the salt of memory stinging and preserving,
a taste to taste each day, a palate of remembrance;
so is the slow parting of our lives, beautified echoes
reaching the untouchable, the things *mas ayá*, beyond

the closed frame and glass seal of the gift I gave you,
some December years ago, when I first took four petals.

—Richard Blanco

Note how the poet varies the repeating lines so that they're not exactly the same when they're repeated. This is the art of writing in fixed form; you don't want an already repetitive form to become boring. You want the reader to remain intrigued and to wonder what you're going to do next, how you're going to make the form "new."

Poet Ron Drummond has invented a fun variation on the pantoum, which he calls the "unitoum." It uses the same basic premise as the pantoum, except that it uses only one word per line. "What distinguishes the unitoum from any pantoum I have come across is that each line of the unitoum is composed of a single word," says Drummond. "Therefore, a unitoum that consists of four quatrains is in fact 16 words in length (and actually consists of a vocabulary totaling eight words). My unitoum, 'Praeludere,' was commissioned for an *a capella* repetitive chant/sung piece for two sopranos, so I focused particularly on the singability of each word. This produced a wholly different character to the form."

Dodging Doggerel

Variety is key to writing well in form. Don't think that you have to remain strict to the form; that can result in archaic sounding verse. Instead, see where you can tweak the form a bit; play with the repetition, line length, meter, rhyme, etc., to make the form your own.

Praeludere

go
wait
follow
stay

wait
maybe
stay
you

maybe
yes
you
me

yes
follow
me
go

—Ron Drummond

Ghazal

The ghazal (*gah-ZAHL*) is a Persian form dating to around 1000 B.C.E. The ghazal, like its French and Italian counterparts, has changed form over the years. Today, the ghazal consists of couplets, usually between 5 and 12 stanzas, all of which use the same end rhyme, and the poet's name in the last stanza. The common rhyme scheme is aa, ba, ca, da, and so on. Some ghazals, including the example here, use a more traditional form in which the poet uses the same word at the end of the second line of each stanza. The primary subject matter of the ghazal is love, mainly sadness or melancholy over parting.

Ghazal from Moscow

Love, your eyes are sunflowers against a green field, filled with song.
One morning they opened on me: green, fleck-gold, pupil-dark song.
*
We belong to each other. But what does it mean to belong?
To hear the sap beneath the bark as song?
*

I've learned the names of trees, but learned them wrong.
Winter, they shed their hair and clap the starkest song.
*
It's cold, my dear. My fingers are wooden tongs
Around this pen, my translations a carcass song.
*
In this country, the sun is weak, grandmothers strong
As vodka. In order to survive you must guzzle its song.
*
When they closed Grandfather's eyes, curtains were drawn—
The sky was cerulean, the lark did not lack its song.
*
The Ferris wheel in Gorky Park always looks still. All along
it's making revolution after revolution, creaks song.
*
When next you open your eyes I'll stay a thousand years long.
Philip promises you. No lie. Mark this song.

—Philip Metres

Haiku and Tanka

You probably remember writing haiku in grade school. The haiku originated from a long, collaborative form called the *renga* and is a fun, short Japanese form consisting of three lines with a syllable count of 5-7-5. Non-Japanese writers of the haiku generally use the 5-7-5 syllabic structure; poets writing in Japanese do not count syllables: They count sounds. Modern writers of haiku often don't count syllables either, but they do continue using the three-line structure, though there are variations on that as well.

The haiku's content traditionally consists of one strong image or imagistic moment, usually considering the natural world (but not necessarily), as in the following haikus by poet Alfred Corn:

October breezes:
The old maple scattering
Haiku on the path.

*

Eating blueberries
While picking them, I notice
No two taste the same.

*

Quicksilver scribbles
On black water: the half moon
Revising its lines.

*

Grand Central Station:
The Brazilian street singer
Mumbles his sambas.

—Alfred Corn

Haikus are not often titled, but you can title them if you'd like:

Postcard from the Park

Petals fall from trees
like pink ashes and the wind brings
the smell of dog poop.

—Guillermo Castro

As a fun project, write 52 haikus, one for each week of the year. Remember that you're trying to focus on an image. Consider the weather, your mood, the movement of the world around you.

Tanka is another Japanese form consisting of five lines of 5-7-5-7-7 syllables, respectively. Traditional topics include: nature, love, travel, the seasons, and lamentation. Like haiku, you can vary this form to be longer or shorter, and you can tinker with the syllable count.

Poetically Correct

A **renga** is a Japanese form that originated as a party game where groups of poets contributed to a single poem, typically consisting of at least 100 lines written by three poets in about three hours; the renga is an imagistic form and is the parent of the haiku, which were considered "warm-up" poems for the renga. Each stanza relates to the one before it, but not to the one before that.

Poems to Dance By

Songs of all kinds are popular forms in poetry—after all, poetry's roots are in music. Many forms of poetry come directly from music: blues, hymns, and rap lyrics, to name just a few. The song is not necessarily a fixed form, but it does contain musical elements such as repetition, meter, rhyme, etc. Here's a selection from Walt Whitman that's delirious with music. Whitman obviously meant this poem to be song-like—he's singing away. Note the repetitions and chant-like quality of this section:

From **Song of Myself**

Singing the need of superb children and therein superb
    grown people,
Singing the muscular urge and the blending,
Singing the bedfellow's song, (O resistless yearning!
O for any and each the body correlative attracting!
O for you whoever you are your correlative body! O it,
    more than all else, you delighting!)
From the hungry gnaw that eats me night and day,
From native moments, from bashful pains, singing them,
Seeking something yet unfound though I have diligently
    sought it many a long year,
Singing the true song of the soul fitful at random,
Renascent with grossest Nature or among animals,
Of that, of them and what goes with them my poems
    informing,
Of the smell of apples and lemons, of the pairing of
    birds,
Of the wet of woods, of the lapping of waves,
Of the mad pushes of waves upon the land, I them chanting,
The overture lightly sounding, the strain anticipating,
The welcome nearness, the sight of the perfect body,
The swimmer swimming naked in the bath, or motionless on
    his back lying and floating,
The female form approaching, I pensive, love-flesh
    tremulous aching,

The divine list for myself or you or for any one making,
The face, the limbs, the index from head to foot, and
    what it arouses,
The mystic deliria, the madness amorous, the utter
    abandonment,
(Hark close and still what I now whisper to you,
I love you, O you entirely possess me,
O that you and I escape from the rest and go utterly off,
    free and lawless,
Two hawks in the air, two fishes swimming in the sea not
    more lawless than we);
The furious storm through me careering, I passionately
    trembling.
The oath of the inseparableness of two together, of the
    woman that loves me and whom I love more than my
    life, that oath swearing,
(O I willingly stake all for you,
O let me be lost if it must be so!

—Walt Whitman

The blues is an American form whose content is generally of a highly personal nature—struggle, sex, anguish, loss, oppression—and it is often bawdy, filled with innuendo. The blues often tells a story, and can be comical, even though the subject matter may be grim. The "classic" blues verse consists of two repeating lines and one line that "speaks" to the previous two. Listen to the blues of Robert Johnson or Howlin' Wolf to get a good idea of what the blues are about. Another type of blues poem is written with the content of the blues and containing musical elements, but without the traditional blues form. See Langston Hughes's poem "Weary Blues" as an example.

Triolet

The triolet (*tree-oh-LAY*), relative of the rondeau, consists of eight lines, two rhymes, and two repeating refrains: AbaAabAB (capital letters indicate repeated lines). Here's an example of a modern triolet:

Triolet

I

The bread bin was empty, the money
  Gone. What was she supposed to do
To feed her kids? Beg? Not likely!
The bread bin was empty, the money
Gone on Guinness for himself, free
  Rounds for the lads. Of course, he knew
The bread bin was empty; the money
  Gone, but what was he supposed to do?

II

The Lord helps those who help themselves.
  My mother took Him at His word.
We stole into the church like elves.
The Lord helps those who help themselves,
So into the poor-box we delved
  And robbed its contents unperturbed.
The Lord helps those who help themselves,
  And mother took Him at His word.

—Connie Roberts

The *rondeau,* related to the triolet, is a French fixed form consisting of 9, 13, or 15 lines (depending on the poet) with a repeated refrain [R] and rhyme scheme: aabba aabR aabbaR or abaR bab abaR. It is also often called *rondel.*

Exercises

Here are some exercises to get you started writing in fun fixed forms. Don't see these as daunting tasks, but as entertaining challenges.

- ➤ Write a Shakespearian sonnet about your first pet—remember the volta—that turn could be the place where you begin to tell what happened to Fluffy.
- ➤ Write a sestina using the following end words: blue, weather, daughter, me, shape, point.
- ➤ Try a pantoum of at least 10 stanzas.
- ➤ Listen to some blues music and write your own blues poem.
- ➤ Get together with two other poets and attempt a renga—remember, you have three hours to do it!

The Least You Need to Know

- The modern sonnet allows for a lot of variation in rhyme, meter, and line length.
- Variation in form is the key to writing form successfully—variation will keep your reader guessing.
- Haiku is a highly imagistic form that doesn't really have to adhere to the 5-7-5 syllable rule.
- Some forms, like songs, can suggest poems without requiring that the poet write in a fixed form unless he or she wants to.
- Form is fun—try it!

Chapter 15

More Fun Forms

In This Chapter

- Acrostics and alphabet poems
- Ars poetica
- Concrete poems and calligrams
- Hunting for Found poems
- Light verse, for better or worse

We looked at fixed forms in the previous chapter, and now we're going to look at other forms that don't have a specific set of requirements, such as repetition or rhyme, but may require particular subject matter or formatting. We've seen that writing in form is fun and challenging, so let's see what else poetic form has to offer us. Onward!

Acrostic

A basic acrostic is a poem where the first letters of each line form a word or phrase if you read them one by one, vertically, down each line. Often, the word spelled down the side of the poem has something to do with the subject matter or concept of the poem. Here's an example that explains the form:

Read Down

Rather than holding your head in pain
Either go from beginning to end
And pay good heed to directions within
Describing the gimmick and then:
Discover the nature of this fair poem.
Or rather: if you're not shy,
When you've read the first letters from up to down—
Never bother to read the last line.

—M. M. De Voe

An acrostic can also have a word formed down the right side of the poem, with each word letter ending the line. A double acrostic has a word formed at the right and at the left, and a triple acrostic has one formed in the center as well. Here's a riddle acrostic by Edgar Allan Poe that challenges the reader to find the form:

A Valentine

For her this rhyme is penned, whose luminous eyes,
 Brightly expressive as the twins of Leda,
Shall find her own sweet name, that nestling lies
 Upon the page, enwrapped from every reader.
Search narrowly the lines!—they hold a treasure
 Divine—a talisman—an amulet
That must be worn at heart. Search well the measure—
 The words—the syllables! Do not forget
The trivialest point, or you may lose your labor
 And yet there is in this no Gordian knot
Which one might not undo without a sabre,
 If one could merely comprehend the plot.
Enwritten upon the leaf where now are peering
 Eyes scintillating soul, there lie perdus
Three eloquent words oft uttered in the hearing
 Of poets, by poets—as the name is a poet's, too,
Its letters, although naturally lying
 Like the knight Pinto—Mendez Ferdinando—
Still form a synonym for Truth—Cease trying!
 You will not read the riddle, though you do the best you
  can do.

—Edgar Allen Poe

That's a tough one to solve. Circle the first letter in the first line. Now circle the second letter in the second line and the third letter in the third line, and so on. You will discover the name of Poe's beloved. Tricky, huh?

An alphabet acrostic, also called an abecedarian, is a poem that uses the letters of the alphabet, either on the left or the right (or both!) to form the poem. This is a really fun form and you can use it when you're feeling uninspired to get you going again. For fun, write an alphabet acrostic from A to Z and then continue from Z to A.

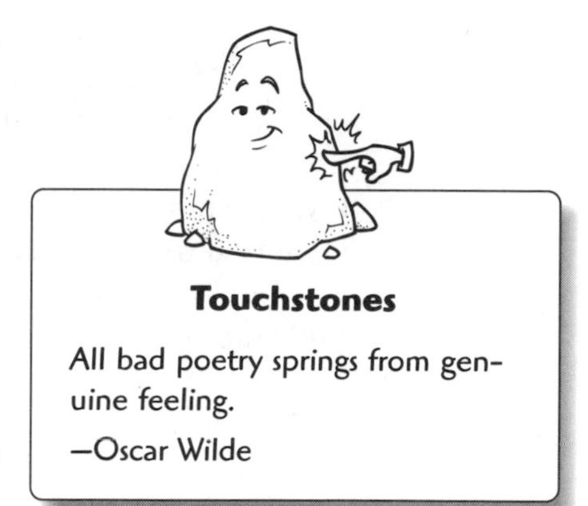

Touchstones

All bad poetry springs from genuine feeling.

—Oscar Wilde

Ars Poetica

An *ars poetica* is a poem praising poetry or written about poetry, or even about the poem a poet is writing at the moment. As poets, we spend a lot of time thinking about poems, reading them, and writing them, so it's natural that the topic of poetry would creep into our writing. Look back at Chapter 1, "What Is Poetry and How Do I Begin to Write?" to see examples of two *ars poetica* poems, "Fragment" and "American Poetry." Here's another example of ars poetica from Walt Whitman:

From **Starting from Paumanok**

The soul,
Forever and forever—longer than soil is brown and
solid—longer than water ebbs and flows.
I will make the poems of materials, for I think they are
to be the most spiritual poems,
And I will make the poems of my body and of mortality,
For I think I shall then supply myself with the poems of
my soul and of immortality.
I will make a song for these States that no one State may
under any circumstances be subjected to another
State,
And I will make a song that there shall be comity by day
and by night between all the States, and between any
two of them,
And I will make a song for the ears of the President,
full of weapons with menacing points,
And behind the weapons countless dissatisfied faces;

And a song make I of the One form'd out of all,
The fang'd and glittering One whose head is over all,
Resolute warlike One including and over all,
(However high the head of any else that head is over all.)
I will acknowledge contemporary lands,
I will trail the whole geography of the globe and salute
  courteously every city large and small,
And employments! I will put in my poems that with you is
  heroism upon land and sea,
And I will report all heroism from an American point of
  view.

I will sing the song of companionship,
I will show what alone must finally compact these,
I believe these are to found their own ideal of manly
  love, indicating it in me,
I will therefore let flame from me the burning fires that
  were threatening to consume me,
I will lift what has too long kept down those smouldering
  fires,
I will give them complete abandonment,
I will write the evangel-poem of comrades and of love,
For who but I should understand love with all its sorrow
  and joy?
And who but I should be the poet of comrades?

—Walt Whitman

Roses Are Red

Form should not be glaring, nor should it be invisible. If your poem is good enough as a *poem* (without the form) a careful reader—you have to assume that your reader is careful—will be able to appreciate what you've written, for both the poem's form and content. Don't bludgeon your reader with the form. With some forms, the lighter your touch the better.

You can see how Whitman discusses his own poetry here and his plans for it, even as he's writing this poem.

Write a poem where you discuss the poem you are writing. It's fun if you write one in a fixed form, like a sonnet, so that you can discuss the sonnet itself as you're writing it. See the poem "My Confessional Sestina" in Chapter 14, "Some Fun Fixed Forms," for an example.

Aubade

An aubade, also called *alba,* is a poem written at dawn expressing the parting of two lovers. Its counterpart is the serenade, celebrating the meeting of two lovers. You'll have to get up pretty early for this one, and find a lover to part with for the best effect. Here's an example of a modern aubade:

Aubade

Rise from indented cushion. Wheeling of pigeons in
　　tandem. Gradual un-numbing
of the right side
of my face. Love

of the beloved's shin, eyes, or the doll-like quality of
　　strangers. Ongoing clichés of feeling:
God walking into a cloud of smoke
He's creating.

For I was a trashcan being wed to another trashcan,
　　trying to understand what was happening.
For I was a mother blue jay banking down the rock-shelf,
　　guiding my young.
For You were a blinking red light atop a building,
warning those in flight.

Though I did know You, I would not speak aloud Your true
　　name. Give lip service,
eye service, hand service, etc.,
for I was a Jew.

　　You hedged me from before and behind,
　　You lay your hand upon me.

Put the music on, boy!
O green turf. O pebbly earth. O teacher's touch. O music
of misunderstanding.

(Strange marriage:
His face so often obscured.)

**Italicized lines are from psalm #139*

—Julie Carr

Cento

A cento is also called a "patchwork poem." It is made entirely of lines from other poets. Here's a part of a long cento I patchworked together from both ancient and contemporary poets:

From **Centos**

You will be aware of an absence presently,
growing beside you like a tree.
Chopped head of crow, strings of white light,
open tail of peacock.
Into the rain-washed evening white with
evangelical fury,
I want to look back and see you in the branches—
there is a part of this poem where you must say it
with me.
You could spend considerable time just concen-
trating,
noticed but unknown, a sleepwalker afraid of
the dark,
walking with no purpose past buildings that
would stand forever.
I think we must give up something, or stop something, or maybe look—
There is a part of this poem where you must say
it with me:
Where the beautiful mingles with the common, it
is the beautiful that suffers.

Try a humorous cento. Centos are traditionally comic in nature. For fun, you can use phrases and sentences from other sources, like how-to books, encyclopedias, and magazines, to make it even more of a patchwork.

Roses Are Red

If you're looking for a title for your poem, try using the name of the form you're using, such as *Ars Poetica, Aubade, Ode to ...* etc. This is an accepted, traditional way to title your poems, especially if you want your reader to immediately recognize your form.

Touchstones

Poetry is the art of understanding what it is to be alive.

—Archibald MacLeish

Concrete Poetry and Calligrams

Concrete poems use their physical appearance on the page to mirror their subject matter. A concrete poem uses formatting, color, and design for desired effects; for example, using a lot of white space around certain words, or setting particular phrases off from the rest of the poem. Here's one example:

[O sweet spontaneous]

O sweet spontaneous
earth how often have
the
doting
    fingers of

prurient philosophers pinched
and
poked

thee
,has the naughty thumb
of science prodded
thy

    beauty   .how
often have religions taken
thee upon their scraggy knees
squeezing and

buffeting thee that thou mightest conceive
gods
    (but
true
to the incomparable
crouch of death thy
rhythmic
lover

            thou answerest
then only with
            spring)

—e. e. cummings

Poetically Correct

A **bestiary** is a poem where animals or inanimate objects are personified and used allegorically, usually with a moral purpose.

The subject matter of this poem is how humans, (called philosophy, science, and religion), try to shape the natural world, but the natural world answers only with what it knows, another season, regardless of the poking and pinching it receives with the expectation of change and answers. The formatting of this poem resembles the pinching and prodding, the unnatural forces on the earth's steady course. You can see how formatting a poem on the page does a lot for its subject matter; however, beware of doing this too much—novice poets often hide inferior poems in fancy formatting.

Calligrams are shaped like their subject matter—I liken them to "packaging" for a poem. For example, a poet may choose to shape their poem like a bird if they are writing about a bird.

Writing a concrete poem takes serious patience as well as a good writer to pull off writing a poem that's solid in both its content and shape—not easy. Often, a poet must force the language to fit the shape, and that can lead to weak poetry. Nevertheless, it's a fun form to try. Here's a concrete poem by Ron Drummond:

Valentine for Terry Ray

Lub dub
lub dub lub dub lub dub:
a double-type bubble pumps red
& blue, a dove coos, a fountain
flows and blossoms sway to
this song, honey: I love
you. I love love
lovelove
you.

This poem, shaped like a heart, is not difficult to appreciate—the recipient of this poem (presumably Terry Ray, as we can see from the title), will understand that the poet intended to send a love poem in this cute little "package." Write a calligram in the form of your favorite food—make the subject matter mirror the form. You will see how time consuming this form is just in terms of formatting, but it's a fun poem to show off to friends!

Dodging Doggerel

When you write in form, don't let the form force you into writing a bad poem—instead, let the form merely "inform" your poem, help the poem be what it wants to be. If you fudge the form so much that it's unrecognizable, but you've written a fantastic poem, great! Keep up the good work!

Found Poems

A found poem is one that you don't really write, but happen upon. You can find poems everywhere if you just look—in advertisements, letters, on television, in magazine articles, and so on. Here's one "found" in an e-mail:

Aunt Toodum's Email

Adapted from the electronic correspondence of Loreta "Toodum" St. Cyr to her nephew Terry

Well, Phillip says he's got his suitcase packed.
Says I'm driving him nuts with this GD computer.
The big deal is he can't use the phone. Ha!
Says he needs a hearing aid because when the phone rings
all he hears is that whistle where Coleen
and me is trying to send a fax. Far as I know
the fax is installed in the modem, right?
You're the computer expert, not me. Like I could know
with my installer click-clicking so fast
she's got the AOL guys crazy signing me on.
And after she sets up my address book
I send a letter to Beverly and (no kidding)
get a 3-page letter from AOL
saying undeliverable, never heard of her.
Come to find out we left off the @ part.
I thought lord they're going to cancel all my free stuff!
Next, my neighbor says my message windows
are stuck so she stops by but never gets them open.
The helpline said to try the on-screen help.
The installer called today and said go out to Sam's
and let him show me how to do it right.
Well I go and, you guessed it, he couldn't get it on.
Then I was playing with it this evening
and found the helpline had faxed me some numbers to call,
so when Wayne's playing golf and Phillip's down
in Lawton, me and Coleen is going to tie up
the phones again. We may be calling you
to help us, but tell your staff if the cost is too high
I'll have to send them towels for payment.
K-Mart had a towel sale Tuesday so I run down
to pick out 2 or 3 but couldn't find
the ones on sale so they told me to pick out some more
of the better ones so I bought me 10
only to find 4 at home from when me and your mom
did Montgomery Wards at the Crossroads.

So get all your staff to tell me the color of their
décor — I'm sure I got one to match. Ha!
Your folks' new car is so pretty, lots of room and rides
real good. I guess you're still standing outside
in the cold trying to flag a bus down so you can
go to work and keep all our computers running —
Heehee! Now that I got your number, you'll probably
be putting the lock on it. Can't blame you!
Still, we're calling if we can't get it right. You're the best.
Coleen says you'll want the dark green towels
but I'm thinking maybe the navy.
        Love ya, Toodum

—Ron Drummond

I went hunting for a poem for this section and found one after ordering Chinese food:

Learn How to Use Your Chopsticks

Tuck under   thumb
and hold firmly

Add second chopsticks
    hold it as you hold
    a pencil

Hold first chopsticks
in original position
move the second
one up and down
now you can pick
up anything!

The spaces and the formatting are exactly like they read on the chopsticks wrapper, but you can play with the formatting if you'd like—in fact, you will probably have to. For fun, you can mix text material that you find with your own material—you can italicize the text that isn't yours or make a small note of it on the bottom of the poem.

Let Me Count the Ways

A movement called language poetry emerged in the 1970s and is characterized by several conventions, including sentence fragments, lack of a unified narrative (no story), and the decontextualization of words (making words mean nothing or changing their meaning), among others. There is a reason for all of these conventions, or lack of traditional conventions, but there's too small a space here to detail such a large topic. If you want to do some research on language poetry, several good anthologies are available today. Language poetry is not simply putting random words together, though it may look like that on the surface.

Light Verse

Light verse is a type of poetry that has "light" subject matter, parodies other poems, or makes serious subjects comical. Often light verse doesn't even make sense or have a point at all beyond making sound. Here's an example that uses sound as its primary strategy:

Turtle Soup

Beautiful Soup, so rich and green,
Waiting in a hot tureen!
Who for such dainties would not stoop?
Soup of the evening, beautiful Soup!
Soup of the evening, beautiful Soup!
  Beau-ootiful Soo-oop!
  Beau-ootiful Soo-oop!
Soo-oop of the e-e-evening,
  Beautiful, beautiful Soup!

—Lewis Carroll

Here's one that tells a funny little story:

Three Young Rats

Three young rats with black felt hats,
Three young ducks with white straw hats,
Three young dogs with curling tails,
Three young cats with demi-veils,
Went out to walk with two young pigs,
In satin vests and sorrel wigs;
But suddenly it chanced to rain
And so they all went home again.

—Anonymous

The primary fixed form in light verse is the limerick. You probably know about this form already—it's very popular and often quite bawdy. The limerick uses an aabba rhyme scheme, and very often the last word in the first and last lines are the same, but not necessarily. The limerick also uses a particular metrical scheme, which is easy to pick up just by reading a few limericks aloud. Writing limericks is a good way of getting the hang of writing in meter. Here are three examples:

There was an Old Man of Calcutta,
Who perpetually ate bread and butter;
Till a great bit of muffin,
On which he was stuffing,
Choked that horrid old man of Calcutta.

*

There was a Young lady of Portugal,
Whose ideas were excessively nautical;
She climbed up a tree,
To examine the sea,
But declared she would never leave Portugal.

*

There was an Old Person whose habits,
Induced him to feed upon Rabbits;
When he'd eaten eighteen,
He turned perfectly green,
Upon which he relinquished those habits

—Edward Lear

Write several of your own limericks. Try to keep them rated PG if you can!

Ode

The ode is an ancient fixed form invented initially as a commemoration on a victory. The themes for odes were supposed to be exalted and stately, often dealing with elements such as mythology. The ode then changed into a more philosophical, personal form, and now it's a little of everything. Because it's such an old form, the ode has gone through many transmutations, and, like the modern sonnet, it has been liberated from a strict form. Here's part of a famous ode by John Keats:

Ode on a Grecian Urn

Thou still unravish'd bride of quietness,
Thou foster-child of silence and slow time,
Sylvan historian, who canst thus express
A flowery tale more sweetly than our rhyme:
What leaf-fring'd legend haunts about thy shape
Of deities or mortals, or of both,
In Tempe or the dales of Arcady?
What men or gods are these? What maidens loth?
What mad pursuit? What struggle to escape?
What pipes and timbrels? What wild ecstasy?

Heard melodies are sweet, but those unheard
Are sweeter; therefore, ye soft pipes, play on;
Not to the sensual ear, but, more endear'd,
Pipe to the spirit ditties of no tone:
Fair youth, beneath the trees, thou canst not leave
Thy song, nor ever can those trees be bare;
Bold Lover, never, never canst thou kiss,
Though winning near the goal yet, do not grieve;
She cannot fade, though thou hast not thy bliss,
For ever wilt thou love, and she be fair!

In this ode, Keats is reflecting on the antics going on in the painting on the side of a Grecian urn. The language in this poem is compact and generally elevated, and the subject matter is classical in nature. This might be a tough one for the novice poet to understand, so let's look at another poem. I've never heard this next poem officially called an ode, but it seems to me that it does largely the same thing that the Keats poem does. Take a look for yourself:

Mending Wall

Something there is that doesn't love a wall,
That sends the frozen-ground-swell under it,
And spills the upper boulders in the sun;
And makes gaps even two can pass abreast.
The work of hunters is another thing:
I have come after them and made repair
Where they have left not one stone on a stone,
But they would have the rabbit out of hiding,
To please the yelping dogs. The gaps I mean,
No one has seen them made or heard them made,
But at spring mending-time we find them there.
I let my neighbour know beyond the hill;
And on a day we meet to walk the line
And set the wall between us once again.
We keep the wall between us as we go.
To each the boulders that have fallen to each.
And some are loaves and some so nearly balls
We have to use a spell to make them balance:
"Stay where you are until our backs are turned!"
We wear our fingers rough with handling them.
Oh, just another kind of out-door game,
One on a side. It comes to little more:
There where it is we do not need the wall:
He is all pine and I am apple orchard.
My apple trees will never get across
And eat the cones under his pines, I tell him.
He only says, "Good fences make good neighbours."
Spring is the mischief in me, and I wonder
If I could put a notion in his head:
"Why do they make good neighbours? Isn't it
Where there are cows? But here there are no cows.
Before I built a wall I'd ask to know
What I was walling in or walling out,
And to whom I was like to give offence.
Something there is that doesn't love a wall,
That wants it down." I could say "Elves" to him,
But it's not elves exactly, and I'd rather
He said it for himself. I see him there
Bringing a stone grasped firmly by the top
In each hand, like an old-stone savage armed.

He moves in darkness as it seems to me,
Not of woods only and the shade of trees.
He will not go behind his father's saying,
And he likes having thought of it so well
He says again, "Good fences make good neighbours."

—Robert Frost

Here, Frost is reflecting on a wall and through the reflection the wall becomes exalted, much as the Grecian urn is; in the end of both poems the poet asserts a statement (even if it's through another mouth) about the nature of the world as it relates to the object being discussed—an ultimate truth is revealed. In the Keats poem, the statement is "Beauty is truth, truth beauty—that is all / Ye know on Earth, and all ye need to know."

Write an ode to your favorite season, revealing something larger about the world, a small lesson the season brings, perhaps, by the end.

Pastoral

Pastoral poetry depicts life in the countryside. The classic pastoral involves a shepherd and the concept of idyllic life:

The Passionate Shepherd to His Love

Come live with me and be my Love,
And we will all the pleasures prove
That hills and valleys, dale and field,
And all the craggy mountains yield.

There will we sit upon the rocks
And see the shepherds feed their flocks,
By shallow rivers, to whose falls
Melodious birds sing madrigals.

There will I make thee beds of roses
And a thousand fragrant posies,
A cap of flowers, and a kirtle
Embroider'd all with leaves of myrtle.

A gown made of the finest wool
Which from our pretty lambs we pull,
Fair linèd slippers for the cold,
With buckles of the purest gold.

A belt of straw and ivy buds
With coral clasps and amber studs:
And if these pleasures may thee move,
Come live with me and be my Love.

Thy silver dishes for thy meat
As precious as the gods do eat,
Shall on an ivory table be
Prepared each day for thee and me.

The shepherd swains shall dance and sing
For thy delight each May-morning:
If these delights thy mind may move,
Then live with me and be my Love.

—Christopher Marlowe

The modern form of the pastoral is written from the perspective of someone from the city looking idyllically at life in the country. Try writing a pastoral about the last time you were completely away from any city, or, for fun, "answer" Marlowe's poem in the persona of the loved one—or perhaps even of one of his lambs.

Prose Poem

A prose poem is a hybrid of a poem and a short-short story. Poet Campbell McGrath (whose poem follows) says that prose poetry is like the gulch between a farmer's fields—there's a little of both fields there—corn *and* wheat—as well as wild grasses, rusty tractor parts, tires, and standing water. That's a metaphorical way of saying that prose poetry is a little of each genre, and then some.

Most prose poems are lyrical and narrative, telling a little, personal story, though that's not always the case. Basically, anything goes—a list, blending with another form (ars poetical, ode, etc.), a song. Here's a prose poem of the lyrical, narrative sort:

A Dove

If May is the month of the Mockingbird, September is the season of the dove. On the roof they have gathered to drink from warm puddles of yesterday's rainwater, preening and cooing in the shade, while their brothers the pigeons line the telephone wires in radiant sunshine, waiting for their daily feed to spill forth from Mr. Johnson's sack of seed and cracked corn. Sunday morning, 10 A.M. High African clouds in the west, alamanda spilled in yellow spikes and coils across the fence. In the backyard: a neighbor's cat. At the sound of the opening window it flees, startled, then hesitates at the top of the wall to glance back—at what?—and as my eye tracks its gaze I catch a sudden motion in the overgrown grass, frantic circling too big for a lizard, too desperate, and even as I notice it and begin to speak, even as I call out *Hey, come see something strange in the yard* I realize, in that instant, what it must be—a bird, mauled, its weary struggle for survival—and wish I could unsay it, wish I could avert the gaze of my conscience because already I foresee the morning slipping away—a box, a warm towel, a bowl of water, and the calls to the Humane Society, and the drive to Fort Lauderdale to tender its fragile body to the Wild Animal Hospital, a shaded compound of blackbirds and parrots, box turtles and one eared rabbits—and now Sam has come over to watch with me and I cannot will away the obvious, and he dashes out the back door to investigate, and now the day has been taken from us, seized, wrenched away, a day of rest I would covet even against that ring of blood and spilled feathers, the slender broken bones in the lawn, and now we are drawn into the circle of its small life, obligated by our witness impossible to deny or retract, committed long before the dull slow course of a thought can be born into language, before the image is set into words, as Sam's words come to me now across the hot summer grass: *Dad, it's alive. A kind of bird. It's hurt. A dove.*

—Campbell McGrath

Try writing your own prose poem. Think back to a time when something small but significant happened to you. Stories are all about cause and effect—the little thing that happened has to have caused something else to happen. For example, in the above poem, as a result of the dove being injured and the speaker finding it, the day is lost.

Other Fun Forms to Try

There are dozens of other forms you can use, far more than I can explain in this chapter! Out of the masses of forms to choose from, I've selected a few more forms for you to try:

Know someone who's getting married soon? An epithalamium—also called a wedding song, is a poem written to celebrate a marriage offering good wishes to the bride and groom.

If you don't want your poems to be lonely, write a companion poem, which are two or more poems written as compliments, opposites, or replies to one another. These are really fun to write, and can often get you out of a "slump."

An epic poem is a long narrative poem that traditionally contains a heroic figure and narrates a historical event or some other tale of heroism, conquest, and battle, usually containing elements of myth. Famous epics include the *Iliad,* the *Odyssey, The Divine Comedy,* and *Paradise Lost.* The epic is usually divided into cantos, or smaller units. The epic might look like one big, long poem, but it's special for far more than just its length. The epic is steeped in tradition and has certain formatting and content issues. Before you tackle a poem of this length, read a few and study them for their elements.

Lyric poetry is a type of poetry that has its roots in song and music, and is characterized today by the short, personal, highly imagistic and sensory poem. It is named for the lyre, a small stringed instrument of the harp family, used by the ancient Greeks to accompany singing and recitation. Try a short, perhaps 20-line poem, of a personal nature—try to render an event that happened to you today into verse. Remember, make it short, imagistic, and try to use as many of the senses as you can.

Exercises

Here are a few exercises to get you started writing in the fun forms you've learned in this chapter.

- Take a sentence from a magazine and use it to write an acrostic poem.
- Get up at dawn and write an aubade. Then, that evening, write it a companion serenade.
- Write a found poem with your next three e-mails. Don't cheat—it has to be the very next three. If you don't have e-mail, use the next three letters you get, even if they're bills or junk mail—even better!
- Write an ode to something really ordinary, like a shoestring or a pencil sharpener.
- Write a prose poem about some form of travel: driving, flying, roller-skating.

The Least You Need to Know

- A basic acrostic is a poem in which the first letters of each line form a word or a phrase if you read them one by one, vertically down each line.
- Concrete poems use their physical appearance on the page to mirror their subject matter.
- You can take any of the forms in this chapter and write them as fixed forms, such as sonnets, villanelles, and so on.
- A found poem is one that you don't really write, but happen upon.
- A prose poem is a hybrid of a poem and a short-short story.

Part 4

Poetry and Practicality

Who casts to write a living line, must sweat.

—Ben Jonson

Yes, even poetry has a practical side. If you "cast to write a living line," that is, aspire to write a line with life inside it, you're going to have to work. This part will teach you to avoid poetry's pitfalls, show you some valuable revision techniques, offer advice on workshops and graduate schools, and enlighten you on the wonderful world of publishing your own poems, including a complete how-to section and an "insider's look" at getting published.

You'll also find a chapter full of original exercises from poets who teach, as well as the short course in appreciating poetry. Finally, a frequently asked questions chapter will answer those little things you still need to know.

Chapter 16

Cursed Be He Who Stirs My Bones!: Avoiding Poetry Pitfalls

In This Chapter

- The importance of poetic convention
- Axing the cliché
- Avoiding language problems
- Punctuating properly
- Giving up the sermon

Part of the inscription on William Shakespeare's grave reads, "Cursed be he who stirs my bones." Surely this statement was aimed at grave robbers, but I can't help conjuring the image of the Bard shuddering in his grave each time someone writes a line of bad poetry.

There are as many ways to make a good poem go bad as there are novice poets—using one important skill too often, not using any poetic skills at all, or making an epic out of something that should have been a sonnet, to name just a few. There's a fine balance to be had in the art of making a good poem.

Part of making a poem "work," that is, making it enjoyable to read, making it original, powerful, comprehensible, musical, and so on, is understanding and using the fundamental skills of poem-making the way they are meant to be used. It doesn't take a brilliant poet to throw some lines of rhyme together and call it a poem. The skill lies in making the rhyme fresh, original, and unobtrusive.

Is there such a thing as a bad poem? Is there such a thing as a bad painting, poorly designed building, or terribly acted play? Certainly, and we probably wouldn't even question these other things. This chapter details many of the ways a poem can "go wrong" and gives suggestions on how to avoid them.

Using Poetic Conventions

Poetry is an art, and as an art its creators are subject to certain poetic conventions, certain rules and traditions that are unique to the art, many of which are covered earlier in this book.

Poetically Correct

Poetic conventions are certain rules and traditions that poets follow to create their art; beginners should learn to use the poetic conventions before they try breaking them.

Writing music is a good parallel example to using *poetic conventions:* Composers understand that music has symbols called notes that, when placed in between horizontal lines on a page, signify a song. Each note represents a key and a duration of time; particular notes placed together in a certain way sound pleasant or powerful, for example. When a composer of music writes these notes down, in following the musical tradition, other musicians will know what the song sounds like and be able to play it.

Now, what would you think of a novice composer who decides that he isn't going to use notes or bother to learn about them, but is, rather, going to write a classical symphony the way he wants to, tradition be damned? You might call him innovative, but most composers would call him a fool.

The want-to-be composer defying convention isn't innovative; he's lazy. His written music would be incomprehensible to other classical composers and musicians because he hasn't yet learned the traditions of his craft. He wants to do things his way but, as a result, he will not be taken seriously by anyone in his field. Who could read his jumbled writing, and who would want to? This certainly doesn't mean that you shouldn't be innovative—on the contrary—just be innovative after you've learned the conventions. Editors and other people "in the know" will recognize a lazy poet. Don't let this happen to you!

Many novice poets "go wrong" in their poems because of laziness, wanting to put poetic convention aside and write their way. A poet isn't lazy. A poet *works*. That doesn't mean that writing poetry shouldn't be fun, however. I once had a poetry professor who said, "Poetry should be a body of play as well as a body of work." How many people are lazy when they play? Play takes energy, too.

So, off to work (and play), poets! Poetry pitfalls can be avoided with a little effort and a lot of practice. In the first part of this book you learned about the important skills a poet uses to forge poems, the poetic conventions—a kind of "poetry formula" to help you build verse. It's easy to balk at the notion of using a formula for writing poems. After all, poetry is the most "free" of all the arts, right? Well, yes, to a degree, but not for the beginner. The novice poet must learn how to write within the poetic conventions, just as the novice composer must learn to put the right notes in the right places in order to make a song *before* he or she invents a new kind of music.

This is not to say that you can't write far differently from other poets, ignoring convention altogether. Go right ahead. The sky won't fall and the world won't end. But you just might not learn as much about poetry as you could if you experimented with traditional methods.

Find a poem that uses many traditional poetic devices and write a poem like it, using the poet's "moves." Where the poet writes a metaphor, you write a metaphor; where the poet uses rhyme, you use rhyme, meter, personification, etc. This will help you to get the feel of using convention.

Language Problems

Poems can have problems at all levels of development, from the word level to the overall language of the poem (which begins with the word!). Word choice is integral to how your poem will read. When you write your poems, pay close attention to each word and how that word plays off of the other words. Each word must count toward the overall intention of the poem. If a word doesn't matter to the poem, take it out! You need to have a ruthless streak to be a poet. If a word or a phrase isn't doing its job, hack it right off—leaving "slacker" language, words and phrases that do nothing for your poem, will weaken it. No hangers-on!

For example, here's a poem by poet Langston Hughes that wastes nothing:

Suicide's Note

The calm,
Cool face of the river
Asked me for a kiss.

What if Hughes went on and on about the river, about being depressed, and what worldly goods the speaker of the poem was leaving and to whom? The power in this poem is in what's *left out*. In these 12 words a whole complicated scenario occurs, but Hughes doesn't have to go on at length about it. He is able to capture the power of the suicide in three short lines.

As an exercise, write the scene that the above poem describes. Write in as much detail as you can. What's the difference between what you've written and the Hughes poem? How did you *know* the details you wrote about in your scene?

Clichés

Clichés are dead metaphors, images, ideas, and phrases that have lost their original meaning and are so familiar to us now that we toss them around without stopping to think about what we're really saying.

Take these clichés for example:

- **Flash in the pan.** Today, this phrase means "popularity that is short lived," like that of a boy band. The original meaning of this cliché comes from the gold prospectors that used pans to find gold in streams. A flash in the pan isn't always gold.
- **Rule of thumb.** To us, this phrase means "a practical rule; a rule we should live by," such as not putting your hand on a hot stove burner. That's a good rule of thumb. Before a universal system of measurement was invented, we defined measurements by common objects and body parts, usually the body parts of a king. People used to measure things using the rule of thumb, even though everyone's thumbs are different sizes!

Here are more obvious clichés: dead tired, apple of my eye, sick as a dog, for example. These phrases mean little to us in the literal sense, and as a result they hold little power. A meaningless phrase should never find its way into your poems. Each phrase in a poem should be filled with importance—your job is to find a way to do that without using "stock" language.

How do you know when something is a cliché? If you've heard it said a thousand times, it's a cliché and should not be in your poem. If you are unsure about a phrase, several books are on the market that list clichés and describe their origins.

As an exercise, write a poem in which you use clichés intentionally, changing the cliché in some way. If you can make the cliché somehow "new" you can get away with using it. Clichés aren't terrible to use if you're using them for a *reason*—realize that you're not going to get a whole lot of meaning out of a cliché unless you have a strategy for using it well. Here's a poem that takes a cliché and makes it surprising and new:

[You Fit into Me]

you fit into me
like a hook into an eye

a fish hook
an open eye

—Margaret Atwood

Obvious and Familiar Language

Like using clichés, obvious and familiar language will hurt your poems. Poetry should make the old seem new and make the reader see the obvious in a fresh and interesting way. For example, we know that, generally, grass is green, the sky is blue, and clouds are white. What can you do to make these things more interesting and fresh?

Again, if you've heard a phrase many times before, you probably shouldn't be using it in your poems. What if the grass was the color of plastic hospital bedpans, the sky was kitchen-cleanser blue, and the clouds looked like cheap cake frosting. Better?

Adverbs

Verbs are important to your poems, adding precise action and movement. The adverb is the enemy of the verb and will weaken the verb by allowing it to be lazy and imprecise. Rather than attach an adverb to a weak or imprecise verb, try to make your verbs stronger and more specific.

Here are some examples:

- Walk slowly = saunter, meander, stroll
- Run slowly = jog, trot
- Run quickly = sprint, gallop, dash, fly, scurry
- Pull quickly = jerk, tug, yank

Adjectives

Like the adverb, the adjective may allow your nouns imprecise, and weaken the overall effect of the poem. Rather than using the adjective as a descriptive crutch, use better, more specific nouns.

Look at these, for example:

- A gray dog = schnauzer, Weimaraner
- Fiery planet = the sun, Sirius the Dog Star
- Hard wood = mahogany, oak
- Parched land = Mojave Desert, Australian Outback

Roses Are Red

Include only important action in your poems—action that means something to the poem's intention. Try not to include too many "stage directions," action language that does not mean much to the poem. For example, writing "then he ran across the street to the bar," and "then he walked over to the pool table," may not be as effective as just placing him in the desired locale without having to tell the reader how he got there.

The Verb "To Be"

The verb TO BE = be, is, am, are, was, were, been.

The TO BE verb is the most commonly used verb and is also the least descriptive. It functions as an equal sign and, as a result, is static. Nothing much happens with the verb TO BE. For example, sun = yellow, egg = fragile, feathers = soft. The sun is yellow, the eggs were white, the feathers are soft. Static. Instead of using the verb TO BE, try to use more active verbs. The sun blazes yellow, the eggs appeared fragile, the feathers feel soft. Or, you can change the construction of the sentence to eliminate the TO BE verb:

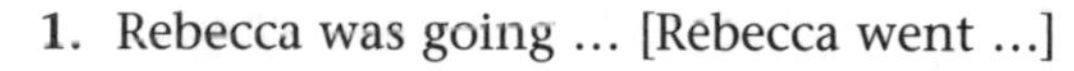

1. Rebecca was going … [Rebecca went …]
2. Mary Ann's cup is red and black. [Mary Ann's red and black cup.]
3. Tony and Steve were walking … [Tony and Steve walked …]
4. Wool blankets are scratchy. [Scratchy wool blankets.]

Dodging Doggerel

Don't try to be deliberately obscure in your poems because that's how you think a poem should be. Try to be as clear as possible in your poems—if you're writing about a pony, your reader shouldn't think you're writing about a light bulb. Instead of using your own code or private symbols for "pony," simply write "pony."

Lack of Focus

The most frequent problem beginning poets have with their poems is lack of focus. Don't try to force too much into any one poem—remember, you can always write several poems on the same subject. Try to focus your poems as much as possible—write on *one* topic, use just *one* extended metaphor, and so on. As an exercise, write several poems focusing on a single part of a larger unit—for example, a poem about one feather on the wing of a finch, the knob on your toaster, or a letter in the name of a loved one.

The "Little" Words

Since part of poetry is using the best words possible, you will want to condense and compress wherever you can. Look at the "little words" you use—*and, but, a, an, the, of, in,* and so on, and try to eliminate as many as you can. Try changing the structure of your lines or using better verbs and nouns—this will help cut the "fat."

Noun-of-Noun Construction

The noun-of-noun construction is not completely avoidable, but it must be written such that the phrase you use is not silly or ridiculous. For example, "leaves of the tree" and "legs of the chair" make sense and are logical constructions, while the "dog dish of anger" and "the sun porch of pain" are not. You want the connections in your poems to make sense, or you will risk losing the reader.

Touchstones

Don't use such an expression as 'dim lands of peace.' It dulls the image. It mixes an abstraction with the concrete. It comes from the writer not realizing that the natural object is always the adequate symbol.

—Ezra Pound

Overwriting

Many beginning poets become so enthralled with the things they are learning that they "overwrite." This is like using a cake recipe and, seeing that it calls for one cup of sugar, pouring two cups in the batter, thinking that more of a good thing will make the cake better. Often, messing with the recipe only makes goop. The same idea works in poetry. You want your poems to have a subtle flavor, using only so much rhyme, music, and repetition. Keep the batter at the correct consistency.

Sure, you could argue that Poe used a lot of rhyme, and Hopkins was crazy for alliteration, but they were highly practiced and skilled poets by the time they managed to use these elements well. As a beginning poet, I encourage you to experiment with all kinds of elements and forms. Go wild. Eventually, you will learn what works and what doesn't.

Punctuation Problems

Most poets today use regular punctuation. Some poets choose not to use punctuation because they may want the poems to be read a certain way, and the lack of punctuation may warrant that. However, eliminating punctuation just because you feel like it might not be a good enough reason.

Poet e. e. cummings (1894–1962) either dropped punctuation altogether in his work, or used it in nontraditional ways. He had antiestablishment leanings and used punctuation as a statement to bring readers to a different level of awareness—or frustration. It's fine for you to use whatever kind of punctuation you feel comfortable with—as long as it's right for the poem. You'll be able to tell how punctuation works in your own poems through experimentation and practice—for now, try to use "proper" punctuation until you get the hang of some of the other important elements of poetry.

Grammar in a Poem?

Even poets have to think a little bit about grammar. Thought you'd get away from it, didn't you? Yes, you can break the rules of grammar in a poem—as long as you do it consistently, which means you will have to know the rules to begin with.

Twisting regular grammar is one of the fun parts of being a poet, but if you do it inconsistently in a single poem, a reader might think that what you're doing is unintentional—you'll look dim-witted, not inventive. Be consistent with your capitalization (or lack of it), punctuation (or lack of it), and other grammatical conventions. If you don't know a lot about grammar, pick up a good grammar handbook.

Telling, Not Showing

Some poems go bad because they are based in concepts rather than in "things." Showing your reader what you're trying to convey is far more effective than telling it with a concept. As you write, try to use images rather than abstractions—try to paint a picture for your reader. For example, "I like Andrew," might be better conveyed in a poem by making a metaphor for Andrew, as in, "Andrew is a (type of flower, favorite season, favorite food, etc.)." See Chapter 5, "Painting with Words: Imagery," for more on creating great images.

Touchstones

Go in fear of abstractions.

—Ezra Pound

Avoiding abstractions is one way to tell if you're *showing*. Scan your poems for "big" conceptual words: life, pain, conscience, soul, and so on, and see if you can make these into images. "My soul aches" might be turned into "I'm a tenement torn down today."

Musical Matters

Beginning poets often don't realize that professional poets are out there writing today, and, as a result, often use the poets of antiquity as their masters. This is a good idea only if you are trained to know what to take and what to leave in these poets' work. Because the beginning poet is not this astute yet, a lot of silly things can creep into their poems—not the least of which are bad rhyme, meter, and repetition.

This is easily avoided by reading as much modern and contemporary poetry as you can—say, poetry from the last 100 years to poets living today. But don't eliminate older poets from your reading list altogether—they are a necessary and integral part of your history as a poet. As you learn how to discriminate between techniques, and as your poetic touch becomes lighter and more sophisticated, you will be able to draw from poets of all eras.

Wretched Rhyme

Beginning poets pick up bad rhyming habits early, and they are difficult to break. I often suggest to my students that they don't rhyme for several months until they get the hang of other techniques. It's easy to use rhyme as a crutch—if it sounds good, it must be a good poem, right? Wrong!

- Avoid moon/June rhymes—if a rhyme is too familiar, you don't want to use it.
- If you must rhyme, try to use some slant or off-rhymes—these are less obtrusive.
- Rhyming should not be more important than what you are trying to say in your poem.
- Forcing rhyme will distort the syntax of your lines and will seem awkward. For example, the second line in this limerick by Edward Lear has its syntax distorted so that the poet could force a rhyme:

  There was an old Person of Chester,
  Whom several small children did pester;
  They threw some large stones,
  Which broke most of his bones,
  And displeased that old person of Chester.

  The line, in regular syntax, should read: "Who was pestered by several small children." Distorting syntax in this way draws attention to a certain line or phrase, which may not be to the benefit of the poem—not that it could hurt a limerick!

Monotonous Meter and Rotten Repetition

Meter, when done well, is a delight to read and is often unnoticeable. Read a lot of Robert Frost's poems and you'll get the idea. When done badly, meter can be awful and monotonous, like a child beating on a drum. Poets often use variations in their metrical patterns, adding depth and texture to their poems. See Chapter 9, "You've Got Rhythm: Metrical Poetry," for more on meter.

You should also handle any repetition with some variation. It's dreary to read something over and over with no break in the pattern, especially when it's not clear how the repetition adds to the poem. Make your repeating elements important.

Here are a couple short sections of *The Song of Hiawatha* by poet Henry Wadsworth Longfellow. Read these sections aloud and you will hear the monotonous metrical repetition—like the beating of drums. It goes on exactly like this for hundreds of lines. Clearly Longfellow wrote in this meter and used these word and syntactical repetitions for his own reasons, but it's a tedious poem to read, nonetheless:

Should you ask me, whence these stories?
Whence these legends and traditions,
With the odors of the forest
With the dew and damp of meadows,
With the curling smoke of wigwams,
With the rushing of great rivers,
With their frequent repetitions,
And their wild reverberations
As of thunder in the mountains?
I should answer, I should tell you,
"From the forests and the prairies,
From the great lakes of thc Northland,
From the land of the Ojibways,
From the land of the Dacotahs,
From the mountains, moors, and fen-lands …

Round about the Indian village
Spread the meadows and the corn-fields,
And beyond them stood the forest,
Stood the groves of singing pine-trees,
Green in Summer, white in Winter,
Ever sighing, ever singing.
"And the pleasant water-courses,
You could trace them through the valley,
By the rushing in the Spring-time,

By the alders in the Summer,
By the white fog in the Autumn,
By the black line in the Winter;
And beside them dwelt the singer,
In the vale of Tawasentha,
In the green and silent valley. …

Touchstones

Verse in which there is nothing but the beat of the meter furnished by the accents of the polysyllabic words we call doggerel. Verse is not that. Neither is it the sound of sense alone. It is a resultant from those two.

—Robert Frost

Subject Matter Matters

Some poems go wrong in their subject matter, whether it's because the subject matter is treated inappropriately or because the poet is using subject matter that really doesn't warrant a poem. You will want your poems to have "good manners." By that I mean you should question a poem that deliberately tries to shock, disgust, or alienate the reader. This is not to say that you can't challenge or even frustrate a reader. Just try not to make your reader put down the poem, never to pick it up again.

There's not much you can't write about in a poem, though the things that beginners like to write about, such as love, death, pain, sorrow, and so on, are often the most difficult. Using concrete language will help these subjects to become more easily rendered into poems.

Touchstones

Sentimentality is a failure of feeling.

—Wallace Stevens

Melodrama and Sentimentality

Melodrama happens when the poet is trying to hard to persuade the reader of some emotion or action. This can lead to serious overwriting. Melodrama can make the serious ridiculous.

Sentimentality uses stock images or phrases to convince the reader of some emotion. For example, using the words "tears" and "crying" will no more move the reader than "dump truck" will. Sentimentality makes emotion and idea simple and unsophisticated, especially if the poet obviously doesn't feel it. Imagine wanting to write about a battle but having no feeling for the battle. You might include the blood and the screams of dying men, but these are stock images of the battle, and the reader will notice.

Touchstones

Don't imagine that a thing will 'go' in verse just because it's too dull to go in prose.

—Ezra Pound

Touchstones

No tears in the writer, no tears in the reader. No surprise for the writer, no surprise for the reader. For me the initial delight is in the surprise of remembering something I didn't know I knew. ... Step by step the wonder of unexpected supply keeps growing.
—Robert Frost

Here's a poem that borders (well, maybe it's dipped beyond the border) on the melodramatic and the sentimental:

Dead Love

Dead love, by treason slain, lies stark,
White as a dead stark-stricken dove;
None that pass by him pause to mark
  Dead love.

His heart, that strained and yearned and strove
As toward the sundawn strives the lark,
Is cold as all the old joy thereof.

Dead men, re-arisen from the dust, may hark
When rings the trumpet blown above:
It will not raise from out of the dark
  Dead love.

—Algernon Charles Swinburne

Sermonizing

You are not a teacher of life; you are a poet. Okay, maybe being a poet makes you a kind of guru, but, nevertheless, your poems should not be didactic, meaning that you shouldn't have an overt lesson in your poems. In the bygone days, poets often sermonized and moralized when writing about the Church or about how one should live one's life. We've come a long way, baby. Don't try to teach anything in your poems; if you have an agenda, and if you're a good writer, it will emerge naturally.

The "Guess What It Is" Poem

Sometimes, beginning poets feel that their poems have to be mysterious. This often comes from the fact that they haven't read a lot of poetry and it's a mystery to them. Better that your reader understands what you're writing about than be mystified and put down your work. Unless you're writing a riddle, come right out and say what you mean. If you're writing about a person, go ahead and let the reader know the *who, what, where, when, why*, and *how* of that person, or your reader might think you're writing about an umbrella. Don't be afraid to use a name and a specific place, and tell the reader *exactly* what's going on in your poem.

Too Much, Too Little, Too Late

Sometimes, novice poets say too much about their subject and sometimes they don't say enough. With poetry, a little goes a long way. Trust that your reader is intelligent and will get what you're saying. Beginning poets often want to toss everything *and* the kitchen sink into a single poem. Many poems suffer from this lack of focus. Instead of trying to fit *everything* in, write several poems on the same subject matter. Instead of writing about a year, write about a minute. Instead of writing about a minute, write about a single moment.

Many beginning poets will concoct a great metaphor and then explain it in the very next line: "My love is like a red red rose/a rose that is really red and beautiful in a beautiful garden." There's no need for the second line, we get it—your love is beautiful. Move on.

Or, the beginner will say too little: "I had a blue teacup/then I went to Paris." Okay, this could potentially go somewhere, but if the teacup and Paris aren't linked somehow later in the poem, the reader will wonder what those two images were doing there. This might be a kind of private symbolism, but rather than expecting your reader to understand a private symbol or an inside joke, let your reader in on your intention.

Exercises

Here are some exercises to get you working toward great poems. Remember, poets work hard at forging poems; and if you want to be a great poet, you've got to put the work in, too.

- Write a really bad poem. Use sing-songy rhythms, lots of needless repetition, bad rhyme, melodrama, and so on. Then write the poem's good counterpart.
- Take a good poem and add to it or subtract from it to make it really bad. What did you have to do to ruin it?
- Write a poem about a political or moral issue that you feel strongly about, but do not sermonize. Let your images inform the reader.
- Write a poem in strict meter (like *The Song of Hiawatha*) and break the lines such that the reader will not be able to read it in a monotonous fashion. Next, add several lines to the poem that are not in meter at all.

The Least You Need to Know

- Using the poetic conventions will help you to become a better poet.
- Try to eliminate cliché and familiar language from your poems.
- Sermonizing and moralizing—trying to teach a moral lesson in your poems—will turn a reader off.
- Use punctuation unless you are eliminating it for a good, poetic reason.
- Remember: Show, don't tell!

Chapter 17

How Do You Get to Carnegie Hall?: Revision, Revision, Revision

In This Chapter

- Why revise?
- Killing your darlings
- Letting your poems rest
- How not to revise the "life" out of your poems
- When a poem dies—poetry funeral?

Unless you're a poet of the Beat Generation (which in all likelihood you're not), who lived by the motto "first thought, best thought," revision is not a matter of choice—you have to revise if you want to be a serious writer.

Revision is the most important thing you can do as a writer. A poet who won't revise does his or her poems a grand disservice. Even if you use every single poetic skill to perfection, you may as well toss all your poems in the trash if you're unwilling to rework them to make sure they are in the best possible shape they can be. Your first thought is generally not your best thought, but you can rework your thoughts and make them even better. In this chapter, we'll discuss the best approach to revision.

Revise Away!

Revision means re-seeing your poems (hence the root word, "vision"); it entails asking your poems how they can be improved and listening for the answer. Once you've written a poem, it has a life of its own; you're in service to *it*, not the other way around. If you force your poem to be something it's unwilling to be, the opposition could be deadly—for the poem! Be kind to your poems. Give them the chance to improve! Revision is not about running spell-check, fixing punctuation, or changing a word or two—it's about seeing your poem objectively and changing it significantly enough to make it "work."

For example, if you've written a metrical rhyming poem and something just isn't right, you have to be willing to take it out of meter and ditch the rhyme to make the poem better. If you're married to the meter and the rhyme, you might be missing out on a way to make your poem far better than its original form.

Dodging Doggerel

If you truly want your poems to be good (or better than they have been in the past), consider doing quite a lot of revision on them if they need it. Look at them keeping all the poetic conventions in mind. Ask yourself: How can I make this poem better?

Murdering Your Darlings

The novelist William Faulkner said to "murder your darlings." He did not mean that killing your loved ones will make your writing better; he meant that you shouldn't become so attached to something in your work that you can't cut it out to make your work better. That's not so strange a theory as it sounds.

This sounds cruel, doesn't it? Take a look at a lovely poetic line of yours—does it really belong there? Does it add something important to the poem? Why do you love it so much? Is it the only line holding an otherwise poor poem together? Why have you been reluctant to remove it, or to use it somewhere else?

The wonderful thing about revision is that you don't have to really "kill" your lines—you can simply "retire" them for a while and use them somewhere else. Good lines of poetry never die—they get reborn in other poems.

Let Me Count the Ways

Revision is one of the most important gifts you can give your poems. Some poems seem to come from a divinely inspired source, and may not need a lot of revision, while others will need a total overhaul. Great writers revise.

Why Revise?

You revise to make your poem better. A careful poet makes sure that every word is in the "proper" place, that everything in the poem has meaning, and that the poet's intention was revealed. You're a careful poet. You revise.

Your first thoughts in your first draft may not be as polished as your second thoughts, and those will not be as tight as the images and ideas in your third. Keep working a poem until you can't look at it objectively anymore. Then show it to someone else. Then revise again. Revision will help you avoid writing *doggerel*—poems only fit to be fed to the dog!

Poetically Correct

Doggerel is hackneyed, trivial or bad poetry, usually using a monotonous rhythm and rhyming pattern.

What About Inspiration?

Okay, don't whine. Inspiration is great, but not all inspiration is created equal. If you can't begin to think of poetry as a real art with real work involved, you're going to miss a large part of what it means to be a poet.

The words that come to you when you're writing poetry do come from somewhere, but I can't tell you from where. Perhaps it's different for each of us. I do sometimes think that some of my poems are the product of some kind of divine inspiration or fortune, but that doesn't mean that they are sacred relics. They, too, need polishing, just as a rare coin does when it's brought up from a shipwreck. If you're lucky enough to find the coin in the first place, don't you have the obligation to shine it up?

Touchstones

Some poets actually say they don't revise and don't believe in revising. They say their originality suffers. I don't see that at all. The words that come first are anybody's, a froth of phrases, like the first words from a medium's mouth. You have to make them your own.

—James Merrill

Letting a Poem "Rest"

Sometimes poems need to rest a bit before you revise them. They are tired from being wrought so fiercely, and they just want to be left alone.

Allowing yourself to gain some distance from a poem is a great way to begin to see it objectively. When a poem is fresh, a poet may not be able to see its weaknesses. Put the poem in a drawer for a while and forget about it. In a week, a month, or even a year, drag the poem out and see what you can do with it. Chances are you've become a better poet in the meantime (if you've been practicing) and will be better able to use your poetic skills on it. Trying to revise it too soon can lead to frustration. You'll get better at revision the more you do it.

When Good Poems Go Bad: The Quick Fix

If you're "hot" to revise your poems right away, here are a few quick-fix tips you can try:

- Try breaking the lines differently. Doing so may help you find the place where the poem took a wrong turn.
- Try writing the poem without your initial strategic skills, such as its rhyme, meter, or repetition, and see if it gets better.
- Eliminate all clichés—unless you've used them for a reason or in some unique way.
- Try to eliminate all TO BE verbs.
- Eliminate most or all adverbs.
- Question every adjective. A good exercise is to eliminate half of them and see what that does to your poem.
- Try different stanza or line lengths.
- Reorganize your poem entirely—try changing the order of the stanzas. Perhaps the last stanza would be great as the first stanza.

Enough Is Just Enough

Sometimes revision can revise the life out of a poem. If you revise a poem too much, you can actually make it worse.

How do you know when it's time to stop revising? Well, you really don't. Some poets will revise poems even after they've been published in book form for years. A poet is rarely completely satisfied with his or her work.

I've heard criticism of poets who "love their work too much." I think this is unfair—it's okay to love your work, but it's not okay to be so self-satisfied that you stop putting in the effort to perfect the eternally imperfect. That's the big mystique of poetry that keeps poets coming back for more. Poetry is not something you'll ever perfect; the key is all in the trying.

No such thing as a perfect poem exists. Since that's the case, there's no real time to stop revising. However, here are some signs that you should leave a poem alone and move on:

- You become obsessed with one poem to the point of neglecting other poems or stopping writing until the revision is "done."
- The poem gets published in a very high-quality literary magazine. This doesn't mean that you can't revise it again, but it means that you might want to move on to new work. Publication is a nice reward for a well-crafted poem—now make that published poem some brothers and sisters.

- Your workshop leader, workshop, 174 editors, your significant other, and your mother hate every revision you've done on this single poem in the past 12 years. Let this one rest a bit and write other poems.
- Every new draft of a poem makes it worse and worse. Put this poem aside for a while and come back to it later.

What Does Your Poem Want to Be When It Grows Up?

Another thing to keep in mind is that sometimes poems have minds of their own. You want your poem to be a haiku but the poem wants to be a villanelle. So let it. Do what the poem wants. If you set out to write one type of poem, and in revision the poem begins to find another form, let the poem take that form instead. Better to write a good unintended poem than a bad forced poem.

The Theory That You'll Keep Getting Better

I'm here to tell you that if you practice a lot, read reams of great poetry, and don't become too self-satisfied with your work, you WILL get better at writing poems.

This is a great theory, because it means that you'll be able to help your first attempts to be better poems. As you learn to write, you'll learn to revise, too. Poems that you once felt were helpless may become your best work. Don't scrap anything—but don't get stuck either.

Roses Are Red

It's a good idea to keep drafts of your work. This way you have a "study" of what you did during the revision process so that you won't forget how you accomplished a certain move. Buy a portable file cabinet where you can easily stuff your drafts. You may have to buy more of these as the years go on, or upgrade to a larger version, but you'll be glad that you've kept all the versions of your work.

The Death of a Poem

There's something to be said for letting a poem you love slip into the ether, never to be seen again. Every poet I know has hundreds of good poems that will never see publication—or even see one other reader. Sometimes even a good poem is just a practice poem. What you're striving for are *great* poems.

"Dead" poems can be fun to come back to years later and revise, or just to study. As you write, you will see yourself improve, and it's fun to go back and look at your "former poetic self"—it's a little like looking through an old photo album. You will be charmed by seeing yourself as a "baby."

Roses Are Red

Keep a file (either a computer file or paper file) with all of your "dead" poems in it—poems that you're not going to revise any further and are not going to send out for publication or use in a manuscript. This is a good place to look when you're revising another poem and need a line or an image. This is called cannibalizing. Bon appétit!

The Benefit of Moving On

Getting stuck in the revision process means that you're not writing anything new. If I had the choice between writing a new poem and revising an old one, I'd choose writing. That way I'd have two poems to revise for the times that I didn't feel like creating new poems.

When inspiration clobbers you, don't revise—write! One day, when you're feeling "dry," you can drag out all of your creations and revise. Or, you can set aside a certain time each day or each week for revision. Moving on from a group of poems that you're having trouble revising will help you to create new and potentially better poems.

A Sample Revision

Here is an example of a poem going through a few revision stages. The poet, Maura Stanton, began with handwritten notes that she didn't save, but she did save the drafts she wrote on her computer. Here they are:

Draft One:

Juxtaposition like a surreal painting
Calling up the comparisons to

Where a photographer
And so the zoo sheltered the wild birds here,

The caption states, and so the zoo herded
Wild birds in here

A hurricane is coming, the caption states,
And so the zoo sheltered the wild birds here
Spreading straw, filling the sinks with water.

But the caption describes a hurricane alert.
Someone's strewn this tiled floor with fresh straw
And herded these wild, dazed birds through the door.
Still, someone with a camera looked hard, and saw
Something else. This photo was flashed from shore to
shore.
At kiosks, we readers smile at the juxtaposition,
Surprised by an ancient delight in comparisons.

Draft Two:

They look like ballerinas fluffing skirts
To me, I say to a friend. Look at the mirror.

Pleased to make our own delicious comparisons.
Forced to our own strange, dreamy comparisons.

At kiosks we stop, surprised by the juxtaposition,
Pleased to make our own delicious comparisons.

At kiosks we stop, pleased by the juxtapositions,
Encouraged to make our own delicious comparisons.
Teased to make our own delicious comparisons.
Surprised at our own delicious comparisons.

At kiosks, we smile over the juxtaposition
Pleased to make our own delicious comparisons.

Like a corps de ballet fluffing up skirts
And stretching to see themselves in the mirror?
Think up some similes. It's hurricane alert.

Someone's strewn this tiled floor with fresh straw
And herded the wild, dazed birds through the door.
And someone else has snapped this photograph
And sailed it straight into every newsroom.
At kiosks we stop, and look, and wonder
Struck by the beauty of all comparisons.

Draft Three:

Invent to explain this delicious pleasure
Reflected in the

We should be out there locked up in a care
While the birds
That makes this photo funny, one that unites
People and birds, making us all alike

The person and the bird, making them seem
Equal on the earth for the space of a dream.

The person and the bird, leveling both
Or raising them to new levels of growth

People and birds, or is it men and women

Through the mind of the

Final Poem:

Pink Flamingoes

Crowded between the stalls and rows of sinks
In the men's bathroom at the Miami zoo
Three dozen gaudy pink flamingoes shrink
Against each other, a dazzling rendezvous
Of skinny legs, long necks, and feathery stir:
They look like ballerinas up on their toes
Stretching to see themselves in the mirror
Of twirling about to pose for this photo.
The caption explains how a big hurricane
Threatens Florida, but this surreal view
Of public toilets hits us all the same,
Making us grin at something that seems true
And wonderful about the human way,
Though what it is, we really couldn't say.

—Maura Stanton

While it didn't begin that way, this poem ended up being a Shakespearean sonnet. As you can see, the poet began with a few images, and even made notes to herself to "think up similes." You can see here how the poet really worked this poem; she didn't just turn on her spell-checker. If you keep your drafts, you can evaluate your revision process and see if you're doing enough to make your poems better, shaping them into what *they* want to be.

Exercises

Here are some valuable revision exercises to get you thinking about revising your own work.

- Have a friend type out several published poems for you without the line breaks. Next, try to see if you can figure out where the line breaks belong. This may help you to get an idea of the line as a unit and will help with your own line breaks.
- Take a poem that you've recently written and use the "kill your darlings" theory on it: Remove everything you love. What does that do to the poem? Is it better or worse?
- Take an antiquated poem and read it several times, to the point where you are positive that you understand the meaning of each line and the meaning of the poem in general. Next, revise it into a modern poem, using your own lines and moves. If the poem takes off on a tangent, let it.
- Take the last poem you've written and cut it up with scissors so that each line or "idea" is on a scrap of paper. Move the scraps around like you're working on a puzzle. Perhaps the lines or ideas belong in different places or don't belong at all. This is a good way to test each little part of your poem. Have a friend put the scraps together the way they see the poem fitting together. If you don't have a friend, feed the scraps to your dog—all the scraps he doesn't swallow should go into the poem. Okay, I'm kidding about the dog-as-critic idea! Though you never know ... here, Fluffy ...

The Least You Need to Know

- Revision is not a matter of choice—you *must* revise your poems.
- Revision is about re-seeing your poems, not just running spell-check!
- Letting your poems "rest" may enable you to see your work more objectively and will help the revision process.
- Sometimes even good poems die. This is part of writing. Let them die with dignity and move on. You can cannibalize them for later poems.
- Rather than get stuck in the revision process, move on and write more poems. Then you'll have more to work on when you're in the mood to revise.

Chapter 18

To Slam or Not To Slam?: Reading Your Poetry in Public

In This Chapter

- Why read poems in public?
- Where to read your poems
- What to expect at a reading
- The short-course on slamming
- Starting your own reading series

The history of poetry includes a long period of time when poetry wasn't a written art, but an oral one. Poets were the historians of the tribe, passing down legends and stories for future generations. This is poetry's legacy, rooted deeply in the spoken word. As we've seen, poetry has its roots in song, chant, and ritual—all forms of poetry meant to be heard.

Poetry needs an audience. Part of the art includes creating and sharing. Sure, you could publish a book (if you're very patient, a great writer, and believe in Lady Fortune), but reading your poetry in public is far easier and is a gift granted to you more often than publication. You'll find that many opportunities are popping up all around the country; all you have to do is find one and show up.

This chapter will help you to get over the fear of reading in public and offer you tips on making your performance the best it can be.

Why Should I Read Poetry in Public?

You should read in public to share your work with others and to contribute to poetry's oral tradition. Only after you've faced an audience can you really know what your poetic ancestors did for the art. Ultimately, you should read your poems in public because you want to. No one's forcing you. But I can tell you that it's a lot of fun.

Poetically Correct

Open mic is a reading where anyone from the audience is invited to read his or her poetry.

When you read your poems in public, you get feedback that you won't get in a workshop (or sitting alone in your room), most of it positive. You'll meet other people who love and write poetry, especially if you become a regular at a particular *open mic,* which is the term for a reading where anyone from the audience is free to read his or her poetry.

Reading your work aloud in front of an audience (no matter how small the audience is) can also help your writing. You will begin to hear where your poems may need tweaking in their line breaks and musical elements. If your tongue trips over a line again and again, it probably should be changed. If you're breathless after reading a particular poem, perhaps you need to add some punctuation or break the lines differently.

Where to Read

If you're in a big city like New York or San Francisco, you're in luck—poetry readings are plentiful. If you live in a college town, it shouldn't be difficult to find them either. If you make your home in a more rural area, you might have to travel a bit and do some research to find a reading or a regularly scheduled reading series near you.

Most bookstores offer open mics or scheduled readings. Call around to find out when they are held. Call your local university's English or creative writing department as well; they're bound to have a reading series. Most colleges also have a poetry society, a couple of poetry journals, and a cultural society, all of which may offer reading series or open mics.

Some cities celebrate National Poetry Month in April with a variety of poetry events. You are bound to find dozens of readings at that time. Keep an eye on the local newspaper around April to see if they list readings. This is a good time to begin making contacts.

What to Expect at a Reading

Poetry readings are usually small affairs, with the exception of those of the "famous" poets, usually highly published prizewinners who draw decent-sized crowds. I've seen open mics with as few as 6 people in the audience and as many as 40. Remember, you're not going to get famous doing this, but you will have fun. Even if only six people are in the crowd, and they're all your siblings, read anyway. Be a good sport. Remember, any type of reading is good practice, even if everyone in the audience is related to you (or sleeping).

Most reading locations offer a microphone so you won't have to shout your poems, but some rooms are small enough that you won't need one. Hearing yourself the first few times over the mic is uncanny; however, realize that you sound normal to your audience, so just pretend that you can't hear your own voice, strange as your poems sound to you reverberating over the speakers.

If you're at an open reading, it's likely that other people will be reading their poetry as well. A sign-up sheet will probably be at the front. If you don't want to go first you can try to sign your name below the others, but that doesn't always work, as some MCs will choose from the list at random.

You might find a lot of distractions at a reading, especially if it's at a commercial establishment like a bookstore, coffee shop, or bar. For one, a cash register is bound to be ching-chinging away; most places host readings in the hopes of bringing customers in, so you can't blame them. There might also be a phone ringing, uninterested customers walking in and out, and people talking. In cases like this, try to have some poise. The people who want to listen will make every effort to hear you.

Touchstones

All poets who, when reading from their own works, experience a choked feeling, are major. For that matter, all poets who read from their own works are major, whether they choke or not.

—E. B. White

Audience Etiquette

Being a member of an audience at a poetry reading comes with certain rules. Here are some basic guidelines:

1. Don't talk while another poet is reading; that's just plain rude.
2. No heckling, unless you're at a slam (we'll get to that in a bit).
3. If you have to get up to use the restroom or buy a grande skim mocha latte, wait until the reader has finished, or at least until a pause between poems.

Roses Are Red

Readings have no real dress code, but if you can dust off that old black beret, you'll really fit the part. A black turtleneck is optional. Try to learn to enjoy coffee if you can—smoking is not obligatory these days.

4. If you must eat, do so with as little noise as possible, and avoid the rustling of wrappers.
5. You don't need to applaud after each poem unless it was such a show-stopper that the rest of the audience breaks into applause as well. Clapping after the poet has finished is traditional.
6. If you liked the poet's work, it's great to go up to them and say so—but don't use this time to critique their poems.

Reader Etiquette

You, as a reader, have some protocol to follow as well. Here are some tips to make your reading go smoothly:

1. If you have time, begin your reading with another poet's work, a poem that you really admire. I like beginning my readings like this, though you don't have to. It's simply a nice way of recognizing and sharing a poem you love and exposing it to others.
2. Thank your audience for coming before you begin.
3. Read to your time limit (find out what it is before you read) and don't go over—that takes time away from other poets.
4. Read slowly, clearly, and pause a moment between poems. A little chatter doesn't hurt, but you should be spending your time reading your poems rather than talking about them.
5. To indicate line breaks, hesitate slightly at the end of each line. This hesitation is usually equivalent to the duration of half a comma.
6. Don't apologize for your work. Have confidence, even if you have to pretend to have it.
7. When you're done reading, thank your audience again.

Dodging Doggerel

Don't explain your poems thoroughly before you read each one. Expect that your audience is there to hear poetry, not to hear a summary of your poems. If you feel that a few of your poems need a bit of explanation, do so briefly. Better to read more poems in the time allotted than ramble on about how and why you wrote them.

Slamming and the Spoken Word

The "spoken word" forum and the poetry slam have become popular in recent years and have been the focus of a lot of media attention, including major motion pictures and MTV.

A poetry slam is a cross between a poetry reading and a gladiator competition with only metaphorical bloodshed. Poets get on stage and read a poem while judges chosen randomly from the audience score their poems. This might sound completely antithetical to the spirit of poetry, but this kind of competition actually has its roots in ancient Greek and Roman times.

According to the book *Poetry Slam: The Competitive Art of Performance Poetry,* by Gary Mex Glazner (Maniac D Press, 2000), the poetry slam began in earnest around 1986 in Chicago. In the next few years, poetry slams sprung up in larger cities around the country and, in 1990, Glazner produced the first-ever National Slam in San Francisco. National Slams have been produced every year since.

Roses Are Red

Practicing in front of a mirror may help to calm your nerves before a reading. Try out your jokes between poems, time your reading, and shuffle the order of your poems to hear how they work best.

Let Me Count the Ways

I moved to New York City during the heyday of the poetry slam at the Nuyorican Poetry Café on 3rd Street between Avenues B and C. I became enamored with the energy and feeling of the place, and found myself attending or participating in slams almost every week. This is where I discovered that I'm a poet of the written word—I never came in above fourth place, and, in fact, came in dead last once—the MC quipped that if the slam was golf, I'd be winning. One of the mottos of the poetry slam is "The best poet always loses." I think they say it so that the ultimate loser doesn't feel too badly about being squashed, but I'm going to believe it anyway!

What Is Spoken Word?

Spoken word is a form of poetry that's written to be read aloud. Because it is meant for an audience of listeners, spoken-word poems often contain a predominance of musical elements (repetition, rhyme, alliteration, etc.) and may even call for foot stomping, hand clapping, singing, or other physical elements that add emphasis to the poem.

Spoken-word poems tend not to work as well on the page as they do read aloud, though that's not necessarily the case. The spoken-word poet is concerned largely with the oral quality of the poem and how the audience will receive it—a slam is, after all, a competition.

Subject matter for spoken-word poems tend to be highly personal or political, often using material that will titillate the audience. The poems are largely narrative, telling a story that the audience (and the judges) will have some kind of reaction to.

How a Slam Works

The "slam open" is for anyone who wants to participate and try for a chance to move up to the invitational slam (made up of the winners of the slam open), the participants of which may move up to the semifinals, the finals, the Grand Slam, and ultimately, the National Slam. At the slam open, poets read one poem in round one that they hope will get them into round two. Poets who don't make it into round two have to come back the following week if they want another chance.

Before the slam begins, the MC will choose judges at random from the audience. These judges need not be versed in poetry; they just have to be willing to judge, which can be a harrowing experience if you judge an audience-favorite poet or poem too low. Judging is from 0 (low score) to 10 (high score), and uses decimal points so that there's less of a chance of a tie.

Poems are judged on content and performance, but mainly on performance, in my experience. Often there's a poet who's "famous" at the slam, one who is loved by the audience, and this poet tends to win frequently.

Poets who read first are at a disadvantage; the crowd is not warmed up yet (not tipsy enough, in some cases) and tends to score the first few slammers lower than they would have later in the evening. If you can help it, jockey for a reading position as late in the slam as possible, when the scores tend to be higher.

While this might sound like very serious stuff—and it is for many of the poets—the slam is downright fun. People are hyped up to hear great poems, and there's a lot of laughter, general silliness, heckling, and the occasional very powerful poem. Even if you don't have the guts to participate (and it does take some courage), try to attend a slam—you'll get a real kick out of it.

Let Me Count the Ways

Rules for The National Poetry Slam (from the book *Poetry Slam: The Competitive Art of Performance Poetry,* by Gary Mex Glazner):

1. **The three-minute rule:** Poems must be read in three minutes or less.
2. **The no-prop-or-costumes rule:** No props or costumes may be used.
3. **The who-wrote-the-poem rule:** Each poet must have written the poem he or she performs.
4. **Scoring poems:** At the Nationals, five judges each score the poems from 0 to 10, with 10 being the highest possible score.

For complete rules, refer to the book listed above or go to www.poetryslam.com and request the full set of rules.

Writing for Listeners

Part of reading your poetry aloud involves considering how the audience will react to your poem. You are not the ruler of the room just because you're at the mic; when you read your poems aloud, you are making a transaction with the audience. You're giving them something, hopefully in the best possible form, and they're giving your poems their attention and appreciation. Many performance poets understand the need to connect with the audience. They are experienced in writing for and handling an audience. Here's a poem that includes sounds beyond the written words. Try to imagine what it would sound like aloud:

The Sound of Metal

For the Sailors of the submarine Kursk
(symbols are to be performed as Morse code)

... — ...
... — ...

... — ...
... — ...

The sound of metal ringing in the sea.
A map to speak of possibility.

Concentric tones of need.
A rhythm charged with want.

Where does it come from?

A steel pulse calling
rising to the surface
clinging to any ear.

Reaching up an atlas of why.
What language is this?

How to explain the density of air?

This is the speech of ocean.
This is the breath you are not taking.

Calling out—free us. Calling out—find us.
We are not hidden.
We are simple sailors,
Won't you gossip about survival?

He has always loved swimming in the river
and it was impossible to pull him out of there.

We know that they are still alive,
because they knock on the walls.

Carbon Dioxide hatches every dream exhaled.

The absolute truth of lungs.
The fierce work of depth-charge.

Claustrophobic frontier.
This foul moment of union.

We are listening.
They are banging an alarm of devotion.

They tell us who to wait for.
 A multitude of pounding.
  The drum composed of life.
   An instrument of clarity.

Singing of consummation.
A bell clinging to the shape of its chime.

Sound quick as water.
Tone thicker than time.
A tapping faint as forget.
Buoyant into the fracture.
Floating up like prayers.

... — ...
... — ...

... — ...
... — ...

—Gary Mex Glazner

You can see that the poet here used Morse code as a part of his poem—directions to the reader are just after the title. I imagine that the code could be stomped or played on two metal sticks, or rendered any other creative way the poet has in mind. Also notice that almost every line is end-stopped, creating a dramatic effect when read aloud. You can use these kinds of effects in your poems, too. I have a poem that uses a bit of dialogue and every time I read it aloud in front of an audience I use voices for the three different characters—this always gets a laugh and people pay more attention to the rest of the poem.

Roses Are Red

Record yourself doing a practice reading to hear how you sound to an audience. Realize that when you play the recording back, you are far more critical of your voice (and of your poems) than is the audience. You'll want to listen for your reading "style." Do you have long pauses between poems? Do you explain too much? Do you consistently trip over lines? Hearing yourself may help you to smooth out your performance.

Starting a Reading Series or a Slam

If you can't find a reading series, open mic, or slam near you, or you feel that your community could use another one, consider starting one yourself. You can approach coffee shops, bars, and bookstores for the space, most of which will be happy to comply if you can promise them some new customers.

Roses Are Red

Before you read your poetry in public or before you compete in a slam, go to several readings and slams and just listen. Try to get a feeling of the room, the audience, and the amount of time you have to read.

Advertise in the local paper, make up flyers, and contact your local radio stations for some free press. If you can offer something like free coffee or cookies for the first few readings, you might find yourself with some loyal attendees. Though they might be the homeless people who live in cardboard boxes near the coffee shop, they may turn out to be the best poets attending!

If you start your own series, you can invite published poets to read, and have your open mic after the reading—that way you will have a built-in audience for the open mic. Starting a series is one way to begin to create a little press for yourself in your poetry community—but remember, it's all about the poetry, first and foremost.

Exercises

Here are some ideas to get your poetry floating on the air. Have courage—get out there and read!

- ➤ Call your local university and write down the dates of some upcoming poetry readings. Try to attend at least one.
- ➤ Practice reading some of your poems in front of the mirror. How do they sound to you? Choose the five best-sounding poems and take them to an open mic, even if you don't plan to read.
- ➤ Read your poems at an open mic. Come on: Get brave!
- ➤ Attend a slam. You may have to go to New York, San Francisco, Portland, or another city to do it! Pack the car, kids—we're going to the Big Apple!

The Least You Need to Know

- ➤ Reading your poems in public can actually help you write.
- ➤ Poetry readings are usually small affairs, but you should read anyway—even if the audience is made up entirely of your family.
- ➤ Spoken word is a form of poetry that's written to be read aloud.
- ➤ The poetry slam is a kind of poetry competition where poems are judged on their performance as well as content.
- ➤ If you have no reading series in your area, begin your own!

Chapter 19

Writing in a Vacuum: Workshops, Colonies, Conferences

In This Chapter

- What is a workshop?
- Finding your own critic
- Workshops on the WWW
- The lowdown on writers' conferences
- The graduate degree in creative writing

We become very attached to the poems we write. In fact, some poets feel their poems are akin to children. Whether they're beloved darlings or wayward rebels, it's often difficult to see our poems objectively for what they are: machines of sound and meaning working toward a purpose beyond their creator. That's a complicated way of saying that they are not really kids.

It's difficult to see our poems for what they are; how can we tell if they are good or not, if they're "working toward their purpose," if they have potential? Very often we can't. That's why it can be helpful to show our poems to other people, especially if we're still working the poem, trying to shape it into its perfect form.

Showing a poem to another person completes the poem's transaction with the world. Poems weren't really meant to sit in a drawer by themselves—that's a lonely life for a poem. Sure, publication allows our poems to go out into the world and find their audience, but publication isn't always easy. Besides, if you're shooting for publication, you're assuming that your poems are ready for that stage, when you might be missing a step—critique.

Having someone critique your poems can be a valuable experience. You will hear things about your poems that you never even considered. You will come to realize that your poems have lives of their own, and that you, as creator, have little to do with how they are perceived once they're in someone else's brain. Critique may help your poems to fulfill your intentions for them and may even give you the "strokes" you need to keep using the skills that you're using well. Not all critique is aimed at pointing out the things that aren't working in your poems. A good critic will point out the poem's strengths, too.

Critique can be scary, especially the first few times you offer up your "children" to the chopping block. Not much will alleviate the fear of critique except for experience. Unless you're the famous poetess shut-in, Emily Dickinson (and I'm going to assume you're not), you have countless outlets for showing your poems to other poets for constructive feedback.

Do you *need* a workshop to be a good poet? Absolutely not. Does a workshop help? Sometimes. Is a workshop fun? Yes, a workshop can be a lot of fun—you'll meet other people passionate about poetry and you'll learn how to critique other people's poems, which will help your own work. I encourage you to seek out a poetry workshop or other venues where you can receive some commentary on your "babies." This chapter will help to take the anxiety out of having your poems discussed and critiqued.

What Is a Poetry "Workshop"?

A poetry workshop consists of a group of poets sitting around in a circle, talking about one another's original work. That's it. A workshop isn't a group of your fans sitting around ready to praise you, nor is it a gang of poetry thugs waiting to rip your poems (and your fragile ego) to irretrievable bits. In a perfect world, the other people in the workshop are as concerned about making your poems better as they are about improving their own work.

Touchstones

I like criticism, but it must be my way.

—Mark Twain

A poetry workshop may meet once a week or more, depending on where the workshop is located, and is run by a "workshop leader." This leader is usually trained to run workshops in a certain manner, and each leader has a slightly different style. If you don't like the style of a workshop leader (perhaps you've become used to another leader's style), try to stick it out in the workshop anyway. You may be surprised by the end of the class that you gained a lot from the difference.

The workshop leader is not your mother, father, sibling, friend, lover, rival, demigod, or pet. The leader is simply there to guide the class in the discussion of poems. All too often, the workshop leader is being well underpaid for the job. Try to be pleasant. If you truly have an aversion to the leader, simply drop the class.

In many workshops, one group of people will be experienced in the workshop format and another group will probably not have taken a workshop before. If you are part of the latter group, don't worry. After a few sessions, you'll be critiquing like one of the pros.

Touchstones

If there's one word that sums up everything that's gone wrong since the War, it's *Workshop*.

—Kingsley Amis

Critique

The idea of a workshop is to critique poems, sometimes called *workshopping*. Because there are generally so many different types of poets in the class, you will receive a wide range of critiques on your poems. You may even get conflicting critiques. For example, half the class may love lines one and three of your sonnet while the other half thinks that those are the lines you should change. You might look to the workshop leader for guidance, but he or she may not give it to you directly. The workshop leader often allows the class to express itself fully before jumping into the fray.

Poetically Correct

Workshopping is the act of critiquing a poem in a workshop. This word often makes workshop leaders wince.

Part of having your poem critiqued is learning which suggestions to take and which to leave. My thoughts on this are that 2 percent of any given critique is generally going to work for any given poem—but that's 2 percent of feedback that you didn't have before. Take the 2 percent and be grateful for it!

A workshop is often a room full of egos. This can make the critique difficult, but a good workshop leader will defuse those egos and make sure that the class is all about the poems, not the people. Make sure that you're not the student griping about the critique of your poem. You will get more out of the experience if you shut your mouth and open your ears.

What happens if you perceive that the entire workshop thinks your poem is terrible? So what? Feel free to think they are all stupid clodheads who wouldn't know a good poem if it poked them in the eye. After you're done feeling hurt and secretly plotting to let the air out of all of their tires, take a look at their suggestions again. Is there anything you can use? Did you really write the perfect poem and they didn't recognize it, or is there some improvement to be made? I thought so.

One main thing you have to realize about a workshop is that the other participants are *not talking about you* when they offer up their critique. They are talking about your poem. There's a difference. Sure, you created the poem, but once it's written it has a life of its own. As you get used to having your poems discussed, the critique will sting less and help more.

Dodging Doggerel

Some beginning poets feel they don't "need" critique on their poems. Often, these fearful or overconfident poets are writing verse that could benefit from a little tweaking—or a lot of tweaking. If you're scared of a workshop or of critique because you haven't done it before, talk openly to your workshop leader about your fears. Allowing your work to grow and yourself to grow as a poet might mean that you show your work to someone else and openly take his or her suggestions into consideration.

How a Workshop Works

A workshop can run in several different ways, but it has one basic structure, so that's the one I'll discuss here.

Roses Are Red

Always address the voice in the poem as the "speaker." Don't assume that the voice in the poem is the poet's voice. Looking at the poem as a separate entity from the poet is the first step in learning how to critique a poem correctly.

Everyone sits in a circle or semicircle. This is so that everyone can see one another. Sitting this way makes the room friendly. This isn't algebra, remember?

There are two ways to distribute poems—the *class before* and the *day of class*. If the class has had the poem for a week or several days, the leader will choose one of the poets to read his or her poem aloud and someone else, not the poet on the "hot seat," will begin the discussion. Having read the poem in advance gives the class the opportunity to really study the work and write their comments down. The pitfall of this method is that the members of the class are often more concerned with sounding smart in their critiques than with helping the poem discussed to improve.

If the poems are passed around the day of the class, the leader will choose one person to read his or her own poem aloud, and may even ask another class member to read it aloud as well. Someone will then begin a discussion of his or her impressions on this "new" poem. The benefit to this method is that the poet gets to hear how others interpret and feel about the poem seconds after they read it. The pitfall is that the class has less time to spend really musing on the poem and all its intricacies. This is often remedied by having the class take the poems home to write further comments on them.

Once the discussion has begun, the poet in the "hot seat" sits quietly listening and taking notes on what the other members of the class are saying about his or her poem. Some workshop leaders will insist that everyone comment on each poem, going around the room or choosing students randomly to speak, while other leaders take a more hands-off approach.

After the discussion of the poem ends, the workshop leader may allow the poet to ask one question of the class. Use this question wisely. Don't try to explain what you think your poem is about, insult the class by calling your classmates ignorant, or stomp out screaming "You'll pay for this!" Simply ask a question about something they discussed that you didn't understand.

If you have no questions, thank the class and move on to the next poem in the stack. Some workshop leaders don't even allow this question—and for good reason. There is a common feeling that the poet in the "hot seat" should not be allowed to speak about his or her poem, because many people will try to defend or explain their work rather than ask a question.

Become an Active Critic in Your Workshop

A big part of getting the most out of a workshop is learning to become good at critiquing other poets' work. You get no Brownie points for sitting there, week after week, with your mouth shut. Doing so may cause resentment in your classmates who may then stop commenting on *your* work. Even if you are fearful of offering critique, try your best: Commenting will help you in your writing, too.

Poetically Correct

Critic: a necessary evil
Criticism: an evil necessity.
—Carolyn Wells

Poetry, like any other pursuit, is filled with jargon. Learning as much as you can about poetry and reading a lot of poems will help you to develop the language you'll need to critique others' poems. Reading the first section of this book will give you some of the tools you need to begin talking about poetry. Don't worry if you're a little confused by all the jargon. Chances are that most of things you will want to discuss about someone else's poem are pretty basic.

Take your cues from the more experienced members of the workshop or from the leader. Even if you only have one comment, say it. You never know how much your comment will help the poet to make his or her poem better.

Workshop Etiquette

Now that you know how a workshop works, here are a few workshop etiquette tips to help you be an outstanding member of any poetry group:

- Talk about the "speaker" of the poem, not about the poet. The "I" in the poem may not represent the poet at all.
- Don't address the poet directly. Direct your critique to the entire class.
- Don't ask the poet questions about the poem during class—reserve your questions for outside the classroom.
- Using phrases such as "I liked it" or "I didn't like it" are meaningless in a workshop. No one cares about your aesthetic opinion, unless it's backed by a concrete example. "The metaphor opening the poem works for me because it strikes me as original yet it reminds me of Shakespeare's sonnet …," for example.
- Don't give a poem back to the poet without having written your critiques on it. This is rude and you're likely to start getting your poems back blank as well. If you haven't written on it, simply tell the poet that you didn't have time and that you'll have a written critique for them next week.
- Always sign your name to a critique.
- Don't doodle on other people's poems. Try not to leave coffee rings on them, or let your dog eat them.
- Don't keep a poem that isn't yours unless you ask the poet first.
- Try not to curse if you can help it, unless you stub your toe on the way out of the classroom. Definitely try not to curse *at* the other people in your workshop.
- If a poem offends you, try to bring your critique down to the poem's elements. Discuss metaphor, rhythm, etc. After you've done that, you can mention that you were offended by the content and tell the class why.
- If your own poem is taking a heated beating, you've probably done something right! Often, the poems that get the most criticisms are the ones that intrigued the class the most.
- Don't talk, flail, mime, gyrate, drool, or otherwise try to get your workshop's attention while your poem is being critiqued. Take notes instead.

- Try, if you can, to begin your critique with the aspects of the poem that you believe are working. Often, learning what *works* helps the poet to improve more so than learning what doesn't work.
- Take some time before you decide that your workshop hates you, your poems, and your critiques. It's sometimes difficult to listen to a critique of your work—your workshop probably doesn't hate anything about you. You'll have to take a look at your behavior in the workshop to determine that for sure!
- You're in the workshop to help others with their poems, not to attack them.
- Do unto others ... while still being honest.

Touchstones

You do not get a man's most effective criticism until you provoke him. Severe truth is expressed with some bitterness.

—Henry David Thoreau

Workshop Pitfalls

You might find pitfalls to perpetual workshop attendance. You may become reliant on deadlines and on the strokes and critique of others to write anything at all; some poets will learn to write for their workshop and not for themselves, in both quantity and quality. Eventually, everyone must wean off the workshop. However, this is not something you should worry about now; there are plenty of more pressing things to concern yourself with! If you've taken, say, 10 or more workshops in a row, consider taking a break and trying to write on your own. You can always come back to the workshop if you need it.

There's also the dreaded "workshop poem," the "perfect" poem with the clean ending, the poem taking little risk, perfectly comprehensible at first reading, whose form is obvious and whose moves are predictable. The workshop tends to favor these poems because they are easy and middle-of-the-road; groups in general tend to favor the mediocre. Why are there so many bad fast-food restaurants out there? Everyone understands that each McDonald's is going to have the same McMuffin, whether it's in Tacoma or Anchorage. The workshop poem is the McMuffin of poetry; your poems should be fine cuisine. If all of the members of your workshop adore every word of your poems,

Touchstones

Poetry is what is lost in translation. It is also what is lost in interpretation.

—Robert Frost

week after week, consider taking some risks in your work or consider trying a new workshop. Read Donald Hall's famous essay, "Poetry and Ambition," for more discussion of the dreaded McPoem.

Workshops and Other Poetry Forums on the WWW

If you can't get to a live workshop, there are plenty of poetry forums on the Internet where you can receive feedback on your work. Some of these are structured, paid classes, having a workshop leader, deadlines, and so on, while on other sites anyone can comment on your work.

Touchstones

To judge of poets is only the faculty of poets; and not of all poets, but the best.

—Ben Jonson

A poetry workshop or forum on the Internet has the advantage of being available 24 hours a day and enables people from all around the world to participate. The forums have the disadvantage of your not being able to choose who sees your work, but most forums have leaders watching out for misbehavior. See Appendix B, "Resources," for a list of poetry workshops and forums on the World Wide Web.

Some poets worry about someone stealing their work if they post it on the Net. Yes, there is a danger of plagiarism, but most poets have too much ego to steal other poet's work. Poetry is also not all that lucrative. You have just as much chance of your poems being stolen on the Net as you do if you publish them in a literary journal.

Starting a Workshop

If you have no workshop near you and you're not a fan of the Internet, you can begin your own poetry group. All you need is a group of people who write poetry and want critique. They have to be willing to show up at a certain time and certain place. This is not always as easy as it sounds.

First, find a place that will host your group. You can hold the workshop at someone's house or in a coffee shop if the manager will allow it.

Next, advertise. Put up flyers near a college if there's one nearby, and post your new workshop on poetry forums on the Net. Make some calls to poetry clubs and societies if there are any in your area. If you're really serious, take out an ad in *Poets and Writers' Magazine,* or one like it. You can begin a workshop with as few as three people if you'd like. Perhaps you'll be lucky and find more.

Finding Mr. or Mrs. Critic "Right"

If you've had your fill of workshops (or perhaps you don't even like the idea of them in the first place) you can search for your very own critic: one person who is "good" for your work, who understands what you're trying to do, and has a way of critiquing you that you appreciate and can use.

Finding this person isn't always easy. Generally, your very own critic will want you to be his or her critic as well—a reciprocal agreement. That means you must fit his or her idea of the "perfect" critic as well. It could take years to find such a dedicated person, or you may not find one at all. Or maybe you'll find your perfect critic at your very first poetry workshop!

You don't need a workshop to work on your poems, but having someone "in the know" looking at your work and offering suggestions can make the difference between a poem that ends up in the bottom of the barbecue grill and one that ends up published in a good literary review.

Let Me Count the Ways

Most poets whom you admire didn't have a writing program or a poetry workshop to attend. They wrote in solitude, or they studied on their own or corresponded with one or two like-minded poets who offered them critique. There were no grades, no workshops, no professorships after publication. What that tells us is that creative writing programs aren't as important to the art of poetry as the poets are. Whether you can attend a writing program or not, just keep writing.

Writers' Conferences

Writers' conferences are like summer camps for adults. They generally last a few days to a week, and are usually set someplace where an adult with a few hundred bucks to spend would like to go anyway—the High Sierras, Italy, Key West, and so on.

Writers' conferences are great places to meet other like-minded writers from all over the world, people you wouldn't otherwise have exposure to. Some conferences require a sample of poetry for their strict admissions procedure, while others have an open-door policy.

Most writers' conferences include seminars, workshops, lectures (and lots of parties!), and some even include daily writing exercises. They generally take place in the summer, when professors are on summer break and most novice writers can get some time off from their jobs. I've been to several of these summer conferences and they are a lot of fun.

You can find out about the wide variety of writers' conferences in *Poets and Writers Magazine* or in the book *Poet's Market.*

Writers' Colonies

A writers' colony is a space set up for serious writers at a more advanced stage in their writing. Most colonies offer space to writers for a few weeks up to a few months. Some offer scholarships, while others require a small per-day fee. They generally have a submission requirement and sometimes a publication requirement. A colony will often accept a writer early in his or her career under special circumstances, and some colonies do so regularly.

Colonies offer a quiet space for writers and provide meals and in-house workshops; the writer only needs to work on his or her writing. Again, you can find out about the wide variety of writers' conferences in *Poets and Writers Magazine* or in the book *Poet's Market.*

The Creative Writing Degree

During the past 20 years, the graduate creative writing program has become something of a phenomenon. New programs are springing up all over the country every year, churning out more and more "professional" poets. It must seem that the natural thing for a poet to do after getting a BA degree is to jump into a creative writing program. Certainly, thousands of people are following that track or already brandishing those degree-letters after their names, your humble author included.

The creative writing program offers students a kind of apprenticeship before being thrust into the "real" world where very few people value poetry. Academia is a place where practicing poets create a community in which poetry is the focus. Creative writing programs also enable younger poets to work closely with poets they admire.

Do you need a degree from a writing program to be a great poet? Not really. A degree may help you to get a teaching position after you've gotten some good publications, if that's what you want to do. Mainly, a creative writing degree will give you two or three years of concentration in your area of interest—and its only that valuable time that helps you write great poems, not the letters behind your name.

Types of Writing Programs

The most common degrees available in creative writing are the MA (Masters of Arts), the MFA (Masters of Fine Arts), and the Ph.D. (Doctorate). The MFA is the most common and is considered the "terminal" degree, meaning that it's the highest you can go in that realm of education.

Each program gives its students a different ratio of creative writing versus academic study. The Associate Writing Programs describe the types of creative writing degrees as follows:

Graduate writing programs are listed in *The AWP Official Guide* in the following descriptive categories: Studio, Studio/Academic, and Traditional Literary Study and Creative Writing. Although the aims and specific curricula of programs within each category differ considerably, the following general distinctions may be fairly made:

- **Studio** writing programs place primary emphasis on the student's writing experience within the program. In this way, they most closely parallel studio programs in music, dance, and the visual arts. Most of the degree work is done in workshops, independent writing projects or tutorials, and thesis preparation. The study of form and theory, and of contemporary writers, may be incorporated into workshops or offered through separate courses. Faculty of such programs are selected for their achievement in the creative forms and not for scholarly work. Students are admitted to such programs almost wholly on the basis of a writing sample, and, in turn, the significant degree criterion is the quality of the thesis manuscript.
- **Studio/Academic** writing programs usually place equal emphasis, in their curricula, on the student's writing and literature coursework, believing that the study of literature is crucial to one's development as a writer. These programs vary considerably in the structure and amount of literature requirements, but frequently rely on the regular English department faculty, noted for scholarly achievement, for many of the literature course offerings, while writers on the program faculty offer form and theory courses, workshops, and thesis direction. Studio/Academic programs often require some kinds of comprehensive examinations, and candidates are expected to be equally well prepared in literature and in writing. Admission is determined primarily by the quality of the original manuscript.
- Programs in **Traditional Literary Study and Creative Writing** offer work in writing with experienced writers on the faculty, and allow a creative thesis, but also expect that a significant amount of the degree work will be completed in the study of literature, usually in courses taught by English department faculty. Such programs tend to align themselves firmly with the academic tradition, and

> emphasize training their students as literature teachers as well as writers. Often, they actively use the same criteria for admission and degree award that are applied to candidates in literature, including the comprehensive examinations and the language requirements (Associated Writing Programs).

When you begin thinking about where you want to apply, you can ask the schools you'd like to attend what type of program they offer. If you want to teach, realize that a more academic program may help toward that goal. If you want to spend most of your time writing, choose a more "studio" type program.

Roses Are Red

Most creative writing programs require the GRE examination for entrance. This is because most creative writing programs are affiliated with English departments. Don't be daunted by this test—most creative writing programs don't use the scores from the GRE as the primary criterion for acceptance. Your portfolio of poems is the most important part of your application, so make sure that it's as strong as it can be, especially if your GRE score isn't as high as you had hoped.

The Top Writing Programs in the United States

When choosing a writing program, one of the things you will want to look at is the program's reputation. How many of that school's students go on to publish their own books and win prestigious awards? Is the faculty well known, and more important, do you like their work?

Newsweek has a ranking system of most colleges in the nation, including creative writing programs. The criteria for these rankings may not be at all the criteria you will want to use to make your decision on which schools to apply to, but it's interesting to see where the schools fall in the ranking. Here's the lowdown on writing programs from *Newsweek:*

Rankings of master's and doctoral programs in the arts, sciences, social sciences, and humanities are based on the results of surveys sent to academics in each discipline. The questionnaires ask individuals to rate the quality of the program at each institution as: distinguished 5); strong 4); good 3); adequate 2); or marginal 1). Individuals who were unfamiliar with a particular school's programs were asked to select "don't know." Scores for each school were totaled and divided by the number of respondents who rated that school.

Creative Writing—Master's Degree (1997)	
Average reputation score (5 = highest)	
1. University of Iowa	4.5
2. Johns Hopkins University (MD)	4.2
2. University of Houston	4.2
4. Columbia University (NY)	4.1
4. University of Virginia	4.1
6. New York University	4.0
6. University of California—Irvine	4.0
6. University of Michigan—Ann Arbor	4.0
9. University of Arizona	3.9
10. Boston University	3.8
10. Cornell University (NY)	3.8
10. University of Massachusetts—Amherst	3.8
10. University of Montana	3.8
10. University of Washington	3.8
10. Washington University (MO)	3.8
16. Brown University (RI)	3.7
16. Indiana University—Bloomington	3.7
16. University of Arkansas	3.7
16. University of Utah	3.7
20. Arizona State University	3.6
20. Emerson College (MA)	3.6
20. George Mason University (VA)	3.6
20. Hollins College (VA)	3.6
20. Sarah Lawrence College (NY)	3.6
20. Syracuse University (NY)	3.6
20. University of Florida	3.6

continues

Creative Writing—Master's Degree (1997)	
20. University of Maryland—College Park	3.6
20. University of Pittsburgh	3.6
20. Warren Wilson College (NC)	3.6
30. University of California—Davis	3.5
30. University of Southern Mississippi	3.5
30. University of Texas—Austin	3.5
33. Iowa State University	3.4
33. University of Missouri—Columbia	3.4
33. University of Oregon	3.4
33. University of Southern California	3.4
37. Bennington College (VT)	3.3
37. CUNY—City College of New York	3.3
37. Florida State University	3.3
37. Ohio State University	3.3
37. Ohio University	3.3
37. Penn State University—University Park	3.3
37. University of Alabama	3.3
37. University of Denver	3.3
37. University of North Carolina—Greensboro	3.3
46. San Francisco State University	3.2
46. University of Cincinnati	3.2
46. University of New Hampshire	3.2
46. Western Michigan University	3.2
50. American University (DC)	3.1
50. Colorado State University	3.1
50. Eastern Washington University	3.1
50. Georgia State University	3.1
50. New Mexico State University	3.1
50. Saint Mary's College of California	3.1
50. San Diego State University	3.1
50. Southern Illinois University—Carbondale	3.1
50. Temple University (PA)	3.1
50. University of Colorado—Boulder	3.1
50. Virginia Commonwealth University	3.1
50. Wichita State University (KS)	3.1

Creative Writing—Master's Degree (1997)	
62. Brooklyn College (NY)	3.0
62. California State University—Fresno	3.0
62. Mills College (CA)	3.0
62. Purdue University—West Lafayette (IN)	3.0
62. SUNY—Albany	3.0
62. University of Georgia	3.0
62. University of Hawaii—Mano	3.0
62. University of Illinois—Champaign-Urbana	3.0
62. University of Minnesota	3.0
62. Vermont College of Norwich University	3.0
72. Binghamton University (NY)	2.9
72. Bowling Green State University (OH)	2.9
72. Cleveland State University	2.9
72. Kansas State University	2.9
72. Michigan State University	2.9
72. Old Dominion University (VA)	2.9
72. University of Alaska—Fairbanks	2.9
72. University of Illinois—Chicago	2.9
72. University of Nebraska—Lincoln	2.9
72. University of New Mexico	2.9
72. University of Wisconsin—Milwaukee	2.9
83. Goddard College (VT)	2.8
83. Miami University (OH)	2.8
83. New College of California	2.8
83. Oklahoma State University	2.8
83. Rutgers (NJ)	2.8
83. School of the Art Institute of Chicago	2.8
83. University of Kansas	2.8
83. University of Miami	2.8

Newsweek

Realize that you can get a great education at a school that's not "ranked." Your education in writing depends on how open you are to learning and how much you practice. Don't judge a school solely by this ranking system. Do some research of your own.

Choosing a Writing Program

You have many ways to choose a writing program beyond reputation. You will want to consider location, cost, faculty, etc. Here are some things you should consider when making your application decisions:

- Is there someone at the school that you really want to work with? Have you read any of the faculty's writing? If not, do so immediately!
- Do you want to live in the town where the school is located? If you can schedule a visit, do so.
- Does the program give financial aid in the form of fellowships or scholarships? If only a few select students receive departmental aid, expect a certain tension within the student body. Some programs give all of their students aid, which allows for a less competitive feeling in the program.
- If the school does not give aid, can you afford it?
- Does the program offer teaching experience?
- What's the student-to-faculty ratio of the program? If there are many students per faculty member, don't expect to get a lot of individual attention.
- Does the program have classes other than the workshops that you are interested in taking? Call for a catalogue or check out the program on the Web.
- Can you take classes outside of the English department? Many programs will accept the credits from classes other than inside the program.
- Ask if the professor you want to work with is a full time faculty member at the university—often, professors are flown in from other places for short seminars. A professor can also take a grant to work elsewhere or a sabbatical. Ask if the professor you want to work with will be there, at least some of the time, while you're in attendance.
- The more "famous" the faculty, the less likely that you will find a close, personal mentor. Well-known writers are pulled in a zillion different directions and you'll just be another task on their list. Imagine—theirs is the life you might be striving for!
- Choose your writing program carefully—realize that you will be spending at least two years of your life there. Once you've committed to going, it's often difficult to turn back.

Roses Are Red

Tips for your creative writing program application ...

1. The most important part of your application is your writing portfolio. Make sure it's as strong as it can be, and place your best poems on top.
2. Your statement of purpose should be succinct and should indicate how you would be a productive member of the graduate program.
3. Get letters of recommendation from the people who know your work best. Make sure you give them enough notice to write the letters and send them on time.
4. Apply early, if possible. Don't wait until the week before the application is due to begin gathering your materials.
5. Don't call and nag the head of the department. You will be notified along with the other applicants. Nagging might create bad feelings, and you might want to apply again if your first application didn't gain you entry into the program.

Exercises

Here are some exercises to get you thinking about workshops, conferences and colonies, and creative writing programs.

- Call the local college in your area and find out when their next beginning workshop is going to be held.
- Search online for workshop and poetry forum resources (see examples earlier in the chapter).
- Approach someone in your workshop and set up a "poetry date." Meet with the person and exchange poems and critique. You can do this with an online poet as well.
- Look in *Poets and Writers Magazine* or *Poet's Market* and find a conference that you would like to attend. Call and request informational materials for the conference.
- Check out some creative writing program home pages on the Web and download some applications.

The Least You Need to Know

- Having someone critique your poems can be a valuable experience.
- You don't need a workshop to make your poems better, but it couldn't hurt all that much to try one.
- Becoming an active critic in your workshop will help your own poems to become better.
- The Web has many places where you can receive critique on your poems—and from the comfort of your own desk chair!
- If you can't find a workshop, begin your own!

Chapter 20

Your Name in Print: Getting Published

In This Chapter

- How to get your poems published
- The big no-nos of submitting poems for publication
- Organizing your submissions
- The low-down on rejection
- Self-publishing?

The big day: You get your first poem published. This is the day that many poets look forward to with anticipation. I'm not going to lie to you: It feels great! You get a nice sense of validation in getting poems published. An editor or group of editors (not just your mother) thought that your work was good enough to publish. You get to share your work with an audience. You have a document to show that what you're doing is serious and good—at least to the editorial board of the literary journal where your poem appears.

All of this is wonderful. But there can be disappointment to publication if you have unrealistic expectations about it. You will not get rich; no one will be nicer to you at the post office or offer you a book contract; you are not "officially" discovered at this point. You have a poem published. It's all part of the journey.

And not all places that publish poetry are created equal. This chapter will guide you in choosing places for publication and show you how to send out your poems properly.

Why Do You Want to Be Published?

First of all, ask yourself why you want to have your poems published. This is a tricky question. Publication does a lot for the ego, but not much for the pocketbook. You won't be interviewed for *Entertainment Tonight* as a poet, no matter how much you publish. Publication, for a working poet, brings professional validation. Now, why do *you* want to publish?

Historically, poetry is supposed to have an audience, which may be the best reason of all to try for publication. Presumably you aren't writing just for yourself but also to express your feelings and ideas to others. Publication will offer you a greater audience than your friends—but perhaps not that much greater!

How to Get Your Poems Published

Your second step (after examining your motives) is to have great poems ready. Don't *ever* send out poems before they are as "perfect" as you can make them. If you send out sloppy poems enough times to the same places, you may get a reputation as the person who writes sloppy poems, and the editors won't take your work seriously when your writing gets better.

Once you've determined that your poems are good enough—perhaps you've won a small contest at your school or writing group—you can begin to think about sending your poems out for publication. There's a real art to the submission process, and if done carelessly or without decorum, can lead to more rejection slips than you can wallpaper your bathroom with.

Where to Send Your Poems

Start by sending your poems to literary journals and reviews. These are the primary places that publish poetry. Some glossy magazines, such as the *New Yorker, Harper's,* and *The Atlantic Monthly* publish poetry as well, but you're better off saving your stamps in the beginning and sending to more realistic places to start. These glossy mags are difficult for first-time authors, and often don't accept unsolicited work—many of these magazines will ask poets they appreciate to submit poems but won't look at poems submitted without this request.

To get a feel of what the different literary reviews and journals look for, visit your local bookstore's writing section where you should find the "little mags." These magazines and journals will often be named after states and colleges, and many of them are run entirely by graduate students.

Choose a few from the stack and read them. Does your poetry look and sound like the poems in the review? If so, you might have a shot at publication there. Remember, the editor has a certain taste in poetry and decisions regarding acceptance are largely subjective. The good news is that editors at the college magazines generally change every two years or so. If your poems are drastically different from the poems in the mag, don't send them there. In most cases, you'd be wasting time and postage.

Touchstones

Nothing stinks like a pile of unpublished writing.

—Sylvia Plath

While you're at the bookstore, buy yourself one of the poetry submission "bibles," such as *Poet's Market,* published by Writer's Digest Books, which publishes a new edition of the book every year, or the *Directory of Poetry Publishers* and the *International Directory of Little Magazines and Small Presses* (both published by Dustbooks). Books like these list thousands of magazines that publish poetry, as well as their submission guidelines, contact information, reporting times, payment information, kind of poetry desired, difficulty of getting published there, and other necessary information. These are invaluable guides to getting your poetry published; you could spend years trying to accrue all of this information by yourself.

Roses Are Red

If you want the latest on what's happening in poetry today, or you want a detailed listing of contests and guidelines, you might want to subscribe to *Poets and Writers Magazine.* Check them out at www.pw.org/. They are located at 72 Spring Street in New York City.

Once you've purchased one of these books, take some time to go through it and highlight all of the magazines that look promising. If you're just beginning to publish, you may want to stick with the smaller mags until you've gotten some publications to show the larger mags on your cover letter.

If you're a detail-oriented person (okay, a control freak), you can use a system of colored highlighters with each color representing a level of mag—A level, B level, C level, etc. The A-level mags are the places where you'd really like to see you work right now. B-level mags are more realistic, and C-level mags are probably where you'll get your first publication (but not necessarily). In any case, this system will help you to further organize your submissions. The fact is that you'll probably have hundreds of places you'll want to submit to.

Roses Are Red

If you live in New York City or plan on visiting there, make sure to spend an afternoon at a library dedicated just to poetry, Poet's House, at 72 Spring Street. There you will find thousands of volumes of poetry, as well as all of the latest journals and reviews. Poet's House is a beautiful space, quiet and inviting, and you can bring your lunch. Check Poet's House out at www.poetshouse.org.

When to Send Your Poems

You will find submission deadlines in the *Poet's Market*. It's best to follow these deadlines or your work will come back to you or get lost.

Poetically Correct

Lag time is the time it takes for your poems to be either accepted or rejected; this can take a week to over six months.

In my experience, the best times to submit your poetry is in the early fall, around September/October, and early spring, around late January/February. This is when editors gear up to fill their magazines and your work will have the best chance of being accepted, as long as the poems are good and right for the magazine.

Only send to a particular magazine once a year, unless asked to send more poems for consideration, or unless you received a very nice hand-written rejection note. Never send to a magazine that is still considering an earlier group of your poems: Don't double-dip! Your copy of *Poet's Market* will list a magazine's *lag time*, the time it takes for a journal to consider your poems, so you can easily keep track of your submissions.

How to Send Your Poems

Submit your poems on clean, white paper, one poem to a page, with your name and address typed in the upper-right corner of each page. You will usually submit four to six poems per magazine, though some magazines specify a number, so you'll want to find out and comply; you can find this information in *Poet's Market* and other similar books.

It's best to send your poems in a large manila envelope, which keeps the pages looking crisp and clean. Otherwise, the editors would have to struggle with pieces of paper that don't want to give up their folds.

If you have not been published before, you don't have to submit a cover letter. Instead, let your poems speak for themselves. If you want to include a cover letter, it should read as follows:

> (date)
>
> (your address)
>
> (magazine's address)
>
> Dear Editor (put name here if you know it):
>
> Please consider the following poems for publication in (name of mag here): (list your poems here).
>
> Thank you for your time and consideration. I look forward to hearing from you.
>
> Sincerely,
>
> (your name)

If you have been published before, you can add a paragraph to this letter listing your previous publications. If you have any special education in poetry, you can list that as well. That's it. Simple. Editors don't care about your hobbies, your family, or your fetishes. All they care about are good poems—that's what matters most.

Along with your cover letter and poems, you MUST include a SASE—self-addressed stamped envelope—with the proper postage attached. This will enable the editors to send you an acceptance letter or a rejection slip without expending much energy. If you don't include this, most editors will not consider your submission, and it might be tossed into the trash. You can't expect magazines to pay for all that postage. If you just want to receive the letter of acceptance or rejection, indicate that on your letter by writing, "Please recycle manuscript; use envelope for correspondence only," and include a business-sized envelope with the proper postage.

Submission No-Nos

You can avoid many submission *faux pas* by "keeping it simple" and letting your poems do the work. Here are a few serious submission no-nos:

- Using any color paper other than white. Sure, your poems may warrant rainbow or gold-leaf paper, but the editors will not take them seriously. Don't distract the editor from your poetry.
- Using any color ink other than black. Sure, your love poem might look good in red ink, but please try to restrain yourself.

- Including cutesy pictures, drawings, or stickers on your poems. Just say no.
- Enclosing lengthy cover letters with unnecessary information. To do so is deadly, especially if the poet sounds cocky and arrogant.
- Explaining your poems in the cover letter—don't do this! Let the poems speak for themselves. Explaining how great they are is even worse.
- Misspelling the review's name, the editor's name, or getting either wrong altogether, i.e., sending to the *Mississippi Review* when the cover letter says *Georgia Review*. Ouch! If the editor has a gender-neutral first name, don't use Ms. or Mr.—opt for using their whole name.
- Including your headshot. No one cares what you look like.
- Making crazy statements in your cover letter. You can't frighten the editor into publishing your work.
- Including money. You can't bribe your way into publication. If you have a lot of money, just self-publish your poems and have done with it!
- Sending a nasty letter when you receive a rejection. This is a great way to alienate an editor and make sure that you're never published in that magazine.
- Calling a magazine and harassing the editors. You may call if you haven't heard from them in at least six months; they may have lost your poems or are still seriously considering them. Be polite when you call.

Simultaneous Submissions

Most magazines say that they don't like simultaneous submissions, meaning that they want to be the only place to be considering your work at the time. This is certainly the polite thing to do because editors take pains to choose the best poems for their magazine, and if they take the time to accept yours, and it has already been accepted somewhere else, you've just wasted their time.

In a perfect world, there would be no reason to simultaneously submit poems, but we don't live in a perfect world. Long lag times and the desire for publication make simultaneous submission almost a necessity. To be fair, you should include a line in your cover letter stating that your poems are also under consideration elsewhere.

It doesn't happen often that two places will want the same poem, but I know of a few people who have had it happen, with embarrassing consequences. If you do choose to submit poems to more than one publication, and one gets accepted, be sure to send a letter to all the other editors and ask for the return of the entire group you sent them. Don't just tell them to toss the one—that's very tacky. Take back the whole submission and try again next year with your unpublished poems.

Paying for Publication

You should never, ever have to pay anyone to publish your poems, unless you are self-publishing them or entering a reputable contest. Any organization or journal that accepts your work and then asks for money before they will send you the book that the poem will appear in, or offers you the privilege of buying a plaque or certificate, is ripping you off. Sure, they are publishing your poem, but they publish everyone's poem! That's how these companies make money. They prey on the fact that we all want our poems published and they know that many people will shell out the $45 for the "anthology" that they produce, just because their poem is in it. Better to have your poem published in a little staple-bound mag photocopied by a few dedicated editors than to dig into your wallet to buy a plaque. If you really want to spend your money, buy subscriptions to the little mags.

Dodging Doggerel

Don't expect publication—the world doesn't owe it to you. Don't stop writing just because you aren't getting published easily, either. Some of the most well regarded poets had a difficult time publishing in their day—take Emily Dickinson, for example. Just keep writing and practicing—eventually, if your poems are good enough and you send them out for consideration, they will be published.

Organizing Your Submissions

Once you've chosen the poems that you're going to send out, chosen the right places to send them, self-addressed your stamped envelopes, and said a little prayer, you will need to organize your submissions. If you're proficient on the computer, you might find it easy to use an Excel file for this purpose. Me, I use an old-fashioned card file and three-by-five cards from the office supply store. Because I like to complicate things (I feel this makes life easier somehow), I use color-coded cards—a different color for the different "levels" of magazine, just like I do with the highlighters in the *Poet's Market*.

I write the name and the address of the magazine on the back of each card, as well as deadlines and other important information. On the front, I write the magazine's name and then list the poems I'm sending, along with the date. Then I file the card and wait. Once I get a response, I mark it on the card, draw a line, and use the space below to record my next submissions. When a card fills up, I staple another card to the front of the original and write the magazine's name on that card as well. Rinse and repeat.

Each year when the new *Poet's Market* comes out, I update my existing cards and create new cards. This is an easy system that anyone can use. If you don't organize, you will soon forget where you sent particular poems and when you sent them.

An Insider Look at the Acceptance/ Rejection Process

I have degrees in English and creative writing from three different universities, and I worked on the literary magazines of all three, either as a reader or an editor, so I'm going to give you the inside scoop on what really goes on in the editorial process. I can only speak for the places that I worked, but the experiences were similar, and, I think, typical.

The first question people usually want answered is if their submissions are really being read. The answer is yes. Your work is probably read by at least three people, unless it's so obvious that it's not for the particular magazine that the first person reading it sends it back right away; that happens often. Sending your work out only when it's ready and only to appropriate publications will help prevent it from coming back right away.

Once two or three people have read and taken notes on a submission, it will go into a pile slated for an editorial meeting. Generally, editorial meetings are held when the pile gets unwieldy—maybe once a month. Remember, most of these magazines are run by people who are doing this as a part-time gig. That's often why lag times are so long.

At the most recent university review I worked on, the editorial meetings would go as follows: About 8 to 10 of us would meet at a local diner and sit around a long table. (If you get your poems back with coffee rings on them, this is why.) We would go through the stack of poems, first reading the notes various editors and readers had written on the envelopes. Generally, we were considering one or two poems out of a submission, so the person who liked them the most would read them to the group. Then the debate began. Half of the people would hate the poem and half of the people would love it, with each person getting the chance to say something about the poem in an attempt to convince the others. The main editor at the time was in favor of the democratic method, so we'd have a show of hands after the debate, and the most hands up won. What this means is that your poem could have had a few people fighting fiercely for it and *still* have gotten rejected.

Rejection ... and More Rejection

Rejection is built into the process of trying to get published. It's not something you're going to avoid, so get used to it now. Your poems will be rejected. Big deal. If you think of it as a part of the journey, you won't be disappointed when you find that little rejection slip in the mail. Buck up—you're a poet!

Brian Leung, former editor of Indiana Review and Assistant Professor of Creative Writing has this to say about rejection: "A rejection note from an editorial staff should not be taken personally. Indiana Review receives thousands of submissions each year. For a variety of reasons, including space restrictions, my staff and I were forced to reject work with real merit. Unfortunately, the volume of rejected submissions doesn't allow for detailed explanations of why the work has not been accepted. Not infrequently, I received replies from upset, sometimes irate writers who took their rejections personally. At its worst, this kind of response can poison a potential relationship with an editor. Patience and perseverance are better tools for getting published. Remember, a rejection means 'not now' but it does not mean 'not ever.' "

Stages of Rejection

Yes, rejection is so much a part of the process of getting published that there are stages to it! You can even have "good" rejections ... rejections that you can be proud of, rejections to brag about to your poetry pals!

- **Stage One Rejection:** In this stage, your poems will come back quickly, accompanied by a small rejection slip or card. Printed on the slip or card it will say: "We're sorry that your manuscript does not meet the needs of *Miserable Review* at this time. Thank you for your submission. Sincerely, the Editorial Staff." What this will look like to you is: "We're sorry (for you) that your work sucks. Please don't write any more of this schlock." It will look like the review couldn't even spare a whole piece of paper for you. Don't despair. Keep writing, keep going, keep sending out your poems!
- **Stage Two Rejection:** In Stage Two, you will begin to get little hand-written notes on the rejection slips asking you to send again or telling you that they liked your work. Don't discount this praise. An editor would not take the time out to send you a note if he or she didn't mean it.
- **Stage Three Rejection:** Once you receive a genuine letter from an editor, you are in Stage Three. A letter written on a whole sheet of paper (wow!) and discussing one or more of your poems is a very good sign. This editor will remember your work later and will be inclined to give it extra notice. A good sign indeed!

Let Me Count the Ways

Things to do with rejection slips ...

1. Wallpaper for your bathroom.
2. Drawer and cabinet liner.
3. Kindling.
4. Compost (white slips only).
5. Voodoo rituals.
6. Confetti fodder.
7. Scrap paper by the phone.
8. Wipe dog poo-poo off your shoe.
9. Tear angrily into bits (paper therapy).
10. Use them to wipe your tears.

The Big Day: Publication!

Publication will come to you in a letter disguised as a rejection slip. You will open the zillionth returned SASE to find—not a little slip—but an acceptance letter stating what poem the journal wants as well as the terms of acceptance. A journal usually wants first-time rights, meaning that you must agree that the poem be published there first (which is why you must write a letter to all of the other places that have the poem in question and ask them to send back the whole group).

You might be asked to sign a form and send it back. Do so right away, with a little note thanking the editor. When you send more poems to the journal, mention that you are a recent contributor in your cover letter.

Has fame come yet? Fortune? Well, no. You'll probably receive a couple copies of the journal when it gets published, and maybe even a subscription for yourself, and sometimes a gift subscription. Occasionally you'll receive a small payment, perhaps $15 to $30 a poem, and maybe more depending on the place.

But you've done it! This is a big deal. A few people will read your work, perhaps be moved by it or learn something. Your poem has a public life!

Contests

Literally hundreds of poetry contests run each year, many with significant cash prizes and prestige. The majority of these contests cost money to enter, though it can be worth the entry fee if you are relatively sure of the quality of your poems. Reputable contests are generally run by a magazine, university, or poetry organization and will often tell you who the judges are and give the names of some of the past winners.

You can find out about contests and their guidelines in *Poet's Market, Poets and Writers Magazine, Writer's Digest Magazine,* and the *Associated Writing Programs Chronicle,* to start.

A First Book

I don't know a single practicing poet who doesn't want, eventually, to have a book published. And if they already have one published, they want another. It's fine to want to publish a book, to want people to read your work—part of poetry's job is to reach another person.

A first book isn't simply a collection of poems that you've written over the years (or months!) and have placed into a pile. A book of poems is an organized work of art, as much as a single poem is. Books of poems are sometimes organized thematically, or have some other type of order. A book is made of great poems, one after another. Until you have that many great poems, hold off thinking about publishing a book.

The market for poetry is pretty small. You're not going to get rich off of publishing a book of poems unless you're a rock star. Generally, a first book of poems is published through a contest judged by an esteemed poet and run by a university or poetry organization. You will have to pay to enter the contest, usually $15 to $25, with the potential of winning $500 to $5,000, plus publication. You can find out about first-book contests and their guidelines in *Poet's Market, Poets and Writers Magazine, Writer's Digest Magazine,* and the *Associated Writing Programs Chronicle.*

A great way to tell if your first book is ready for publication is to find and read the winners of some of the contests from the last two years. Also, some contests announce their judges—take a look at their work as well, or the work of past contests that they've judged. Do you think the judge might like your poetry?

A first book can be difficult to place with a publisher. I've known people who have gotten their books published after just two years of trying, and

Touchstones

Publishing a volume of verse is like dropping a rose-petal down the Grand Canyon and waiting for the echo.

—Don Marquis

others who needed more than 20 years. Are you writing for publication or because you can't not write? When you get discouraged, it always comes down to that question.

Chapbooks

A chapbook is a little book, about half the number of pages, or fewer, than a full-length book. You will find chapbook contests in the same places that you find full-length book contests. A chapbook is a great way to get your poems to readers without losing the option of entering a first-book contest. Again, the chapbook contests are difficult to win—your poems better be great!

Self-Publishing

If you begin to get frustrated with the process of trying to publish a first book, or you're in need of instant gratification, you can self-publish your book. You can find hundreds of vanity presses and desktop publishers to work with, and the printing process is getting cheaper as technology advances.

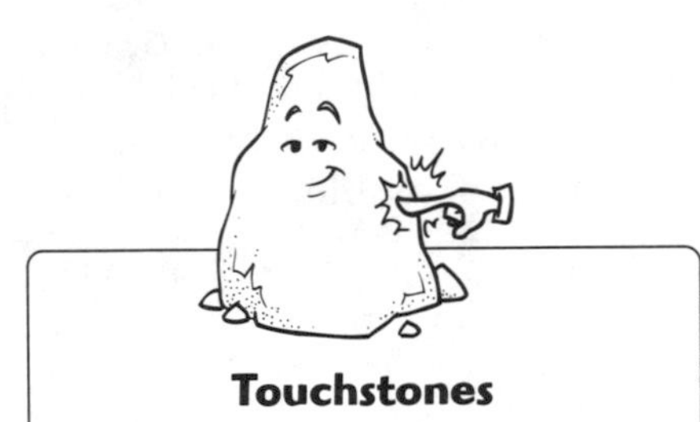

Touchstones

Publication is the auction of the Mind of Man.

—Emily Dickinson

The problem with self-publishing is in the marketing and selling of your book. You will not be able to get your book widely marketed, though you can get it listed on some of the large Internet booksellers, and you might convince your local independent book store to stock a few. You can always put up a Web site for your book and try to sell it that way.

Self-publishing lacks the prestige of having your book win a contest or be accepted by a publishing house. Of course, poetry has a long history in self-publishing, and many of our most revered poets published their own work and then went on to become well-known poets.

What a Tangled Web We Weave

The World Wide Web offers a publishing opportunity to poets unlike any other time in poetry's history. By simply putting up your own poetry Web site, you can attract thousands of readers a day to your work. Many published poets have their own sites and offer sample poems and links to their poems on other sites on the Web.

Some Web-based poetry magazines publish poems on their sites and even pay upon publication. Publishing on the Web is still not as accepted, in terms of prestige, as the paper book or literary review is—this may change in the future. See Appendix B, "Resources," for some poetry sites that accept submissions.

Exercises

Here are some suggestions to get you on your way to publishing your own poems.

- ➤ Buy this year's *Poet's Market* or another, similar book, and make a list of 10 places you would like to see your work.
- ➤ Take an hour and surf the Web for poetry sites.
- ➤ Make a pile of the poems you think are ready for publication. Remove 50 percent of the poems—take out the weaker poems, even if they are "good." Submit the remaining poems to literary magazines and Web sites.
- ➤ Read five new first books and try to get an idea of how they are organized.

Roses Are Red

Reading interviews is a great way to discover how other people became published poets. Many books and magazines feature interviews, or you can go to www.poetry.org or www.4betteror4words.com to find great online interviews featuring poets.

The Least You Need to Know

- ➤ Publishing your poems won't make you famous, but it will give you a thrill!
- ➤ Submit your poems on clean, white paper, one poem to a page, with your name and address typed in the upper-right corner. Don't deviate from this!
- ➤ Organizing your submission process will help you to submit your poems more effectively.
- ➤ Rejection is part of the process of publishing—don't let it get you down.
- ➤ Putting up your own poetry Web site can draw thousands of people to your work each day—that's quite a readership!

Chapter 21

Pen Out of Ink?: Beating Writer's Block

In This Chapter

- What is writer's block?
- Exercises from poets who teach
- Tips on getting over the fear of writing
- More exercises ...
- Even more exercises ...

There's no such thing as writer's block. That's a hefty assertion, isn't it? You can always write something: a letter, an e-mail, a diary entry, a page in your journal, a very bad poem—something that gets pen to paper. Writer's block isn't the inability to write, but rather the fear of writing poorly.

I hereby give you permission to write the most wretched verse that poetry has ever seen—poetry that really stinks. Then I give you permission to revise it. Just get it written.

No one is good in the first draft. Get over the fear of writing, climb over the block, and get your fingers tapping on those keys. This chapter will help you to get your creative spirit roaring again. Here you will find original, inventive exercises from poets who teach poetry to people much like yourself (you can find their short biographies in the contributor notes section of this book). Take these exercises as fun challenges, and I hope you write many fine poems from them.

Exercise #1: I Gotta Use Words When I Talk to You: From Diann Blakely

Many beginning poets use language as a kind of code, as a means of emotional withholding and evasiveness, which finally baffles and excludes its readers. In art as in life, such exclusion is a failure of intimacy. This doesn't mean that poetry is confession, or even autobiography. However, poems in which the author has little stake won't hold anyone's attention, not even the poet's; and poems that don't present their material—tell rather than show—through sensory means don't allow readers to engage with the poet's own. Of course, poems can also show off, usually when the poet substitutes overabundant imagery for grappling with the subject and its language.

Thus, my favorite exercise nudges writers toward finding a balancing point between disclosure and privacy, urgency and craft, ache and image, showing and showing off. Write a poem about the worst thing you've ever done without telling me what that thing is. It might be helpful to think about how you would film this scene, but remember that movies can depend almost wholly on imagery, whereas poems depend on imagery—and not just visual imagery—as revealed through form, style, diction, tone, word choice, and so on. Here's an example:

Story Hour

Near the parking lot, a few last red leaves swirl
catch me, catch me if you can—toward twilit skies
scarred with late autumn's frozen bits of cirrus.
Or are they contrails? A jet's roar lifts my eyes—

catch me, catch me if you can—toward twilit skies
and I walk too close to a kid-crammed car,
which swerves and tailspins. Snow White lifted her eyes,
still drugged with sleep, for a smitten prince;

but walking too close to a kid-crammed car,
my eyes updrifting with those red swirled leaves,
is dangerous. Like sleeping with a smitten prince—
but that's a fairy tale. Here's a true story,

one that little kids, driven home through leaves
from neighborhood libraries, shouldn't hear—
it's a scary tale—though this true story
ends with justice done: last night at a bar

near the library, my friend said she'd just heard
that the man who's raped ten local women
has been arrested, been locked behind bars.
Married, a father of twins, he lives nearby,

this man who's raped ten local women
(I've seen him around, mowing his backyard
or tossing balls for kids who live nearby);
he's described and named by the newspaper
I found this morning in our frost-flecked yard,

the grass like crystal. My friend talked of his wife,
also described and named in the newspaper,
then sipped her red wine. "She'll never be the same."
We looked at men and talked of being wives,

and lipstick, but kept other secrets. Last week
a man I can't forget said he felt the same,
looking at me in this library parking lot
(I've kept secret about this since last week)

as he did when looking at old pictures
of his ex, who'd worked at the library
and lived with him but without warning moved
to Colorado, which she'd looked at in pictures.

My friend, an alarmist, once said rapists
often stalk victims at libraries or movies.
But in this parking lot, that man's eyes shone lonely,
and I've walked back here every day. A rapist,

or a prince, who might return with a kiss?
This empty parking lot now shines lonely
with the half-swallowed sun, cars bound for home.

Should I hope he'll return with a kiss,
having trailed me here? A jet's roar lifts my eyes.
I'm wearing red lipstick, which I don't at home.
Catch me, catch me if you can, beneath twilit skies.

—Diann Blakely

Roses Are Red

If you really get stuck in a writing rut, take yourself to another location. Often, changing scenery can help get your writing going again.

Exercise #2: A *Rose* Is Not a *Rosa:* From Richard Blanco

Your ear is drawn to a couple speaking French at the table next to you at Starbucks, or you cry the first time you see an opera even though the only Italian word you know is "ciao," or you sing along in Spanish to "Que Sera Sera" or "Living La Vida Loca."

It is clear that foreign languages excite and intrigue us when speaking or listening in our own language. For one, we delight more in the sound rather than the strict meaning of language; we are reminded of the importance of sound and respond to the purer pleasure of its melody or cacophony.

Since language is not only a code for communication, but also a mode of thought that reflects the cultural consciousness of its speakers, we are also engaged by the possibility of deciphering and understanding other realms, other perceptions of reality, alternate modes of expression. The purpose of this exercise is to challenge our "normal" perceptions and dynamics of language by engaging with the foreign, using that challenge to create poetry, which stretches the "comfort zone" of our native English. Try one or all of the following:

- **Translitic.** A translitic is a "translation" of a poem that concentrates not on the meaning of the words but on their sounds. For example, *verde* in Spanish (meaning "green") could be translated phonetically to *bare day* in English. Select a short poem in another language (preferably in a language you don't know either formally or informally) and write a translitic. After the first version of the translitic, feel free to revise and edit as you wish. Your ultimate goal is to produce a poem of your own that has been "seeded" through the sounds of another language.

Roses Are Red

If you're blocked and you've been keeping a journal (hooray for you!), go back and see if you can extricate a good line or two from what you've already written and begin a poem with it. Or challenge yourself and use it at the end of a poem. That means you have to write to get to it!

- **Translation.** Whether you know another language or not, translation is a valuable exploration of the dynamics of syntax and the how meaning is invested. Again, select a short poem in another language and write a strict word-for-word translation using a dictionary or your own knowledge of the language. Then "shape" your translation, stitching the pieces of language together. Notice what works or doesn't work, and what figures of speech or images are not "translatable." Then use your original translation to seed a poem of your own. The aim is *not* to provide a "good" translation of a poem, but to explore and examine the intricacies and workings of language and produce your own poem.

- **Interlingual.** Interlingualism incorporates words or phrases from another language that can be translated either explicitly or implicitly within the context of the poem. For this exercise, select a phrase or line from a poem in another language (or any foreign-language phrase or word of your choice) and incorporate it into a poem of your own. Examine what the phrase or word means, not only literally, but figuratively with respect to the cultural context and tradition of the other language/poem. The aim is to incorporate this idea into *your* poem, to translate it, as it applies, into your realm of experience.

Exercise #3: About the Author: From Catherine Bowman

Years ago I received this unidentified questionnaire in the mail. I saved it, and I use it as a fun springboard to imagine different lives, personalities, and worlds. I also like the interview format, one of the most popular forms of our times.

Instructions: Answer the following questions. (They can be true or you can make them up.) Write a poem based on the answers that most strike your imagination.

Sex: F _____ M _____

1. Describe in a few sentences a most intimate moment and why it is intimate.
2. Describe in a few sentences something you really fear and why.
3. Describe a really embarrassing moment and why it was embarrassing.
4. Describe one of your fantasies.
5. Describe something you do when nobody is around, when you are all by yourself.
6. Describe your favorite food and why you like to eat it.
7. Describe something you find disgusting and why it is disgusting.
8. Describe something you daydream about.
9. Describe a habit or habits you have.
10. Describe a secret wish or longing you have.
11. What can you tell me about the inside of your refrigerator, or your clothes closet, or your medicine cabinet, or your kitchen cabinet, or any drawer in your house, or the glove-compartment in your car?

For a variation, you could answer these questions as if you were speaking in the voice of another person. For example, you might imagine what the contents of Emily Dickinson's refrigerator would be in contemporary America. You could also answer the questions as if you were speaking in the voice of a color, a tree, a type of weather, or a number. Another variation would be to answer the questions with bits of found text from reference books, catalogues, cookbooks, and newspapers.

Exercise #4: The Swing Shift Blues: From Richard Cecil

If you aspire to be a poet, chances are that you're quite familiar with the technical details of several humiliating, low-paying, dead-end jobs. Here's how to put that knowledge to work for you:

Write a soliloquy or a dramatic monologue spoken, or thought, by a worker leaning on a broom, or placing the dishes in the dishwasher, or ducking outside for a smoke on break, or taking an order from a customer or a boss, etc. Shakespeare has provided lots of excellent examples of soliloquies of kings and princes meditating on the problems of the rich and powerful, but his lower-class characters usually talk and think like clowns and fools. Contemporary poets with greater experience of life at the bottom provide much better examples of the potential for this exercise to illuminate the human condition. Here's one of the best models for this exercise—Maura Stanton's "The All-Night Waitress."

The All-Night Waitress

for Gail Fischer

To tell the truth, I really *am*
a balloon, I'm only rubber, shapeless,
smelly on the inside …
I'm growing almost invisible.
Even the truckers admire my fine
indistinctiveness, shoving their fat hands
through my heart as they cry,
"Hey, baby! You're really weird!"
Two things may happen: if the gas
explodes at the grill some night,
I'll burst through the greasy ceiling
into black, high air,
a white something children point at
from the bathroom window at 3 A.M.
Or I'll simply deflate.

Sweeping up, the day shift will find
a blob of white substance
under my uniform by the door.
"Look," they'll say, "what a strange,
unnatural egg, who wants to touch it?"
Actually, I wonder how I'd
really like being locked into orbit
around the earth, watching
blue, shifting land forever—
Or how it would feel to disappear
unaccountable in the arms of some welder
who might bust into tears
& keep my rubbery guts inside his lunch box
to caress on breaks, to sing to ...
Still it would mean escape
into a snail's consciousness, that muscular
foot which glides a steep shell
over a rocky landscape, recording passage
on a brain so small how could it hurt?

Exercise #5: Obsessive Definitions: From Denise Duhamel

First I ask that you DON'T read on through this whole exercise at once. Instead, do each step one at a time. It may spoil some of the fun if you read ahead. Give yourself about 45 minutes to complete it.

1. Freewrite for 10 to 15 minutes, just to get limbered up. Write everything that comes into your head, as though you were writing in a journal.
2. Now, on a separate piece of paper, write down 20 words you absolutely love, 20 words you always want to use in a conversation or a poem, but that never seem to come up often enough—whirligig, prong, Babel, curlicue ...
3. Now, go back and read your freewriting. In one word, define what's going on. What is your obsession at the moment? It may be a vodka and tonic, a crush, a movie star, guilt .... Write that one word down at the top of the paper that has your 20 words on it.
4. Now the really fun part begins. Define the 20 words in front of you in terms of your obsession. When you're finished, put the words in alphabetical order. You can title your poem "Glossary of Gloria" (if you're thinking about Gloria) or "An Interpretive Dream Dictionary of Pall Malls" (if what you wrote about is wanting a cigarette).

Here's a poem I wrote in this form (I used 26 words instead of 20)—the obsession is "dieting."

The Last Page of a Jenny Craig Seminar Booklet

(Glossary of Terms Used)

abacus: ancient device of torture used to count food groups, precursor to Richard Simmon's Dial-a-Meal

Byzantine Empire: where history shows the first calorie was counted

cloister: religious food, lowfat wafers; also black baggy clothes

diphthong: underwear for small butts, spiteful underwear, underwear that scoffs the food-obsessed

ennui: the smell of warm bread

Francophile: highly caloric tarts, gravy, baguettes

goatee: facial hair most often sported by skinny men whose very presence scares chubby women

horticulture: the study of steamed vegetables

igloo: a place so cold that even heavy-duty spoons cannot penetrate ice cream

Jacob's ladder: an invention used by Biblical exercisers, similar to our modern day StairMaster

kooky: the best friend of the ingénue, often overweight

lascivious: eating until one is completely full

maiden: a woman who loves dairy products (including ice cream, sour cream, heavy and whipped cream)

North Star: a distant dream and where weightlessness is possible

oblique: the kind of comment that hurts a fat person's feelings most

praying mantis: a supermodel-thin green bug that males are attracted to even when they know she's no good for them

queasy: the pulp that settles at the bottom of carrot juice

rococo: period of art that most large women vote as their favorite

sky: a big blue mother, unattainable and unpredictable; why many overeat

taupe: buttery in color, like the perfect grilled cheese

umpire: anyone or anything you feel is judging you; anything or anyone who makes you feel defensive

velveteen: nice soft round stomach, someplace you'd like to rest, a complete lack of self-hate

Waikiki: dreaded vacation spot; vacation spot that caters to bikini-wearers

xenophobia: the fear of someone seeing your XL tag flip out of the back of your shirt collar

yo-yo: stepping up to or away from a doctor's scale

zither: the harmony of strings you hear when you lose your first pound

—Denise Duhamel

Touchstones

American writers drink a lot when they're "blocked" and drunkenness—being a kind of substitute for art—makes the block worse.

—Anthony Burgess

Exercise #6: The Day the Pleasure Factory Broke Down: From Stephen Dunn

Write a poem called "The Day the Pleasure Factory Broke Down." In it you must mention a South American Country, a flower, and the name of a pop song, each in a surprising way.

Exercise #7: Clustering: From Lola Haskins

This exercise is a combination of two things—how-to and clustering. The how-to gives you your focus, the clustering keeps the poem from being linear and potentially boring, especially to a reader who happens to have no built-in interest in the subject of the poem. Take something specific you know how to do—examples: tying flies, cleaning a counter top, playing the sax. Then, take a piece of paper at least 8½ × 11 and write that thing in the middle. Draw an oval around it. Then draw, out from the center as fast as you can think, words

Roses Are Red

Steal a title from another poem, one you particularly like, and let it inform a poem that you write. Then, when you're done, remove the title you've used and replace it with the last line of your own poem.

that answer variations on the question "What's it like?" Don't think. Don't stop until you've filled the paper or hit the point where you think you know exactly where to start your poem.

Here's an example: Say you chose cleaning the counter. That would be in the center of the cluster. Now, what color is that job? Write it: "yellow." What sound would "yellow" make if it made a sound? Write it: "cheep." What rhymes with "cheep"? "Deep," "leap," "sweep." What is the texture of "sweep"? Write "swooshy." What rhymes with "swooshy"? When you run out of gas with one line of association, start over in the middle and work it out to the edge in the same way. Questions are: "What color is this?" "What does it feel like?" "How does it taste?" "What rhymes with that?" "How does it sound?" and so on—in other words, questions connected with the senses. When you've filled the page, look at what's there, and associate words from as far apart in the cluster as possible, words whose creative paths have nothing to do with each other. You'll find that some of these associations go to the heart of the thing you started with. This technique works for any time you get stuck, and with abstractions, too, such as "love" or "anger," but I suggest that the first time you try it you use how-to, because that will start you out concrete.

"To Play Pianissimo and Staccato," from my book *Forty-Four Ambitions for the Piano,* are poems I began like that.

To Play Pianissimo

Does not mean silence,
the absence of moon in the day sky
for example.

Does not mean barely to speak,
the way a child's whisper
makes only warm air
on his mother's right ear.

To play pianissimo
is to carry sweet words
to the old woman in the last dark row
who cannot hear anything else,
and to lay them across her lap like a shawl.

Staccato

The woodpecker drums
about the tree
a rising spiral

until even the highest smallest leaves
cannot help themselves

but shiver, then turn wild
at his bald beak
his head of stopped fire.

Touchstones

I've never been big on the agony of writing. I see no evidence that Tolstoy suffered from it.

—James Mitchner

Exercise #8: Poetic Dialogue: From Dean Kostos

In this exercise, you will be writing a poetic dialogue, but without stage directions. There are various ways of distinguishing the two voices on the page. You may want to italicize, or simply indent one of the voices each time it recurs.

Try to make this a dialogue between opposites; this can be between This and That (whatever qualities you might ascribe to those words), people from history, between adult-you and the child-you, or between abstractions. By that I mean day/night, good/ evil, age/youth, emotions/intellect, war/ peace, and so on. I would suggest that you pursue the latter strategy, inasmuch as it can open up the arena of imagination and thought.

Roses Are Red

When you're really, REALLY stuck, color. Buy a box of 64 crayons and draw your memories: your first, your most powerful, your silliest, your most embarrassing moment—you'll be surprised at all of the poems you can get out of making these memories visual.

When you decide whose voices you'll be invoking, consider the kinds of speech patterns that would give us an accurate sense of that character. Think about diction. Would that character say "To whom am I speaking?" or "Who am I talking to?" or simply "Who is it?" Would they speak in long complex sentences, or short staccato ones? Do they use many contractions and colloquialisms, few, or none? After you make these choices, remain consistent with them. The reader needs to "hear" the voices, and thereby discover more about the personalities and their motives.

Exercise #9: The Best and the Worst: From David Lehman

Buy the "Best American Poetry Anthology" of the year. Choose the poem that you think is the best in the book, and also choose the poem you think is the worst. Then write a poem that is better than the best and a poem worse than the worst.

Exercise #10: What's in a Name?: From Lyn Lifshin

Beginning with your name on your birth certificate, list all the names you have ever been called, including nicknames, nasty names, names screamed at you when someone was angry, pet names, names based on the color of your hair or any other physical quality. Here are mine, for example: Rosalyn Diane Lipman, Lip, Mrs. Lifshin, Ros, Rosie, Lynnie, Fat, Kike, R.D.L., Gitana, Sherrie Liane, Lynn, Lyn, Lifskin Mrs. Lifshin, Ms. Lifshin, Honey, Babe, Lady Lyn, Upstate Madonna, Skinny, Eric's wife, Bob's girl, stuck up, gypsy, La Bella E Magra, Raisel Devora, Miss Middlebury High, Rose Devorah, The Black Rose, daughter, JAP, Cat, Lippy, Garnet Van Cortland, Foxy, Liane, Diane Sweety.

Look at the various names and see what emotions you feel reading each one. Pick one name and flow with it. Do a stream of consciousness, a free association of words, images, feelings: whatever comes to your mind. I took Rose Devorah and found myself writing these words down: old houses, old people, Russia, licorice fire, lace, a wedding, people burned up in the rose fire, roses, special, rarely dying, won't stay long, expensive, fragile, not sturdy like carnations or mums but more wild, intense, special, not anything that can stay, blood colors, raw cheeks, cherries in the snow, apples, wild roses, thorns pricking you, won't let you too near, except for a price.

You can try this with a number of names and nicknames. First you might want to try, with crayons, making a design or a logo—something you might want to use on your stationary or on a T-shirt—and see what drawing makes you think of. Just don't worry about making sense when you write down what comes to your mind—let yourself be crazy, outrageous, fantastic.

From this free flowing of images and words and feelings, try to make a poem or write the beginning of a short story. Write a letter to this particular you or to something that you can pull out of the free flowing, which is a little like scribbling, the looking for a little design you can develop. This is what I did with Rose Devorah—I looked at the free-flowing words and then let myself dream about a made-up person whom I imagined coming from the images, a little like the way dreams often grow out of the things you might see during the day but then emerge in a strange new way.

Rose Devorah

Dreams of old houses
in Russia, licorice hair
fire licks as lace is
scorched, turns ash
before the wedding
and the bride's bones
are dust in the roses
green dies from.

Sun sets in the
afternoon. Some
unknown aunt she
could have been named
for who might have been
wild, intense as rare
tea roses or Rashmi
Rose incense burnt in
a pale room walls
pulled from floats
thru frames that
are like mirrors, her
raw cheeks cherries
in the rain, or
blood from a wild
doe running turning
snow color of plums
Devorah pulls into
A fist of her name,
It sounds like sorrow.
Blood light turns
glass between her and
what she reaches out
toward to ruby. She
won't let you near
except for a price
you can't afford.

Touchstones

When my horse is running good, I don't stop to give him sugar.

—William Faulkner

Exercise #11: Graphing Your Life: From Campbell McGrath

Time and again we speak of the need to create "concrete images" in our poems, seeking to follow the golden maxim of "show, don't tell." And yet, unlike painters or filmmakers, for whom the creation of images is a shockingly literal, plastic concern, poets must struggle with the paradox of forming their images from the exasperatingly fluid, gallingly abstract medium that is language. A devilish task indeed, but such is our lot, and let us not forget the corresponding freedom of the poetic medium—how much simpler to approach the act of creation with only a pencil or computer to depend upon, with no need to stretch canvasses, mix oil paints, argue with cinematographers, to say nothing of studio executives.

Touchstones

Every writer I know has trouble writing.

—Joseph Heller

Back to the question of the image. How, in a nutshell, do we escape the grasp of this paradox, and create these unforgettable, forged-from-iron images? Beats me. But consider, as a counterpart, the power of a graph. Numbers, like words, are abstract; mathematics is a complex symbolic system, a language that to me, at least, frequently reads as impenetrably as classical Greek. And yet even I can appreciate a graph. Even if I have no notion what it quantifies, I can appreciate its vivid arc, its thrust, its energized curve of meaning set against the abstract grid of the void. It speaks in the powerful synaptic language of the image, the delightful mental flashcards of remembered perception.

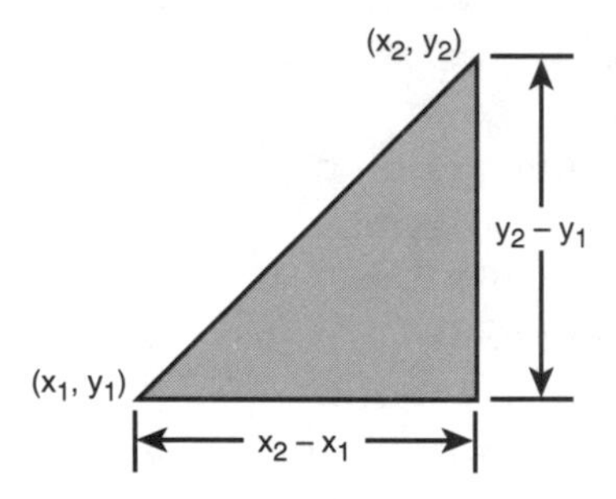

Therefore, your mission, should you decide to accept it, is to write a poetic counterpart to our graph. Let the y-axis signify sorrow, the x-axis signify joy, and the poem be the graphic map of your life. And remember—be concrete.

Exercise #12: Not This, Not This, ... but That: From David Rivard

Write a poem of at least 15 lines that employs the principle of the *via negativa,* either in whole or in part.

The *via negativa* ("by way of denial") is one of the essential devices for any poet's toolbox. Through repetition and resistance, it creates a pressure that can be both dramatic and psychological; through the use of a releasing turn (somewhat like that of the sonnet), it can create surprise and structure. Structurally, it provides the sense of counter-argument and of changed feelings. A famous example is Emily Dickinson's poem #510. Here is the opening movement:

> it was not Death, for I stood up,
> And all the Dead, lie down—
> It was not Night, for all the Bells
> Put out their Tongues, for Noon.

It was not Frost, for on my Flesh
I felt Sirrocos—crawl—
Nor Fire—for just my Marble feet
Could keep a Chancel, cool—

And yet, it tasted, like them all,
The Figures I have seen
Set orderly, for Burial,
Reminded me, of mine—

As if my life were shaven …

Dodging Doggerel

When you're using a poetry exercise and your poem begins to lead you away from it, go where the poem wants to take you. You are in service to poetry, not to the poetry exercise.

The basic idea is to create an impulse to deny some facts or events or feelings, and to deny repetitively, so that pressure builds. Then you release all that pent-up energy by reversing direction and admitting to something. Dickinson says "It was not this … It was not this … It was not this … Nor this … And yet …" The turn the poem takes is clear. The pleasure of the device lies also in how it enables you to bring something up while dismissing it—ironically, the denied fact or feeling or thought still enters the world of the poem, a kind of ghost presence. Another famous example, Wallace Stevens's "Disillusionment of Ten O'Clock," literally does create some ghosts (or at least ghostly nightgowns!).

In my favorite example, Marina Tsvetaeyeva's "Homesickness," the poet's resistance to admitting her longing for Russia while in exile flows suddenly and movingly into the simple image of a rowan bush by the side of a road. This poem points to the *via negativa's* great usefulness in handling especially emotional material in an unsentimental way. Once you are aware of the device, you'll begin to see its use—in ways strict and loose—all over the poetic landscape of the last 500 years.

Exercise #13: Detail Scavenger Hunt: From Maureen Seaton

Here is a good way to gather details to make a rich and textured poem. You can do absolutely anything with the details once you've "found" them (written them down)—write a rant, translate them into another language and write a pantoum, collaborate with a group or go solo. Use all of the details in your poem, or a few, or just one. You can make up your own Scavenger Hunt—try a City Hunt, a Suburb Hunt, a Cornfield Hunt, a Seaside Hunt, a Cyber Hunt. Wherever you are, come up with a list of things to "find" and then go looking. Or use the same list everywhere and see how the details and poems shift. Here's one I suggest for cityscapes. Go to the corner of your street and prime your senses. Notice the eccentric and neglected details. Really search for something no one else might find. Walk around. Poets don't go outside enough. This exercise will put cherries back in your cheeks. I call it the Scavenger Hunt.

Something red

A headline

An interesting window

A bright light

A quiet smell

Your favorite word(s) today

Something not orange that reminds you of orange

Something that rhymes with "juniper"

Something you overheard

A childhood memory

Fascinating footwear

The moment it got colder

A loud song

Exercise #14: Two Exercises: From Reginald Shepherd

This first exercise involves two things: trying to break down students' proprietary sense of their own work, and distracting them from what they plan to say, to allow a chance for the surprising things words might do to sneak up on them. I divide the class into groups of four or five, depending on the size of the class, and have each group write a poem collaboratively. I give each group 10 nouns and 10 verbs; they can change tense and number, but the nouns have to stay nouns and the verbs have to stay verbs. I also give each group a title for their poem and ask them to somehow relate their poem to the title; I find that some of Wallace Stevens's more outlandish titles work well for this, as they don't suggest obvious topics or subjects.

Roses Are Red

When I need some inspiration, I open a book of one of my favorite poet's poems and I choose a poetic fragment at random, sometimes just a word, and use it to write a poem—I generally embed it in the poem rather than begin or end with it. This method has never failed me.

Each group's poem must be 20 lines long, each line must be 10 syllables long, and one of the assigned words must appear in each stanza. I usually ask that each member of a group (depending on the number of people) write a stanza, either four lines or five lines, to make sure that everyone in the group contributes equally, but they all go over their group poem as a whole. I find that the combination of different voices and the fact that they have to concentrate on fulfilling so many requirements can produce some very interesting and surprising results: They often surprise themselves with what they come up with. It's a way to open them up to possibilities of things that can happen in poems, which they may not have thought of on their own, and also to show that inspiration (if I may dare use such a word) can come out of restriction. The collaborative nature of the exercise is also a way to help them see that words don't belong to any of them, or to any writer: They're the writer's medium, but no one invented them or has a special claim on them.

My second exercise is a bit more of a "see what happens" exercise; it asks, "What if you were someone else, something else?" Its main point is to take one out of oneself and take a literally different perspective. Based on the formal, though not the thematic, model of Elizabeth Bishop's "The Prodigal," I ask them to write a poem in two sonnets, the first of which involves a person looking at and interpreting a landscape, projecting his or her feelings into it. The second sonnet then involves giving that landscape a voice, speaking back to the viewer in its own terms. This involves asking the students not only to imagine themselves as another person, but also to imagine themselves as another kind of thing altogether, and what that would feel like.

Exercise #15: Bedroom Catalogue: From Maura Stanton

If you want to be a poet, you're about to give up the luxury high-rise condo where you now live for a more precarious but more fulfilling existence. Or perhaps you're already living in an artist's garret with your parrot, computer, stained mattress, cereal box, coffee cup, and popcorn popper (a gift from your co-workers when you quit). Describe yourself by describing your surroundings. Include a lot of the real details that are right there around you in your bedroom, the one with the balcony overlooking the sea or the one with the 17 spiders and the single light bulb. Let your reader get to know you through the things you own—or don't own.

A Portrait of the Artist's Bedroom

Dirty glasses, coffee cups,
a VCR/TV remote,
and a shaky stack of books
crowd the night stand at arm's length
from the unmade, crumb-strewn mattress
set crookedly upon a box spring
whose claw-ripped undercloth sags down
from the weight of a sleeping cat—
safe, there, from the vacuum cleaner,
though it hasn't passed through lately
judging from the matted dust balls
clinging to discarded socks
wadded up like waste paper
tossed among haphazard shoes.

A trapezoid of winter sunlight
focused through frost-covered panes
illuminates a rumpled rug
off angle to the wooden floor's planks.
Dust, like snow, falls through the sunbeam,
slowly turning the black rug
and the pine-yellow floor light gray,
which is the color of the cat fur
scattered here and there in clumps,
some floating free, like tumbleweeds,
some clinging to the dresser's legs.
One of the dresser drawers, half open,
leaks white socks, jockey shorts,
and a slender, black-tail—
don't close that drawer! Above the dresser
hangs a mirror framed in wood
with pictures wedged into each corner:
one of a black cat, one of a gray cat,
one of the two together and
a postcard of Van Gogh's café.
The mirror mirrors two corner closets
across the room, their doors wedged open.
One's crammed with shirts and pants and sports coats,
one with dresses, skirts and blouses,
half a dozen empty hangers,
and a tower of shoe boxes,
the three top ones turned on their sides,
open, stuffed with tissue paper
which shows the hollow where the shoes
nested till removed and packed
into the overnight bag which
isn't hanging from its nail.
Also in the mirror there's
the image of the sloppy bed
and night stand with details reversed,
and in the bed, in the real room
and in the mirrored one, there's me
with Nobody beside me, who
comforts us when she's away.

—Richard Cecil

One Exercise: From Charles Harper Webb

Take a page of a newspaper and circle six words (or phrases) that you like. Then write a poem incorporating the six words. The goal is not just to use the words; anyone can do that. The goal is to let the words guide you in directions that you would not normally go. Don't try to use all of the words right away. Feed them into the poem gradually. Many successful poems written via this exercise don't use the first word until halfway into the poem.

Roses Are Red

Buy a couple of old, obscure reference books, perhaps a book of military quotations and a book of scientific bird names and blend bits and pieces of the information in both of them to make a poem.

A variation is to begin writing a rough draft of a poem, and every so often (two minutes, five minutes, depending on how fast you write) incorporate one of the words into the poem. You'll be amazed at how your mind finds ways to connect the words to whatever you're writing.

Once you've finished with the draft, you owe the words no more allegiance. In future drafts, leave the words in or take them out as you see fit.

Exercises

Here are some more exercises to get you unblocked and writing!

- Choose one of the preceding exercises and use it to write a fixed form such as a sonnet, villanelle, or pantoum.
- Make up your own poetry exercise from a successful poem that you've written and use the exercise to write a new poem.
- Write a poetry exercise based on a poem that you really like (not your own). To do this you'll have to really look at what the poet did to make the poem work.
- Take two of the exercises in this chapter and blend them to write a single poem.

The Least You Need to Know

- There's no such thing as writer's block—you can always write something, even if it's not great.
- You can use poetry exercises to help you get a poem started.
- If your poem wants to take a path away from the poetry exercise, let it.
- If you're really "blocked," try to change your location, writing utensils, or poetic process.
- Just keep writing!

Chapter 22

Poetry Appreciation 101

In This Chapter

- Finding the good poems
- "Feeling" a poem
- Understanding author intention
- Interpreting a poem
- How history can help

Classes for beginners that focus on the arts generally have the word "appreciation" somewhere in their title (or at least in the course description): art appreciation, music appreciation, poetry appreciation. The word "appreciation" is important to the way one looks at works of art by other artists. You probably know a lot about the *who, what, where, when,* and *why* of your own work, but the work of other poets can be baffling if you don't know what to look for or what to appreciate.

The ability to write great poems stems directly, I believe, from the ability to appreciate great poems. Note that I'm not saying you must understand them, like them, or carry them around in your back pocket. I'm saying that knowing what makes them "great" is the first step toward making your own work great, too. Most poets begin their love affair with poetry by finding something they love about a certain poet's work. For me, it was Robert Frost in the eleventh grade. He was the first poet I took the time to appreciate, and I still love his work today.

In this chapter, you'll learn some of the things to look for when "appreciating" a poem. I could not possibly, in the scope of this single chapter, give you a lesson complete enough to encompass the entirety of how to "read" a poem. There are so many poems, so many schools of poetry and schools of thought, that all I can give you are the basics. But that's a good start.

Appreciating a Poem

You can follow certain steps when you set out to appreciate a poem, and these steps will help you become a better poet, too. In fact, if you've read this book to this point, you probably already know some of the things you're looking for. Once you've found your subject—perhaps a poem that has previously baffled you—you can begin. Onward!

Follow the Pack: Finding Good Poems

Begin by reading the poets that other people have determined are good. If that advice seems a bit like distasteful pack behavior to you, you're going to miss out on a lot of good poetry. I've seen a lot of beginning poets become snobbish when faced with the literary canon (that's a body of "accepted" literature, not a cannon, like on a ship). "What's so great about Emily Dickinson?" my students whine, finishing with a sarcastic "Why is Shakespeare considered so darn wonderful?" Because we said so, that's why. Okay, that's not really why, but it's a good enough answer for now. Just read them. As you become more experienced in judging between what's "good" and what's sloppy, you'll come to see what's so darn wonderful about Shakespeare.

Pick up an anthology of poetry, and begin reading. The editor of the anthology did his or her best to choose the finest poems for inclusion in the book. Of course, the poems in the books are all the editor's opinion of what's great, so read a few anthologies by several editors. If you find that some poets occur frequently, those might be the poets to research further.

Some poets are universally agreed to be "great." Shakespeare isn't a bad start. I've never heard the poetry of Walt Whitman, Emily Dickinson, or Robert Frost questioned, either. There are many, many others, too, so you'll just have to begin reading.

You could read 10 poems every day for the next 100 years and still not touch the surface of all of the valuable poems out there. Remember, this is an ancient art. So, get started!

Let Me Count the Ways

What makes great poems great? Whose definition do we adhere to when it comes to weeding out the doggerel? Well, the easy answer is that great poems stand "the test of time." They are appreciated century after century. The more difficult answer has to do with literary scholarship over the centuries. Basically, the scholars in each era decided (and still do) which poets were important. The more written about a certain poet or poem, the more likely it will stay in the literary canon and be considered "great." The poet was worthy of attention, so therefore he or she still is. Should we trust these scholars? Sure, but that doesn't mean we shouldn't have opinions of our own. For instance, the ratio between men and women in the standard literary canon favors highly on the male side; should we then conclude that women aren't good poets? Nonsense! Women haven't been writing for as long a period as men have—up until the past hundred years or so women were primarily focused on domestic chores and were, for the most part, illiterate. Part of being an artist is challenging the notions of the scholars and the critics. Don't discard the poets who are considered "great," but don't read them to the exclusion of lesser-known poets whom you happen to think are great, too.

"Feeling" a Poem

The first thing you should do is read the poem in question (the one you are trying to appreciate) once to yourself and once aloud. What's the feeling you get from reading the poem? Does it leave you cold or wanting more? Does it make you cry, alienate you, remind you of something? Write down your initial impressions.

A poem should have an effect on its reader. A poem should inform and enlighten—it should *cause* something, even if that something is bewilderment. A poem isn't necessarily going to save your soul, but a poem, if it's good, should be able to make you see the world in a different way.

Blizzard

Snow:
years of anger following
hours that float idly down —
the blizzard
drifts its weight
deeper and deeper for three days
or sixty years, eh? Then
the sun! a clutter of
yellow and blue flakes —
Hairy looking trees stand out
in long alleys
over a wild solitude.
The man turns and there —
his solitary track stretched out
upon the world.

—William Carlos Williams

When I read this poem, my initial feelings are those of being solitary, cold, and contemplative. I feel like thinking more about the poem. I have questions: Who is the man? What's the significance of the snow/hours/anger metaphor? This poem will make me read it again. I may never learn the identity of the man, but I can use my best guesses: He's the author himself; he's a metaphor; he's someone whom the speaker in the poem is angry with. There's no telling for sure. But the poem did have an effect on me. I'm curious about it. I'm struck by the intensity of the solitude in it. I appreciate the image of the hairy looking trees—that makes me chuckle a bit when I think about it. This poem is "working" for me on a number of levels, at least initially. I can make a judgment about this poem: I like it. I won't be able to look at the trees in the early Spring the same way again. When I walk in the snow, and I'm alone, the only set of footprints in the field of white, I may think of this poem, and then think of the man in it. I've been changed.

Dodging Doggerel

The first interpretation of a poem should always be a literal one. Don't look far beneath the surface at a first or second reading. Try to discover what the poem is literally about. Then, after you've done that, you can go back and find the deeper meanings, if there are any to be found.

The Skills I Use, the Skills They Use

If you were attentive to the second part of this book, you will know that poets use several basic skills to create their art. Often, a poem is considered "good" if the poet has used these skills well. When you look at a poem, see if you can pick out some of the poet's strategies and techniques. Is the poet using slant rhyme and quatrains? Terza rima? Is the poem a pantoum? Trying to discover what the poet is doing in the poem is one step toward appreciating the art in the poem.

I Told You I Was Sick

(tombstone engraving, Key West, FL)

Asthma attacks and astigmatism. It doesn't sound like much,
 but I knew what was coming—arthritis, aneurysms,
 Alzheimer's,
back aches and breast cancer. I feared a resurgence of the
 bubonic plague—
common colds are never really common colds! Colon cancer,
 cervical cancer,
diarrhea, disc problems. I never was sure what I'd have
 next—a Down syndrome baby, diabetes, and what about
 that
ecoli breakout? I was always falling—was it epilepsy? I
 was always itchy—eczema and
foot fungus and
gonorrhea. Gall stones tumbled inside me. My lover gave me
herpes, a heart attack, hypertension,
infertility, insomnia,
jaundice, jaw grinding in my sleep,
kidney stones, and a knee replacement! My mother gave me
lock jaw and lupus and leukemia! Don't believe your doctor,
 when he says not to worry about
manic depression, mood swings, multiple personalities,
 multiple sclerosis,
neurological disorders,
osteomalacia, osteomyelitis, osteoporosis,
pneumonia and polyps! Just because I was a gal, that
 didn't mean I shouldn't be concerned about my
 prostate.

Questionable moles are always something horrible.
Rickets, rheumatism,
scoliosis, seborrhea, sickle cell anemia, and shingles—you
    can get them from a sick person's sneeze! What about
TB? No one believed my prediction, but now it's back.
    Check your thyroid, get that triple bypass.
Urinary infection,
VD, vaginitis, and
whiplash. I got them all from just one car accident! Maybe
    it was the
x-ray radiation that finally did me in, that brought on my
    bout with
yellow fever,
zipping through my body, that good-for-nothing quack
    zipping up my body bag so fast.

—Denise Duhamel

What can we glean from this poem? For starters, we read it once and get a first impression. It's a funny poem of morbid humor. I chuckled when I read it (being a professed hypochondriac myself, I could appreciate this poem on another level as well). First thought: I like it.

Okay, now we have to get beyond "I like it." The first thing to do is identify the obvious strategies: This is a list poem. The subject is hypochondria, which is a kind of obsession. The list is perfect for a poem about obsession. We can see that the author chose her form carefully.

Take a closer look at the poem. Is it using a form other than the list? Read the letters on each line going down the left side of the poem; yes, this is an alphabet acrostic (abecedarian). Along with the obsessive quality of the list, the poem is in an ordered form—obsession, especially hypochondria, is all about control and ordering. The form fits the content.

Next, we can look at the title. The speaker in the poem is dead (we learn that in the last line) and the title addresses someone who perhaps could have helped the speaker stay alive, or at least someone whom the speaker had tried to convince of her illness (and maybe it implicates us, the readers, a bit as well). The poem itself is ironic because, as we know, no one but the hypochondriac believes he or she is ill until the person lies cold on the slab. We get further information on the poem from the subtitle telling us that the author found the poem's title on a tombstone in Key West. So this is also a persona poem (well, that's obvious—dead people do little actual writing).

Next, we can look at the even more basic elements of the poem. This poem uses a lot of musical elements: repetition, alliteration, assonance, consonance. Not only do the letters of the alphabet occur in order at the beginning of every line, but the names of the diseases that occur in each line correspond with the letter for that line. This is a poet who's paying attention to every aspect of the poem, from the content to the music and the form. This poem is very "voicey" as well; you can hear the speaker's distinct, rapid, accusatory tone ringing from inside the poem.

Touchstones

Even when poetry has a meaning, as it usually has, it may be inadvisable to draw it out. ... Perfect understanding will sometimes always extinguish pleasure.

—A. E. Housman

Next, you can judge a poem on its originality and fresh language. This is often tough to do with older poems whose metaphors may have been fresh a few hundred years ago but are now considered clichés. Take a look at our subject poem. Is the language fresh, put together in an original way? I think so. I like the way the speaker blames everyone else for her illnesses—and she gets the last word, too, with the inscription on her gravestone—and I like the way all of the disease words sound together when I read this poem out loud.

Finally, I give a poem the "change the world" test. Did this poem make me see the world differently and will I see the world a little differently from this moment onward? That's a lot to ask of a poem, isn't it? I'd have to say yes for this poem. I'll probably remember the inscription the next time I pass a graveyard and remark about it to a friend. I may, unfortunately, remember this poem the next time I visit the doctor or get the flu. And I will probably remember this poem the next time I write a list poem or an abecedarian; it has now become a part of my poetic fiber. That's what a good poem does.

Could you appreciate this poem? Look at all of the work the poet has gone through to create it. The poet used many of the skills at her command and used them well. Even if you don't like this poem, for whatever reason, you can certainly see how it has value as a poem and you can learn from it.

After I wrote this section, I asked the poet to write a short paragraph about her intention in writing the poem. This is a luxury—many poets we like to read aren't around anymore. Here's what Denise Duhamel said about this poem:

> "I was very interested in exploring the absurdity of hypochondria and that incredible anxiety and spiral thinking someone who thinks she is physically ill can fall into. The abecedarian form helped me write this poem, to get to the next word or the next illness. I was initially inspired to write the poem upon seeing a real gravestone—it's seldom that the inscription on such stones is funny."

Roses Are Red

Have some confidence when you approach a poem. Realize that your interpretation is as valid as anyone else's. Trying to interpret a poem can be frustrating if you're not confident that you have the skills to do so. Realize, too, that the more you learn about poetry and poets, the better you will be able to interpret and understand poems. A poem that you analyze today might mean something completely different to you in a year.

Poetry Interpretation

Beginning poets often think that they have to understand what a poem is about for the poem to be good. I'm here to tell you that you can have an appreciation of a poem without having a complete grasp on it. Beginning poets also get hung up on author intention, arguing about what the author intended the poem to mean.

The fact is, none of this matters. The poem has a life of its own once it's cast into the world. When someone reads your poem, you might not always be there, standing over his or her shoulder, explaining what it's about. That's why it's so important for you to make your intentions clear. You're not dumb if you don't understand a poem. It's possible that the poet wasn't clear enough or that the poem wasn't meant to be understood. Here's an extreme example:

A Tetrastich in the Lanternish Language

Briszmarg dalgotbrick nubstzne zos,
Isquebsz prusq: albok crinqs zacbac.
Mizbe dilbarskz morp nipp stancz bos,
Strombtz, Panurge, walmap quost gruszbac.

—François Rabelais

This poem isn't meant to be understood. It's a nonsense poem. Why would an author write such a thing? For the sheer joy of playing with language—for the fun of making noise. Or not. Perhaps the author has serious intentions. There's no telling, and he's not here for me to ask. However, I can appreciate this poem in my own perception of it because that's all I have at the moment.

Some poets have a lot of material written about them. For example, Dante's work has been the subject of scholarship for over 700 years. If you don't know what to make of Dante's poems, you can certainly find books that will tell you what to make of them. Learning a little about the life and history of a poet can tell you a lot about how to interpret his or her poems. However, the poems themselves are ultimately more important than their authors—remember, poems often outlive their authors. Good art should be able to stand alone without history, author interviews, scholars, and critics—though these things can be interesting, too.

Touchstones

When you read and understand a poem, comprehending its rich and formal meanings, then you master chaos a little.

—Stephen Spender

Lost in Language

Sometimes, it's the language itself that trips up our complete understanding or appreciation of a poem. Let's take a look at a poem by Shakespeare. First, from looking at the poem closely we can see that it's a sonnet (we appreciate that) and that it's by the master of sonnets, Bill S. himself. This information tells us right away that it's probably not a horrendous poem; the Bard has some cachet. However, since we know we're supposed to think it's good (or at least appreciate it) from the beginning, it can be kind of nerve-wracking if we don't understand it. So, let's do a little line-by-line translation. Here's the poem for starters:

Dodging Doggerel

Don't think your interpretation is the ultimate "correct" one—or that someone else's is either. Most poems have multiple interpretations.

Who will believe my verse in time to come,
If it were fill'd with your most high deserts?
Though yet heaven knows it is but as a tomb
Which hides your life, and shows not half your parts.
If I could write the beauty of your eyes,
And in fresh numbers number all your graces,
The age to come would say 'This poet lies;
Such heavenly touches ne'er touch'd earthly faces.'
So should my papers, yellow'd with their age,
Be scorn'd, like old men of less truth than tongue,
And your true rights be term'd a poet's rage
And stretched metre of an antique song:
But were some child of yours alive that time,
You should live twice,—in it, and in my rhyme.

With a poem from an era whose language is quite different from ours, it's a good idea to try to tackle the poem in small bits. Take it line by line and see if you can unearth the meaning in small chunks. Here's my "translation," eliminating the metaphors and unearthing the meaning behind them. See if you agree with my interpretation:

Who will believe my flattering representation of you in my poems in years to come? Lord knows that my poems only tell half the story. If I could represent your beauty fairly, readers in the next era would call me a liar. They'd say there could be no beauty such as yours. So my poems would be scorned and your true merits called "poetic license" in an ancient type of verse. But if you had a child living at that time, you would live twice—in it and in my poems.

Touchstones

Poetry is what gets lost in translation.

—Robert Frost

Even if the language is difficult, just about every poem can be boiled down to a pretty simple idea/meaning/story. Of course there are exceptions, but you can try anyway. The concept for this poem, as I see it, is this:

Nothing I write will be able to capture your real beauty.

Sure, Shakespeare, make us all feel inferior, why don't you?

Touchstones

The poem is not made from these letters that I drive in like nails, but of the white which remains on the paper.

—Paul Claudel

If you get stuck trying to decipher a poem with archaic language, try to get hold of a volume of the *Oxford English Dictionary*—you'll find all of the definitions you need there. Don't be daunted by poems like this. You can muddle through the language, count the number of lines and syllables, find something that you recognize and understand in the poem, and come to a kind of appreciation for it.

Exercises

Here are some exercises to get you started appreciating poems.

- Find a poem that you've never really understood and try to break it down to its elements, and then find something to appreciate in it. This may help you to understand it better.
- Try a line-by-line interpretation of the following poem. See if you can write your understanding of the poem into a paragraph.

Spring and Fall

to a young child

MÁRGARÉT, áre you gríeving
Over Goldengrove unleaving?
Leáves, líke the things of man, you
With your fresh thoughts care for, can you?
Áh! ás the heart grows older
It will come to such sights colder
By and by, nor spare a sigh
Though worlds of wanwood leafmeal lie;
And yet you wíll weep and know why.
Now no matter, child, the name:
Sórrow's spríngs áre the same.
Nor mouth had, no nor mind, expressed
What heart heard of, ghost guessed:
It ís the blight man was born for,
It is Margaret you mourn for.

—Gerard Manley Hopkins (1844–1889)

The Least You Need to Know

- ➤ You don't have to understand a poem completely to be able to appreciate something about it.
- ➤ The first thing you can do to begin "appreciating" a poem is to read it for "feeling."
- ➤ Breaking a poem down into its elements and looking closely for the poet's "moves" will help you to find an appreciation for it.
- ➤ Author intention isn't necessarily as important as your interpretation of the poem.
- ➤ Don't get daunted by a poem that contains archaic or complicated language—take the poem line-by-line and break it into its elements.

Chapter 23

Writing Poetry FAQs: Most Frequently Asked Questions

In This Chapter

- Poetic license
- Does anyone take rhyme seriously anymore?
- Why does poetry have so many rules?
- Do I have to copyright my poems?
- When will I be discovered?

We've covered a lot in this book, but I'm sure you still have questions. There's so much to learn, more than any one book can teach you, though this is a good start. Here are some frequently asked questions that might help you to tie up the loose ends.

What Is Poetic License?

Poetic license originally meant that the poet was allowed to deviate from traditional rules of grammar, diction, and poetic content; poetic license was the freedom to counter the norm. Today, poetic license not only means that, but it also involves the freedom to abandon fact and use whatever means necessary to create workable verse. The poet is the ultimate authority of the poem.

Why Does Poetry Have So Many Rules?

Poetry doesn't have *any* rules. What you might consider to be rules are part of the art of poetry. When a painter uses a paintbrush, do we call it a rule? When a violinist uses a bow, do we call that a rule? No, we don't. We realize that using a paintbrush and a bow are part of the respective arts of painting and music. So, when a poet uses slant rhyme, stanzas, and line breaks, he or she is not following some arbitrary set of rules. The poet is using the tools of his or her art.

Do I Have to Capitalize the Beginning Word of Each Line in My Poem?

The convention of capitalizing the first letter of the first word in each line has a long history in poetry, but no, it's not necessary anymore. It's an aesthetic choice.

Why Do Some Poets Shorten Words, as in *O'ercast, E'er, 'Mong, 'Twould, 'Twas,* Etc.—You Get the Point

The blanket name for the shortening of words like this is called *elision,* from the Latin, meaning: "to strike out." Each kind of elision has a specific name, depending on which syllable is removed.

Touchstones

In poetry you have a form looking for a subject and a subject looking for a form. When they come together successfully you have a poem.

—W. H. Auden

Elision was practiced during the time when meter was especially crucial to poetry. Poets often had to fudge around with words to get them to fit into the metrical scheme of their poems, which was a perfectly acceptable thing to do. Here is an example:

Too easily impressed; she liked whate'er
She looked on, and her looks went everywhere.
Sir, 'twas all one! My favour at her breast …

The lines that contain the shortened words are basically iambic, but they wouldn't be if *whate'er* was allowed to be three syllables—the same goes for *'twas*. Each of these lines has 10 syllables, a nice, neat number. Imagine the chaos if some lines had 9, some 10, and some 11! The horror!

Poets don't really use this technique anymore. Metrical poetry has gotten more liberated over the years, and poets don't trouble themselves as much about eliminating wanton variation. Today, variation is highly acceptable and is even part of the convention of writing in meter now. It's probably a good idea to stay away from this technique unless you have a really good reason for using it.

Roses Are Red

If you want to be influenced by great writers, and you're a beginning poet, read great writers of the last century as well as poets writing today. That way you are less likely to pick up ancient conventions. When you get more experienced and learn more about poetry, go back to the older writers and let them teach you what they have to offer.

Someone Told Me I Shouldn't Use *Thee, Thy, Dost,* and Other Words Like Them. Why Not?

Good advice. Often, when beginning poets think of what poetry really *is,* they think it has to sound ancient and use "high" language, like Shakespeare used. What they don't realize is that Shakespeare was using the language of his day, and was even considered a bit vulgar in his time (all those bawdy jokes and innuendo!). You should use the language of your day as well. If, however, you and your family and friends speak to one another using thee and thou, then go right ahead and use those words in your poems! But if you're like the rest of us, avoid those kinds of archaic usages.

Where Should I Break My Lines? Can't I Just Break Them Anywhere I Want?

Well, you can begin that way (you have no other choice), but where your lines break should mean something to the larger unit of the stanza or poem. Writing in fixed forms, like the sonnet, will help you to begin to understand line breaks. The lines will end as a result of following the form, and you'll begin to get the hang of thinking of the line as a unit on its own. Trying to decide where to break lines in free verse is often difficult. Practice and reading other poets will help you learn. I can only offer you some practical advice in the matter:

1. Try not to break on a little word like *a, the,* or *and,* or in the middle of a prepositional phrase, thereby leaving these words at the end of a line.
2. Try not to break all of your lines on the same part of speech.

3. Read your poem aloud many, many times during the process of writing it. You may begin to hear the natural pauses, the places where you could potentially break the line.
4. Of course, disregard all of this advice if it's not working for your poem!

What Do I Do If a Line in My Poem Is Too Long and Runs Over onto the Next Line?

If you like to write long, Whitmanesque lines and your computer won't let you fit the line as a single unit on the page, simply tab over once where the line runs over. This is standard practice and editors will understand what it means.

How Do I Title My Poems?

That's a good question. The title is important to how the poem is read. It can be the key to unlocking the meaning or concept of the poem. The title can be the defining moment, without which the poem would be lost, or it can be simply a line from inside the poem, a word or phrase indicating what the poem is about, or the first line of the poem, adding a bit of repetition.

Some poets write their titles first and then write the poem to fit the title, while others leave their poems untitled. I prefer a poem with a title. It gives the poet a moment at the beginning of the poem to point the right way for the reader, like a map. I can't tell you exactly how to title your poems, but I can suggest that you do so.

Touchstones

Titles distinguish the mediocre, embarrass the superior, and are disgraced by the inferior.

—George Bernard Shaw

Do I Have to Use Stanzas in My Poems?

No, you don't, but why wouldn't you want to? The stanza as a unit can be helpful to illuminate the meaning of a poem, and can add a moment of silence, a breath, where one is needed. Many fixed forms require stanzas. Try them—you might like using them.

I Had an Idea for a Poem but Then I Found Out That Someone Else Wrote One with the Same Subject Matter. Can I Still Write It?

Of course. There's probably not a subject you could write about that hasn't already been tackled, a flower that hasn't been described, a metaphor for the moon, the seasons, and love not tried. But that's okay. Your job as a poet is to take old subjects and make them new. Just about everyone has been in love, admired the ocean, and felt emotional pain over a loss. If you feel it, another human has felt it before, but perhaps you can put a new phrase to your love/admiration/pain that makes your reader think, "Yes, that's it exactly. I've never seen it expressed in such a way."

Dodging Doggerel

When you write a poem "after" a poet by using his or her style and technique, try to make it your own poem. Avoid following the other poem too closely or you could be on the brink of plagiarism.

What Does It Mean When a Poet Writes a Poem *After* Another Poet?

A poem written *after* another poet is a poem in imitation of or homage to that poet. The poet writing the new poem usually writes *after Poet's Name* just after the poem's title or at the end of the poem. Writing a poem *after* another poet is not plagiarism—plagiarizing a poem is when you use the poet's exact words and try to pass them off as your own. Using another poet's work to influence you is not plagiarism. Read Robert Duncan's poem "Poem on a line by Pindar" and John Keats' poem "On First Looking into Chapman's Homer" as examples.

I'm a Free Spirit and I Just Want to Express My Feelings, So Why Do I Have to Know Anything About Meter or Form? Aren't Those Things Passé Anyway?

Meter and form are not passé. In fact, they are quite "in" right now (well, they never really went "out"). Expressing yourself is great, but you can learn a lot about the art of poetry by trying some formal poems. You will learn a lot about compression of language, line, rhyme, and other poetic elements. Some forms are very expressive—try a canzone (see Chapter 14, "Some Fun Fixed Forms").

I Want to Try Writing Some Fixed Forms. Do I Have to Adhere Strictly to the Form, or Can I Play Around with It a Bit? If I Do, Is It Still a Formal Poem?

Playing around with the form and making it your own is great. Readers today are delighted by variations in form, especially if they're done well. For example, you could try a sonnet with very long lines that go off the page, or a triple sestina—whatever gets you going and excited about writing in form.

Does Anyone Still Take Rhyme Seriously?

They sure do. Rhyme is an important skill to try to master as a poet, and it's a crucial part of many fixed-verse forms. Rhyme, when done well, is a delight, and adds depth and texture to a poem. If you have an aversion to rhyme (and I don't blame you), try writing some quatrains in good slant rhymes—that can be challenging and a lot of fun.

Can I Use Modern-Sounding Details (Cell Phone, Coke Can, E-Mail) in a Poem and Still Have It Be Considered a Serious Poem?

Yes, indeed you can. Part of what poetry does includes detailing everyday life. Poetry is a document of a poet's life and times. If your everyday life is filled with popular icons and tech stuff, then go right ahead and use what's around you. In fact, your poems will feel more authentic if you're honest about your world, rather than if you try to mimic the voices and concrete details of past poets.

Let Me Count the Ways

Over the course of the history of poetics, there has been much discussion of imitation in poetry. One feeling is that all poetry, indeed all art, is imitation. Poets don't create anything really new: They imitate the world instead.

I Feel Very Misunderstood by My Workshop. They Just Don't "Get" What I'm Trying to Do. Should I Try to Find a New Workshop or Quit Trying the "Group Thing" Altogether?

Not everyone is going to understand your poetry, even if you win two Pulitzer Prizes and the Nobel. Perhaps your workshop is trying to help you and you're reluctant to listen to them. Try some of their suggestions; maybe it's you who's misunderstanding them and not the other way around.

There is a chance, however, that you're too advanced for your workshop. This does happen. There comes a time when you "get it," when poetry starts clicking for you and you're stuck in a workshop with real beginners. This can be frustrating. See if you can take an advanced class, or find one on the Web.

Touchstones

I don't wait to be struck by lightning and don't need certain slants of light in order to write.

—Toni Morrison

Isn't Poetry Just About Creating Something Beautiful? Making Beauty out of the Language?

Well, yes and no. Part of writing poetry is about creating something aesthetically pleasing, but I wouldn't use the word "beautiful," necessarily. Could you write a poem about the Holocaust that was "beautiful"? That's a tough one. I'd say that a better description for a poem about the Holocaust would be "powerful" or "earnest," perhaps, depending on the poem. Can a poem be beautiful if its subject matter is horrible? Yes, the language itself might be pleasing to the ear, but I wouldn't call the subject matter "beautiful."

Poetically Correct

Plagiarism is the act of taking ideas, writings, and so on from another person and passing them off as your own.

Poetry isn't *just* about trying to create "beauty." It's about trying to get to some larger truth (though using the senses), and about making the reader see/understand/appreciate something that he was not aware of so acutely before. Of course, this is a tiny answer for a huge question.

Do I Have to Copyright My Poems?

No, you don't. The likelihood that someone will steal your poems and call them their own is slim, and if they do, you can't do much about it anyway. Copyrighting your poems (or writing a © on everything you write) is amateurish, and editors and other poets know this. Poetry is simply not lucrative enough to take the time to steal. What would someone do with your poems? Sell them to inferior poets to pass off as their own? Not likely. When you publish a book, your publisher will copyright the poems for you. Before that, don't worry about it. If you are really paranoid, you can do the "poor man's" copyright—mail your poems to yourself and don't open the envelope when it arrives—the postmark will serve as a sort of copyright, but I've heard this doesn't hold up in court. But don't take your legal advice from me—if you want to copyright your poems, go right ahead.

Touchstones

Fame is a bee
It has a song—
It has a sting—
Ah, too, it has a wing

—Emily Dickinson

How Do I Get a Book of Poems Published?

Practice, practice, practice.

Then send your manuscript, when it's ready, to contests that publish first books. Don't bother to send a first book to a publisher unless most of the poems in the book are published in great literary journals and you've won some big prizes. In that case, you can send a query letter to a publisher asking the company if you can send your book for consideration. Do not send your manuscript unsolicited; it will come right back to you, probably unread.

Most presses publish poetry as a courtesy to the art. No press makes the big bucks off their poetry list; that's unfortunate, but true. It seems that many more people want to write poetry than want to read it, which is quite an incongruous state indeed. If you want to write poetry and publish poetry, you've got to read what's out there. Read the great, the good, the bad, and the abysmally wretched. Reading helps you to hone your senses and gives you ideas for new poems.

Touchstones

Whatever has been said well by anyone is mine.

—Seneca

If I Keep Writing Poetry, Will I Be "Discovered"?

Only uncharted islands, new galaxies, atomic particles, and cures for diseases are discovered. You are a poet. You have to work hard, harder, hardest, and then hope that you get a flicker of attention from the poetry community once you have a few books published. Realize that the poetry community is not as large as, say, the motion picture community. Write for the love of the art, not for fame, and you'll be content—or at least you won't be miserable, waiting to be discovered.

I've Never Shown My Poems to Anyone Else Before and I'm Afraid To—but I Want Some Feedback—What Should I Do?

Take a chance that someone will really like your work, or, at the very least, offer you some suggestions for improvement. Fear might be preventing you from making the transformation from a *good* poet to a really *great* poet. Read Chapter 19 on workshops for more information.

The Least You Need to Know

- Archaic language like thee, thou, and dost are better left out of your own poems.
- Tweaking fixed forms is a fun way to make them "new."
- There's nothing new under the sun—write about what you want to write about, even if you've seen it done before.
- If you really want to be published, write as many poems as you can, read as many poems as you can, and have some patience.
- Write poetry because you love to write it—that's all.

Glossary of Poetic Terms

abecedarian An alphabet acrostic. *See* alphabet acrostic.

abstraction Word that expresses an idea (pain, honesty, love) rather than an image.

accentual verse Verse that relies only on the number of accents (or stresses) in a line; it doesn't matter where those stresses fall.

acrostic A poem in which the first letter of each line, the last letter of each line, or an arbitrarily chosen letter in the middle of the poem forms a word, phrase, or sentence.

alliteration The repetition of initial consonant sounds (*b*rown *b*ears *b*eat *b*oats).

allusion A reference to something historical, mythological, or literary in a poem without explaining it.

alphabet acrostic An acrostic poem in which the letters of the alphabet are used to form lines.

anaphora Occurs when the beginning of each line in a poem repeats the same word or phrase.

ars poetica A poem praising poetry or written about poetry, or even about the poem a poet is writing at the moment.

assonance The repetition of similar vowel sounds in successive or proximate words.

aubade Also called alba, an aubade is a poem written at dawn expressing the parting of two lovers.

ballad The ballad form consists of quatrains with four beats in lines one and three, and three beats in lines two and four; content matter usually consists of love, adventure, and tales of fatal relationships.

beat Synonymous with stress and accent in metrical poetry, the beat is the strong (stressed) syllable in a group of two or more syllables.

blank verse Unrhymed iambic pentameter.

blues An American form whose content is generally of a highly personal nature—struggle, sex, anguish, loss, oppression—and it is often bawdy, filled with innuendo. The blues often tells a story, and can be comical, even though the subject matter may be grim.

cacophony Occurs when a group of words or a poem has a harsh, grating sound.

caesura (from the Latin for "to cut") A pause in the middle of a metrical line, having to do with the tempo of a poem; can be syntactic, grammatical, formed by punctuation, or even a bit of white space on the page.

calligram A poem whose words on the page form a shape or an object related to the poem.

canzone The canzone uses repeating end words. The form consists of five 12-line stanzas and a six-line envoi. There are variations to how the end words repeat in this form, but you can use the following pattern as a guideline:

Stanza 1: abaacaaddaee
Stanza 2: eaeebeeccedd
Stanza 3: deddaddbbdcc
Stanza 4: cdcceeeaacbb
Stanza 5: bcbbdbbeebaa
Envoi: abcde

caudate sonnet A lengthened sonnet containing a "coda," usually a couplet, at the end.

cento A poem made up a lines and pieces of other poems; it's usually humorous in nature.

chant A form of oral poetry composed generally, but not necessarily, to be communally performed; it's something between a speech and a song.

cliché clichés are dead metaphors, phrases that have lost their original meaning.

companion poems Two or more poems written as compliments, opposites, or replies to one another.

conceit A metaphor that extends throughout a portion of a poem, and in some cases, throughout the entire poem.

concrete poem A poem in which the words on the page are formatted such that they create emphasis with their positions.

consonance The repetition of consonant sounds within words (better letters litter lighter).

couplet A two-line stanza.

counterpoint Variations in a meter in a metrical poem.

crown of sonnets Seven sonnets, the last line of each sonnet beginning the first line of the one following it; the last line of the crown is a repetition of the first line of the opening sonnet; also called a corona.

curtail sonnet A shortened version of the sonnet, usually around 10 lines.

diction How all of the words in a poem sound once they are placed against one another.

doggerel Trivial or satirical verse, often characterized by monotonous meter and obvious rhyme.

dramatic monologue A poem written in the voice of one speaker, usually telling a story of some kind, and usually a persona.

end-stopped Occurs when a line of poetry ends with punctuation.

enjambed Occurs when a line of poetry runs over to the next line without punctuation.

envoi A short, concluding stanza, mainly found in French poetic forms.

epic poem A long narrative poem that traditionally contains a heroic figure and narrates a historical event or some other tale of heroism, conquest, and battle, usually containing elements of myth.

epistle poem A poem written in the form of a letter.

epithalamium A poem written to celebrate a marriage offering good wishes to the bride and groom: a wedding song.

euphony Occurs when a group of words, or a poem, has a smooth, pleasing sound.

figurative language Language that does not use its original literal meaning, such as a metaphor.

foot A unit in metrical poetry that measures the stresses in a line. The following are the most common metrical feet:

Iamb: U /	Trochee: / U	Anapest: U U /
Dactyl: / U U	Spondee: / /	Pyrrhic: U U

Lines in metrical poetry are measured by how many feet they contain. The most common metrical lines are the following:

- Monometer: 1 foot
- Dimeter: 2 feet
- Trimeter: 3 feet
- Tetrameter: 4 feet
- Pentameter: 5 feet
- Hexameter: 6 feet
- Heptameter: 7 feet
- Octameter: 8 feet
- Nonameter: 9 feet

found poem A poem that you don't really write, but happen upon.

free verse Poetry that is not written in a fixed form and contains no regular meter.

ghazal A formal poem consisting of rhymed or unrhymed couplets that are not necessarily thematically connected; the poet's name appears in the final couplet.

haiku A three-line Japanese form traditionally written in English with the syllable count of 5-7-5; subject matter is primarily about the natural world.

hyperbole A figure of speech that uses overstatement for emphasis, surprise, or humor.

iambic pentameter The most widely used metrical form in the English language; a line of poetry containing five iambs.

imagery Descriptions in a poem that make the reader conjure mental images.

invocation A kind of prayer, generally to a muse or to one of the gods, which tries to invoke, or call forth, the aid of the one being requested.

irony Occurs in a poem when the poet or speaker indicates the opposite of what he or she actually means.

language poetry A school of poetry in which words are detached from their traditional meanings.

limerick A traditional form in light verse consisting of five lines rhyming aabba; content is usually humorous and bawdy.

lyric poetry A type of poetry that has its roots in song and music; it is characterized today by the short, personal, highly imagistic and sensory poem. Named for the lyre, a small stringed instrument of the harp family, used by the ancient Greeks to accompany singing and recitation.

metaphor A figure of speech in which two (or more) dissimilar things are being compared.

meter An ordering and unifying element in poetry that mimics and heightens the rhythms of our speech and the rhythms of the natural world around us; meter involves the stresses of words and how those words are placed next to one another to create a metrical pattern (you will hear the word stress referred to as beat or accent as well—these are interchangeable terms).

metonymy (*met-ON-oh-me*) A type of metaphor that uses a closely associated object as a substitute for the original object, as in, "The White House spoke today with world leaders," meaning that the president spoke with the world leaders.

mixed metaphor Occurs when one or more of the elements of a metaphor don't belong together.

monostiche A one-line stanza.

muse Any one of the nine daughters of Zeus and Mnemosyne (the goddess of memory); poets invoke the muses to help them to create poems.

narrative poem A poem that tells a story.

nonsense verse Poems that don't necessarily make sense, but do use poetic traditions such as stanza forms, rhyme, and so on.

octave An eight-line stanza.

ode An ancient fixed form invented initially as a commemoration of a victory.

onomatopoeia Words that sound similar to their meaning, such as plop, hiss, fizz, skid, buzz, whirr, sizzle, bang, roar, and squeak.

pantoum A poem of indeterminate length (it can consist of just a few stanzas or go on forever) using four-line stanzas, repetition, and braiding, similar to how the villanelle works. The pantoum's pattern is as follows:

Line one
Line two
Line three
Line four

Line two repeated (five)
Line six
Line four repeated (seven)
Line eight

Line six repeated (nine)
Line ten
Line eight repeated (eleven)
Line twelve

And so on indefinitely (or until the poem comes to a natural end).

pastoral Poetry that depicts life in the countryside. The classic pastoral involves a shepherd and the concept of idyllic life.

performance poetry Performance poems are meant to be performed, rather than be read on the page.

persona A voice in a poem that isn't the poet's; for example, when a poet writes in the persona of an animal.

personification A figure of speech that gives human (or animal) qualities to inanimate objects.

Petrarchan sonnet Attributed to Petrarch, this sonnet consists of an octave (eight-line stanza) rhyming abbaabba and a sestet(six-line stanza) rhyming cdcdcd, though there are accepted rhyming variations in the sestet.

prose poem A hybrid of a poem and a short-short story.

quatrain A four-line stanza.

quintet A five-line stanza.

refrain A repeated phrase throughout a poem, it can be one repeating line, a few lines, or whole stanzas that repeat.

renga A Japanese form that originated as a party game in which groups of poets contributed to a single poem, typically consisting of at least 100 lines written by three poets in about three hours; the renga is an imagistic form and is the parent of the haiku, which were considered "warm up" poems for the renga. Each stanza relates to the one before it, but not to the one before that.

reversed sonnet A sonnet that uses one of the traditional rhyme schemes backward.

rhyme scheme The general pattern that rhymes follow in a poem.

scansion The method that poets use to measure metrical patterns.

septet A seven-line stanza.

sestet A six-line stanza.

sestina The sestina consists of six stanzas and an envoi. Sestinas used to have a certain meter and specific number of syllables, though today's sestinas are far less strict. Each of the first six stanzas contains six lines each, each line of which ends in the same set pattern of words, with a three-line envoi. The word pattern goes as follows:

Stanza 1: abcdef
Stanza 2: faebdc
Stanza 3: cfdabe
Stanza 4: ecbfad
Stanza 5: deacfb
Stanza 6: bdfeca
Envoi: bd, dc, fa

Shakespearian sonnet Also called the Elizabethan Sonnet or the English Sonnet, it is the most common sonnet, and is the type that Shakespeare used (hence the name). The main distinction between this type of sonnet and its counterparts is its rhyme scheme: ababcdcdefefgg.

simile A metaphor that uses the words like or as between the tenor and the vehicle.

speaker The speaker is the voice in the poem.

Spencerian sonnet Attributed to Edmund Spencer, this sonnet rhymes abab bcbc cdcd ee.

Spenserian stanza A nine-line stanza.

sonnet A poem normally consisting of fourteen lines in any of several fixed verse and rhyme schemes, typically in rhymed iambic pentameter; sonnets generally express a single theme or idea.

sonnet sequence A string of sonnets containing related or similar subject matter.

stanza A group of lines forming a division in a poem; from the Italian, meaning "room."

syllabics Syllabic verse relies only on the number of syllables in a line, not where the stresses fall.

symbol A thing or action in a poem that has meaning beyond itself.

synecdoche (*sin-EKK-toe-key*) A type of metaphor that uses a part as a stand-in for the whole, as in "There were seven sails on the bay," meaning that there were seven ships on the bay.

synesthesia Synesthesia combines two senses together, as in, "a velvety voice," "sparkling silence," or being able to taste a color, as in "the sharp taste of yellow on my tongue."

tanka A Japanese form consisting of five lines of 5-7-5-7-7 syllables, respectively. Traditional topics include nature, love, travel, the seasons, and lamentation. Like haiku, this form can be varied to be longer or shorter, and you can tinker with the syllable count.

tenor A metaphor has two parts, the tenor, or the main subject of the metaphor, and the vehicle, the thing that the tenor is being compared to, the object "carrying" the comparison.

tercet A three-line stanza.

terza rima A rhyme scheme invented by Dante Alegheri for *The Divine Comedy;* this rhyme scheme resembles a braid: aba bcb cdc ded efe and so on.

triolet The triolet (*tree-oh-LAY*) consists of eight lines, two rhymes, and two repeating refrains: AbaAabAB (capital letters indicate repeated lines).

vehicle A metaphor has two parts, the tenor, or the main subject of the metaphor, and the vehicle, the thing that the tenor is being compared to, the object "carrying" the comparison.

villanelle A French form consisting of five stanzas of three lines each with a sixth four-line stanza; the first and third lines rhyme, as do all of the second lines.

Appendix B

Resources

In this section, you'll find valuable resources to help you write and publish your poetry. Good luck!

Further Reading on Poetry and the Art of Writing Poetry

Addonizio, Kim, and Dorianne Laux. *The Poet's Companion: A Guide to the Pleasures of Writing Poetry.* New York: W.W. Norton, 1997.

Cameron, Julia. *The Artist's Way: A Spiritual Path to Higher Creativity.* New York: Penguin Putnam, 1992.

Drake, Barbara. *Writing Poetry.* Ft. Worth, Texas: Harcourt Brace Jovanovich, 1983.

Fussell, Paul. *Poetic Meter and Poetic Form.* New York: McGraw-Hill, Inc., 1979.

Gioia, Dana. *Can Poetry Matter?: Essays on Poetry and Culture.* St. Paul, Minnesota: Greywolf Press, 1992.

Glazner, Gary Mex. *Poetry Slam: The Competitive Art of Performance Poetry.* San Francisco: Manic D Press, 2000.

Hugo, Richard. *The Triggering Town: Lectures and Essays on Poetry and Writing.* New York: W. W. Norton & Company, 1979.

Jerome, Judson. *The Poet's Handbook.* Cincinnati, Ohio: Writer's Digest Books, 1980.

Kohl, Herbert. *A Grain of Poetry.* New York: Perennial, 2000.

Lamott, Anne. *Bird by Bird: Some Instructions on Writing and Life.* New York: Pantheon Books, 1994.

Lehman, David. *The Big Question: Poets on Poetry Series.* Ann Arbor, Michigan: The University of Michigan Press, 1995.

Mayes, Frances. *The Discovery of Poetry.* Ft. Worth, Texas: Harcourt Brace College Publishers, 1994.

Mock, Jeff. *You Can Write Poetry.* Cincinnati, Ohio: Writer's Digest Books, 1998.

Packard, William. *The Art of Poetry Writing: A Guide for Poets, Students, and Readers.* New York: St. Martin's Press, 1992.

Padgett, Ron, ed. *The Teachers & Writers Handbook of Poetic Forms.* New York: Teachers & Writers Collaborative, 1987.

Pinsky, Robert. *Poetry and the World.* New York: The Ecco Press, 1998.

Pound, Ezra. *The ABC of Reading.* New York: New Directions, 1960.

Preminger, Alex, and T.V.F. Brogan. *The New Princeton Encyclopedia of Poetry and Poetics.* New Jersey: Princeton University Press, 1993.

Shields, Pamala, ed. *Poet's Market 2001.* Cincinnati, Ohio: Writer's Digest Books, 2000.

Twitchell, Chase, and Robin Behn, ed. *The Practice of Poetry.* New York: HarperPerennial, 1992.

Wallace, Robert. *Writing Poems.* New York: Little, Brown, and Company, 1987.

Magazines

American Poetry Review
1721 Walnut Street
Philadelphia, PA 19103
www.aprweb.org

Literary Magazine Review
Dept. of English Language and Literature
The University of Northern Iowa
Cedar Falls, IA 50614-0502
319-273-2821

Poets and Writers Magazine
PO Box 453
Mount Morris, IL 61054
815-734-1123
Web site: pw.org
E-mail: poet@kable.com

The Poetry Connection
13455 SW 16 Court #F-405-PM
Pembroke Pines, FL 33027
954-431-3016

The Writer's Chronicle
A Publication of the Associated Writing Programs
Tallwood House, Mail Stop lE3
George Mason University
Fairfax, VA 22030
703-993-4301
Web site: www.awpwriter.org
E-mail: awp@gmu.edu

Writers' Digest
1507 Dana Ave.
Cincinati, OH 45207
1-800-289-0963 or 513-531-2690
Web site: www.writersdigest.com

Web Sites of Interest

The Academy of American Poets
www.poets.org/

Poetry Society of America
www.poetrysociety.org

Associated Writing Programs
awpwriter.org/

The Atlantic Monthly Poetry Pages
www.theatlantic.com/unbound/poetry/poetpage.htm

Poetry Previews
www.poetrypreviews.com/

W3PX Poetry Exchange
www.w3px.com

The Poetry Center
www.sfsu.edu/~newlit/

Poetry Daily
www.poems.com

Poetry Today Online
www.poetrytodayonline.com

Bookwire
www.bookwire.com/poetry/

Electronic Poetry Review
www.poetry.org/

Poets and Writers
www.pw.org

Teachers and Writers Collaborative
www.twc.org

The Poetry Forum World Wide Registry
www.poetryforum.org/registry.htm

Prose on Poetry
www.northshore.net/homepages/hope/critPoetryPassages.html

NYCPoetry.com
www.nycpoetry.com/

Shocked Poetry
www.shockedpoetry.com/index.html

The International Society of Performing Poets
www.slamnews.com/iopp.htm

Zuzu's Petals Organizations of Interest
www.zuzu.com

The MFA Page
www.bestweb.net/~galleria/mfapage.htm

Poetry Sites Offering Electronic Texts (and More)

The following sites offer poetry texts:

Project Guttenberg
www.promo.net/pg/

Bartelby.com Great Books Online
www.bartleby.com/verse/

The Poetry Archives at eMule.com
www.emule.com/poetry/index.cgi

Everypoet.com
www.everypoet.com/index.htm

Representative Poetry Online
www.library.utoronto.ca/utel/rp/intro.html

The Academy of American Poets
www.poets.org/

Contemporary Poetry at About.com
poetry.about.com/arts/poetry/index.htm?rnk=c&terms=poetry

Classic Poetry at About.com
classicpoetry.about.com/arts/classicpoetry/?once=true&

Shakespeare at About.com
shakespeare.about.com/arts/shakespeare/

American Verse Project
www.hti.umich.edu/cgi/a/amverse/amverse-idx?page=bibl

The CMU Index of Canonical Verse
eserver.org/poetry/

Workshops and Forums on the WWW

The following sites offer workshops or interactive forums:

Gotham Writers' Workshop
WritingClasses.com or www.write.org/

Kalliope Online Poetry Workshop
www.geocities.com/SoHo/8028/intro.htm

The New School Online University
www.dialnsa.edu/

The Original Albany Poetry Workshop
www.sonic.net/poetry/albany/

Zeugma: An Online Workshop for Poets
melicreview.com/zeugma/

Eratosphere
eratosphere.ablemuse.com/index.shtml

The Critical Poet
thecriticalpoet.tripod.com/

Critique Me
www.critiqueme.com/

Interactive Poetry Pages
www.csdco.com/~cantelow/poem_welcome.html

Egroups
www.egroups.com/subscribe/poetry

Inside the Web: Poetry and Critique Message Boards
www.insidetheweb.com/mbs.cgi/mb379523

Every Poet
www.everypoet.com/

The Poetry Thread
www.geocities.com/Athens/Troy/4212/

Sites to Help Craft Poems

Random House Webster's Dictionary
www.infoplease.com/dictionary.html

American Heritage Dictionary
www.bartleby.com/61

Merriam-Webster's Dictionary
www.m-w.com

Cambridge Dictionaries
www.dictionary.cambridge.org

Encarta World English Dictionary
dictionary.msn.com

Oxford English Dictionary
oed.com

The Word Wizard
www.wordwizard.com

A Word A Day
www.wordsmith.org/awad/index.html

Thesaurus.com
www.thesaurus.com/

WriteExpress Online Rhyming Dictionary
www.writeexpress.com/online.html

Rhyming Dictionary Online
www.rhymezone.com

Index

Symbols

A

B

C

D

E

F

G

H

M

N

O

P

Q

R

S

T

U

V

W

X-Z